Top 20

OF EVERYTHING

Published in 2011
by Igloo Books Ltd
Cottage Farm
Sywell
Northants
NN6 0BJ

www.igloo-books.com

B044 0811
2 4 6 8 10 9 7 5 3 1
ISBN: 978-0-85780-096-1

Printed and manufactured in China

Top 20

OF EVERYTHING

igloo

CONTENTS

THE ARTS

Most popular artists	34
Best known art images	34
Most expensive works of art (paintings)	35
Most popular exhibitions at the National Gallery, London	100
Most visited art museums	101
Tenors of the recording era	170
Sopranos of the recording era	170
Most frequently performed operas	171

HISTORY AND WARFARE

Longest reigning European monarchs	84
Earliest presidents of the USA	85
Greatest US presidents	85
Biggest empires in history	110
Earliest civilizations	110
First countries to give the vote to women	111
Longest wars	134
Bloodiest battles	135
Shortest wars	135
Biggest battleships of World War II	150
Military air fleets worldwide	151

LANGUAGE AND LITERATURE

Bestselling adult novels ever	16
Bestselling authors ever	16
Bestselling non-fiction books	17
Biggest selling daily newspapers in the world	32
English language newspapers	33
Countries by newspaper circulation	33
Most widely-spoken languages	52
Most widely-written languages	53
Least-spoken languages	53
Most borrowed books from libraries	64
Largest libraries in the world	65
Paid-for magazines by circulation	65
Bestselling books not in English	88
Bestselling children's books in English	88
Longest novels ever written	89
Most recent winners of the Gold Dagger Award	198
Most recent Man Booker Prize winners	198
Most recent winners of the Nobel Prize for Literature	199

MONEY

Richest people in the world	112
Richest royals	112
Richest celebrities	113
Richest countries by GDP	214
Countries with the most billionaires	214
Poorest countries by GDP	215
Largest gold reserves by country	245

PEOPLE

Most popular boys' names in the US today	18
Most popular girls' names in the US today	18
Most popular surnames in the USA	19
Cheese-consuming countries	78
Milk-consuming countries	78
Countries with the most McDonald's	79
Alcohol-consuming countries	79
Countries with the lowest life expectancy	118
Countries with the highest life expectancy	118
Oldest people	119
Most popular UK boys' names 100 years ago	132
Most popular US boys' names 100 years ago	132
Most popular US girls' names 100 years ago	132
Most popular UK girls' names 100 years ago	133
Girls' names in the UK today	148
Boys' names in the UK today	148
Most common surnames in Scotland	149
Most common surnames in England	149
Highest populations aged under 15	162
World's highest prison populations	162
Largest monarchies	163
Calorie-burning activities	168
Fastest cross-channel swims	169
First climbers to reach the summit of Everest	169
Most recent celebrities who died young	172
Causes of death worldwide	173
Most common phobias	173
Tallest men in the world	176
Shortest people in the world	177
Most obese nations	176
Countries with most native English speakers	190
Countries with most native Spanish speakers	191
Countries with the lowest birth rate	206
Years with the most births in the UK	206
Countries with the highest birth rate	207

SPORT

Highest scores in International Rugby Union 20
Most points scored in total at IRB World Cup 20
Most points scored at IRB World Cup 21
Fastest male marathon runners 26
Fastest female marathon runners 26
Most snooker titles 27
Most international caps (Rugby) 40
Most Rugby League Challenge Cup wins 40
Most grand slam tennis tournament
  wins (male) 41
Most grand slam tennis tournament
  wins (female) 41
Highest earning sportsmen 48
Biggest sports stadiums by capacity 49
Olympians with most medals (Winter Games) 62
Olympic gymnastics gold medals 63
Olympic figure skating gold medals 63
Olympic swimming gold medals 62
Highest transfer fees 82
World Cup goalscorers (finals only) 82
Highest-paid footballers per season 83
Fastest mile runners 86
Fastest men over 100 meters 86
Fastest women over 100 meters 87
Most competitors at the Olympic Games 94
Most Paralympic gold medals in one sport 94
Olympians with most gold medals 95
Most World Series appearances (plus wins) 98
Pitchers with the most strikeouts 99

Most home runs in baseball 99
Most points in an NBA career 102
Most games played in an NBA career 102
Highest annual NBA salaries 103
Highest innings in Twenty20 114
Most runs in a test career 115
Most Formula 1 Grand Prix wins 126
Horses by earnings (USA) 126
All time best rankings in the Tour de France 127
Most successful club sides in European
  competition (football) 140
Most international caps (football) 140
Most international goals 141
FIFA World Cup-winning countries
  and placings 141
Olympic gold medals: Winter Games 178
Olympic gold medals: athletics 178
Gold medals: Paralympic Winter Games 179
Gold medals: Paralympic Summer Games 179
Most test matches in a career 210
Most wickets in a test career 210
Highest innings in One-Day
  International cricket 211
Countries with most Olympic gold medals
  (Summer Games) 216
Olympians with most medals
  (Summer Games) 216
Olympians with most medals
  (Summer and Winter Games combined) 217

TRANSPORT

Busiest rail networks 10
Longest rail networks 10
Fastest train journeys 11
Most expensive cars to insure
  in the US 22
Countries that produce the
  most vehicles 22
Most powerful cars 23
Busiest London Underground
  stations 44
Biggest underground rail systems 45
Busiest underground systems 45
Largest sailing vessels 72
Biggest passenger ships 72
Busiest airports 73

INTERNET AND PHONE

Most downloaded Smartphone apps 38
Countries with most landline
  telephones 39
Countries with most mobile phones 39
Internet retail sites (UK) 152
Most popular online purchases 152
News websites 153
Most followed people on Twitter 160
Social networking sites 160
Countries using the internet 161

UNBELIEVABLE FACTS

Richest dead celebrities 30
Premature obituaries of the last 20 years 31
Most popular pop songs 70
Countries with the highest Scout and Guide memberships 71
Most influential blogs 158
Most popular websites 158
Most unusual deaths of the last two decades 159
Riskiest containers and packaging 200
Riskiest items of clothing and footwear 200
Riskiest items of sport and leisure equipment 201

EARTH AND SPACE

Largest islands 76
Largest oceans and seas 76
Largest lakes 77
Biggest earthquakes 90
Biggest floods 91
Worst avalanches 104
Worst volcanic eruptions 104
Highest active volcanoes 105
World's deepest caves 105
Stars closest to Earth 116
Largest stars observed in the Universe 116
First humans in space 117
Comets' closest approach to Earth 117
Coldest places on Earth 124
Hottest countries on Earth 125
Biggest asteroids 166
Biggest meteor craters 166
Earliest satellites and space probes 167

Longest rivers 180
Tallest waterfalls 181
Deepest oceans and seas 180
Highest mountains 202
Longest mountain ranges 203
Largest deserts 203

ENERGY AND RESOURCES

Oil consumers 14
Natural gas consuming countries 14
Coal consumers 15
Oil producers 15
Gold producers 28
Silver producers 29
Copper producers 29
Coal producers 58
Gas producers 58
Best environmental performance 59
Worst environmental performance 59
Biggest landfill sites 66
Biggest rubbish producers 66
Hydro-electricity consumers 67
Producers of nuclear power 67
Cement producers 186
Biggest air polluters 186
Cocoa (chocolate) consumers 187
Salt producers 187

PETS AND ANIMALS

Most cats per country 138
Most dogs per country 138
Most aggressive dogs 139
Countries farming chickens 142
Countries farming cattle 142
Countries farming pigs 143
Countries farming ducks 146
Countries farming sheep 147
Most popular cat breeds (USA) 174
Most popular dog breeds in the UK 174
Types of fish caught and landed (in tonnes) 175
Chicken-eating nations 175

MUSIC

UK and US hits of the 1950s 36
UK and US hits of the 1960s 37
UK and US hits of the 1990s 42
UK and US hits of the 2000s 43
Ivor Novello Award winners 46
Mercury Prize winners 46
Most MTV Awards 46
Most Brit Awards 47
Most Grammy Awards 47
Longest run in the UK Singles Chart 50
Longest run in the US Singles Chart 50
Longest run in the US Albums Chart 51
Longest run in the UK Albums Chart 51
Most played songs in the US 54
Most played songs in the UK 54
Most number one albums in the UK 55
Most number one albums in the US 55
Biggest concert attendances 80
Longest at the top of the UK chart (singles) 81
Longest at the top of the US chart (singles) 81
Most Platinum Awards in the UK (groups) 92
Most Platinum Awards in the UK (female) 92
Bestselling albums in the USA 93
Artists with the most Platinum Awards (UK) 93
Most number one singles in the UK 120
Most number one singles in the USA 120
Longest at the top of the UK chart (albums) 121
Longest at the top of the US chart (albums) 121
Bestselling singles in the UK 144
Bestselling albums in the UK 144
Top UK single downloads 145
UK and US hits of the 1970s 184
UK and US hits of the 1980s 185
Bestselling albums worldwide of all time 194
Bestselling artists worldwide 195
Bestselling singles worldwide 195
Biggest-selling females in the USA 204
Biggest-selling males in the USA 204
Biggest grossing tours 205
Biggest Beatles concerts 212
Posthumous UK number one hits 213
Most certified awards in the USA (groups) 213
Most Platinum Awards in the UK (male) 218
Most certified awards in the USA (male) 219

FILM, TV AND ENTERTAINMENT

Highest-earning films	24
Biggest film flops	25
TV-owning countries	56
Longest-running stage shows	57
Highest-earning Bond films	60
Films winning most Oscars	60
Highest-earning comedy films	61
Highest-earning horror films	61
Highest-paid actors	68
Highest-earning documentary films	68
Highest-paid actresses	69
YouTube videos	74
Bestselling films on DVD (UK)	75
Longest-running TV shows	75
Most profitable films with a budget under $1 million	96
Most expensive films ever made	97
Highest-earning musicals	122
Highest-earning animated films	122
Highest-earning comic book film adaptations	123
Richest child stars	156
Countries with the most cinemas	157
Cinema-goers by country	157
Longest-running radio shows in the UK	192
Highest-rated TV shows in the UK	193
Highest-rated TV shows in the USA	193

MAN-MADE DISASTERS

Worst rail disasters	188
Worst aircraft accidents	189
Worst maritime disasters	220
Biggest oil spills	221

WILDLIFE

Biggest spiders	12
Biggest fish by weight	13
Longest-living aquatic creatures	13
Fastest land animals	106
Biggest land mammals	106
Fastest birds in flight	107
Longest dinosaurs	128
Heaviest dinosaurs	128
Smallest dinosaurs	129
Most endangered mammals	136
Longest-living land animals	136
Animals most closely related to humans	137
Biggest birds by wingspan	164
Heaviest birds	164
Farthest migrating birds	165
Smallest land mammals by length	182
Biggest bears	183
Longest snakes	208
Most venomous reptiles and amphibians	209
Deadliest creatures	209

PLACES

Largest populations by country	8
Smallest populations by country	8
Countries with longest coastlines	9
Cities with busiest hotels	130
Most populous cities	130
Longest place names in the world	131
Smallest countries in the world	154
Largest countries in the world	154
Least densely populated countries	155

BUILDINGS AND STRUCTURES

Highest bridges	108
Longest bridges	108
Longest tunnels	109
Cities with most skyscrapers	196
Tallest buildings	197

LARGEST POPULATIONS BY COUNTRY

Country / Population

1 China	1,339,190,000	6 Pakistan	170,260,000	11 Mexico	108,396,000	16 Egypt	78,848,000
2 India	1,184,639,000	7 Bangladesh	164,425,000	12 Philippines	94,013,000	17 Iran	75,078,000
3 USA	309,975,000	8 Nigeria	158,259,000	13 Vietnam	85,790,000	18 Turkey	72,561,000
4 Indonesia	234,181,000	9 Russia	141,927,000	14 Germany	81,757,000	19 Congo	67,827,000
5 Brazil	193,364,000	10 Japan	127,380,000	15 Ethiopia	79,221,000	20 France	65,447,374

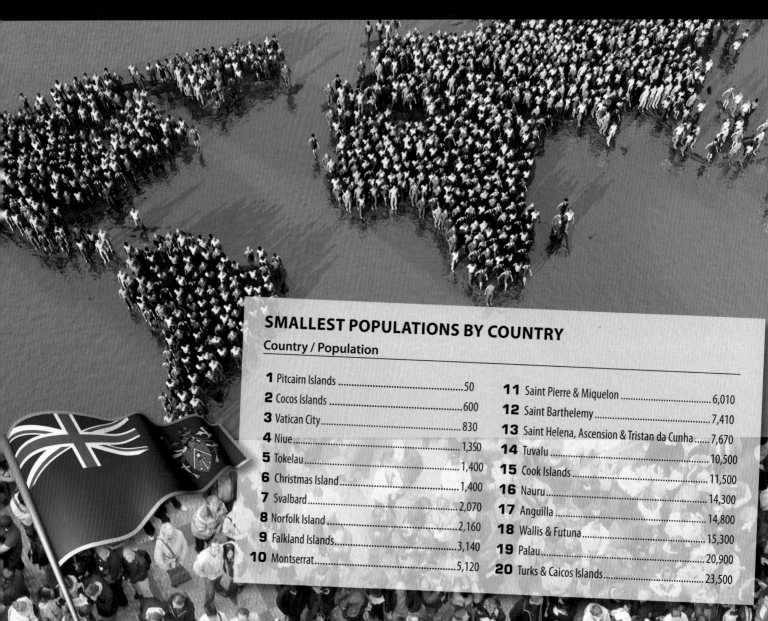

SMALLEST POPULATIONS BY COUNTRY

Country / Population

1 Pitcairn Islands	50	11 Saint Pierre & Miquelon	6,010
2 Cocos Islands	600	12 Saint Barthelemy	7,410
3 Vatican City	830	13 Saint Helena, Ascension & Tristan da Cunha	7,670
4 Niue	1,350	14 Tuvalu	10,500
5 Tokelau	1,400	15 Cook Islands	11,500
6 Christmas Island	1,400	16 Nauru	14,300
7 Svalbard	2,070	17 Anguilla	14,800
8 Norfolk Island	2,160	18 Wallis & Futuna	15,300
9 Falkland Islands	3,140	19 Palau	20,900
10 Montserrat	5,120	20 Turks & Caicos Islands	23,500

COUNTRIES WITH LONGEST COASTLINES

Country / Length of coastline

	Country	Length of coastline
1	Canada	125,567 miles (202,080km)
2	Indonesia	34,000 miles (54,716km)
3	Greenland	27,394 miles (44,087km)
4	Russia	23,396 miles (37,653km)
5	Philippines	22,549 miles (36,289km)
6	Japan	18,486 miles (29,751km)
7	Australia	16,006 miles (25,760km)
8	Norway	15,626 miles (25,148km)
9	USA	12,380 miles (19,924km)
10	New Zealand	9,404 miles (15,134 km)
11	China	9,101 miles (14,500km)
12	Greece	8,498 miles (13,676km)
13	UK	7,723 miles (12,429km)
14	Mexico	5,797 miles (9,330km)
15	Italy	4,772 miles (7,600km)
16	Brazil	4,656 miles (7,491km)
17	Denmark	4,554 miles (7,314km)
18	Turkey	4,473 miles (7,200km)
19	India	4,350 miles (7,000km)
20	Chile	4,000 miles (6,435km)

If you decided to walk around Canada following the shoreline walking at a rate of 12 miles (20km) each day, it would take you 28 years!

BUSIEST RAIL NETWORKS

Country / Number of passengers per km per year (billions)

1 China 876
2 India 838
3 Japan 254
4 Russia 154
5 France 88
6 Germany 77
7 UK 51
8 Ukraine 48
9 Italy 46
10 Egypt 41
11 South Korea 31
12 Indonesia 26
13 Pakistan 25
14 Spain 23
15 Switzerland 17.4
16 United States 17
17 Poland 16
18 Iran 15
19 Taiwan 15
20 Kazakhstan 15

LONGEST RAIL NETWORKS

Country / Length of track miles / km

1 USA 140,810 / 226,612
2 Russia 54,157 / 87,157
3 China 46,875 / 75,438
4 India 39,284 / 63,221
5 Germany 29,959 / 48,215
6 Canada 29,868 / 48,068
7 Australia 23,954 / 38,550
8 Argentina 19,823 / 31,902
9 France 18,250 / 29,370
10 Brazil 18,203 / 29,295
11 Japan 14,586 / 23,474
12 Poland 14,336 / 23,072
13 Ukraine 13,964 / 22,473
14 South Africa 12,969 / 20,872
15 Italy 12,092 / 19,460
16 Mexico 10,997 / 17,665
17 UK 10,294 / 16,567
18 Spain 9,304 / 14,974
19 Kazakhstan 8,513 / 13,700
20 Sweden 7,163 / 11,528

FAMOUS RAILWAY TRAINS

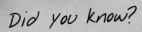

Did you know?

The Orient Express began trips from Paris to Bulgaria on 5 October 1883, and from 1889 went as far as Constantinople (now Istanbul), Turkey. It was the first trans-European train and traveled a total of 1,700 miles (2,736km) across six countries. It stopped running in 1977 but was relaunched five years later.

FASTEST TRAIN JOURNEYS

	Journey*	Train	Distance (miles/km)	Speed (mph/kmph)
1	Lorraine–Champagne, France	TGV 5422	104.1 / 167.6	173.6 / 279.3
2	Okayama–Hiroshima, Japan	Nozomi	190.0 / 144.9	158.9 / 255.7
3	Taichung–Zuoying, Taiwan	7 trains	111.5 / 179.5	152.0 / 244.7
4	Brussels–Belgium–Valence, France	Thalys Soleil	516.8 / 831.7	152.0 / 244.6
5	Frankfurt–Siegburg/Bonn, Germany	Ice 10	89.4 / 143.3	145 / 233.5
6	Madrid Atocha–Zaragoza, Spain	7 Ave trains	190.8 / 307.2	141.4 / 227.6
7	Shenyang Bei–Qinhuangdao, China	D24 &D28	251.0 / 404.0	122.5 / 197.1
8	Córdoba–Puertollano, Spain	7 Ave trains	83.45 / 134.3	122.09 / 196.5
9	Seoul Yongsan–Seodaejeon, S. Korea	KTX trains 410 & 411	100.04 / 161	120.04 / 193.2
10	Ingolstadt–Nürnberg, Germany	Hbf. 4 UCE trains	55.92 / 90	119.86 / 192.9
11	Daejeon–Cheonan Asan, S. Korea	13 KTX trains	39.77 / 64	108.43 / 174.5
12	King's Cross–York, UK	1 IC225	188.40 / 303.2	107.68 / 173.3
13	Alvesta–Hasslehölm, Sweden	X2000 543	60.89 / 98	107.44 / 172.9
14	Roma Termini–Florence SMN, Italy	Eurostar 9484	162.18 / 261	105.82 / 170.3
15	Baltimore–Wilmington, USA	7 Acela trains	68.41 / 110.1	100.10 / 161.1
16	Shenzhen–Guangzhou Dong, China	D' trains	776 / 1249	99.67 / 160.4
17	Tikkurila–Tampere, Finland	10 Pendolinos	109.98 /177	98.49 / 158.5
18	Arezzo–Roma Termini, Italy	Eurostar 9421	123.47 / 198.7	97.50 / 156.9
19	St. Pölten–Linz , Austria	Eurocity & ICE 766	76.24 / 122.7	95.32 / 153.4
20	Lillestrøm–Gardermoen, Norway	Airport trains	16.31 / 30.2	93.95 / 151.2

Source: *Railway Gazette International's* World Speed Survey

*Test journey for each country given; other fast services exist in the same countries

BIGGEST SPIDERS

Spider / Legspan (in/cm)

1

Giant huntsman spider
(*Heteropoda maxima*)
12 / 30.5

2

Brazilian giant tawney red
(*Grammostola mollicoma*)
11$\frac{1}{2}$ / 29

3

Brazilian salmon pink
(*Lasiodora parahybana*)
10 / 25.4

4

Goliath tarantula
(*Theraphosa blondi*)
10 / 25.4

5

North American wolf spider
(*Cupiennius sallei*)
10 / 25.4

6

Bahia scarlet tarantula
(*Lasiodora klugi*)
9$\frac{1}{2}$ / 24

7

Brazilian black and white
tarantula (*Acanthoscurria
brocklehursti*)
9 / 23

8

Purple bloom bird-eating
(*Xenesthis immanis*)
9 / 23

9

Monstrosus
(*Xenesthis monstrosa*)
9 / 23

10

Chaco golden knee
(*Grammostola pulchripes*)
8$\frac{1}{2}$ / 22

11

Brazilian whitebanded
tarantula
(*Acanthoscurria geniculata*)
8$\frac{1}{2}$ / 21.5

12

Avondale spider
(*Delena cancerides*)
8 / 20

13

Columbian giant tarantula
(*Megaphobema robustum*)
8 / 20

14

Giant baboon spider
(*Hysterocrates gigas*)
8 / 20

15

Brazilian red and white
tarantula
(*Nhandu chromatus*)
6$\frac{1}{2}$ / 16.5

16

Mexican redleg tarantula
(*Brachypelma emilia*)
6 / 15

17

Pink zebra beauty
(*Eupalaestrus vampestratus*)
6 / 15

18

Brazilian wandering spider*
(*Phoneutria nigriventer*)
6 / 15

19

Cardinal spider
(*Tegenaria parietina*)
5$\frac{1}{2}$ / 14

20

Brown huntsman spider
(*Heteropoda venatoria*)
5 / 13

* The Brazilian wandering spider is the deadliest of the giant spiders — its venom is more toxic than the Australian funnel web spider.

BIGGEST FISH BY WEIGHT

Fish / Weight (lb/kg)

1 Whale shark (*Rhincodon typus*) 79,366 / 36,000 **2** Basking shark (*Cetorhinus maximus*) 35,274 / 16,000
3 Southern sawfish (*Pristis perotteti*) 5,412 / 2,455 **4** Manta ray (*Manta birostris*) 5,070 / 2,300
5 Ocean sunfish (*Mola mola*) 5,070 / 2,300 **6** Great white shark (*Carcarodon carcharias*) 5,000 / 2,268
7 Beluga sturgeon (*Huso huso*) 4,575 / 2,075 **8** Greenland shark (*Somniosus microcephalus*) 3,007 / 1,364
9 Megamouth shark (*Megachasma pelagios*) 2,680 / 1,215 **10** Kaluga sturgeon (*Huso dauricus*) 2,205 / 1,000
11 White sturgeon (*Acipenser transmontanus*) 1,800 / 816 **12** Tiger shark (*Galeocerdo cuvier*) 1,400 / 635
13 Giant freshwater stingray (*Himantura chaophraya*) 1,323 / 600 **14** Great hammerhead shark (*Sphyrna mokarran*) 1,280 /580
15 Common thresher shark (*Alopias vul pinus*) 1,100 / 500 **16** Blue shark (*Prionace glauca*) 860 / 391
17 Pacific halibut (*Hippoglossus stenolepis*) 800 / 363 **18** Grey nurse shark (*Carcharias taurus*) 660 / 300
19 Siamese giant carp (*Catlocarpio siamensis*) 660 / 300 **20** Mekong giant flatfish (*Pangasianodon gigas*) 645 / 293

LONGEST-LIVING AQUATIC CREATURES

Creature/ **Oldest recorded age (years)**

1 Deep-water black coral (*Leiopathes sp.*)	4,270
2 Gold coral (*Callogorgia elegans*)	2,740
3 Antarctic sponge (*Cinachyra antarctica*)	1,550
4 Icelandic cyprine clam (*Arctica islandica*)	405
5 Freshwater pearl mussel (*Margaritifera margaritifera*)	250
6 Bowhead whale (*Balaena mysticetus*)	211
7 Rougheye rockfish (*Sebastes aleutianus*)	205
8 Red sea urchin (*Strongylocentrotus franciscanus*)	200
9 Koi carp (*Cyprinus carpio*)	200
10 Hydrocarbon seep tubeworm (*Lamellibrachia luymesi*)	170
11 Geoduck saltwater clam (*Panopea generosa*)	160
12 Lake sturgeon (*Acipenser fulvescens*)	152
13 Orange roughy (*Hoplostethus atlanticus*)	149
14 Whale shark (*Rhincodon typus*)	150
15 Warty oreo (*Allocyttus verrucosus*)	140
16 Lobster (*Homarus americanus*)	140
17 Japanese spider crab (*Macrocheira kaempferei*)	100
18 European eel (*Anguilla anguilla*)	88
19 Killer whale (*Orcinus orca*)	80
20 Dugong (*Dugong dugon*)	73

Source: Journal of Natural History

NATURAL GAS CONSUMING COUNTRIES

Country / Consumption of natural gas (billion cubic feet/ meters) / Percentage of world total

1 USA / 22,000 / 647 / 22.2%

2 Russia / 13,700 / 389 / 13.2%

3 Iran / 4,500 / 132 / 4.5%

4 Canada / 3,400 / 95 / 3.2%

5 China / 3,100 / 89 / 3%

6 Japan / 3,000 / 87 / 3%

7 UK / 3,000 / 87 / 2.9%

8 Germany / 2,800 / 78 / 2.6%

9 Saudi Arabia / 2,800 / 78 / 2.6%

10 Italy / 2,550 / 72 / 2.5%

11 Mexico / 2,500 / 70 / 2.4%

12 United Arab Emirates / 2,000 / 59 / 2%

13 India / 1,800 / 52 / 1.8%

14 Uzbekistan / 1,700 / 49 / 1.7%

15 Ukraine / 1,660 / 47 / 1.6%

16 Argentina / 1,550 / 44 / 1.5%

17 France / 1,500 / 43 / 1.4%

18 Egypt / 1,500 / 43 / 1.4%

19 Thailand / 1,400 / 39 / 1.3%

20 Netherlands / 1,400 / 39 / 1.3%

Source:
BP Statistical Review of World Energy

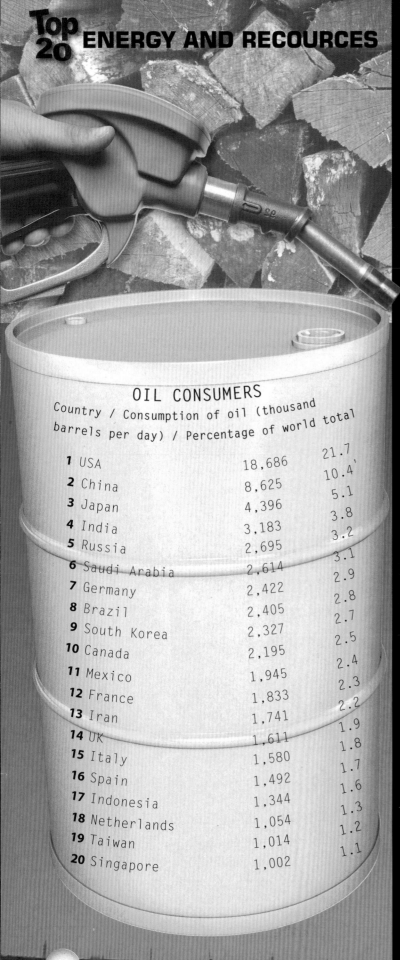

OIL CONSUMERS

Country / Consumption of oil (thousand barrels per day) / Percentage of world total

	Country	Consumption	Percentage
1	USA	18,686	21.7
2	China	8,625	10.4
3	Japan	4,396	5.1
4	India	3,183	3.8
5	Russia	2,695	3.2
6	Saudi Arabia	2,614	3.1
7	Germany	2,422	2.9
8	Brazil	2,405	2.8
9	South Korea	2,327	2.7
10	Canada	2,195	2.5
11	Mexico	1,945	2.4
12	France	1,833	2.3
13	Iran	1,741	2.2
14	UK	1,611	1.9
15	Italy	1,580	1.8
16	Spain	1,492	1.7
17	Indonesia	1,344	1.6
18	Netherlands	1,054	1.3
19	Taiwan	1,014	1.2
20	Singapore	1,002	1.1

COAL CONSUMERS
Country / Short tons annually (millions)

1 China 2,893

2 USA 1,129

3 India 579

4 Germany 276

5 Russia 261

6 Japan 207

7 South Africa 203

8 Australia 146

9 South Korea 106

10 Turkey 93

11 Greece 74

12 Taiwan 73

13 Ukraine 69

14 UK 66

15 Canada 62

16 Indonesia 50

17 Spain 45

18 Thailand 36

19 North Korea 36

20 Italy 28

OIL PRODUCERS
Country / Production (thousands of barrels per day) / Percentage of world total

1. Russia / 10,032 / 12.9
2. Saudi Arabia / 9,713 / 12.0
3. USA / 7,196 / 8.5
4. Iran / 4,216 / 5.3
5. China / 3,790 / 4.9
6. Canada / 3,212 / 4.1
7. Mexico / 2,979 / 3.9
8. United Arab Emirates / 2,599 / 3.2
9. Iraq / 2,482 / 3.2
10. Kuwait / 2,481 / 3.2
11. Venezuela / 2,437 / 3.3
12. Norway / 2,342 / 2.8
13. Nigeria / 2,061 / 2.6
14. Brazil / 2,029 / 2.6
15. Algeria / 1,811 / 2.0
16. Angola / 1,784 / 2.3
17. Kazakhstan / 1,682 / 2.0
18. Libya / 1,652 / 2.0
19. UK / 1,448 / 1.8
20. Qatar / 1,345 / 1.5

TOP 20 LANGUAGE AND LITERATURE

BESTSELLING ADULT NOVELS EVER

Title (date of first publication) / Author / Estimated sales (millions)

1 A Tale of Two Cities (1859) Charles Dickens / 200 +
2 And Then There Were None (1939) Agatha Christie / 100
3 She (1887) H. Rider Haggard / 83
4 The Da Vinci Code (2003) Dan Brown / 80
5 The Catcher in the Rye (1951) J.D. Salinger / 65
6 The Curse of Capistrano (Mark of Zorro) (1919) Johnston McCulley / 50
7 Jonathan Livingston Seagull (1970) Richard Bach / 40
8 Angels and Demons (2000) Dan Brown / 39
9 War and Peace (1932) Leo Tolstoy / 36
10 Kane and Abel (1979) Jeffrey Archer / 34
11 To Kill a Mocking Bird (1960) Harper Lee / 30
12 Valley of the Dolls (1966) Jacqueline Suzanne / 30
13 Gone with the Wind (1936) Margaret Mitchell / 30
14 The Thorn Birds (1977) Colleen McCullogh / 30
15 The Revolt of Mamie Stover (1951) William Bradford Huie / 30
16 Nineteen Eighty-Four (1949) George Orwell / 25
17 The Celestine Prophecy (1993) James Redfield / 23
18 The Godfather (1969) Mario Puzo / 21
19 Love Story (1970) Eric Segal / 21
20 Jaws (1974) Peter Benchley / 20

BESTSELLING AUTHORS EVER

	Author	Estimated sales (millions unless stated)
1	Agatha Christie	4 billion
2	Barbara Cartland	1 billion
3	Harold Robbins	750
4	Georges Simenon	700
5	Sidney Sheldon	600
6	Enid Blyton	600
7	Danielle Steel	600
8	Dr. Seuss	500
9	Gilbert Patten	500
10	J.K. Rowling	450
11	Leo Tolstoy	413
12	Jackie Collins	400
13	Horatio Alger Jr.	400
14	R.L. Stine	400
15	Corin Tellado	400
16	Dean Koontz	400
17	A.S. Pushkin	357
18	Stephen King	350
19	Louis L'Amour	330
20	Eric Stanley Gardner	325

Stephen King has sold 350 million books worldwide

The religious book of Islam, the Quran, was written in the 7th century AD. Many muslims learn sections of the text by heart.

Jackie Collins has written 27 bestselling novels to date.

Title / Date of first publication (if known) / Author (if known)/ Estimated sales (millions unless stated)

BESTSELLING NON-FICTION BOOKS

1 The Bible / 6 billion

2 Quotations from Chairman Mao (1966) Mao Tse-tung / 1–2 billion

3 The Qu'ran / 800

4 New Chinese Character Dictionary (1957) Xinhua Zidian / 400

5 The Book of Morman Joseph Smith Jr. / 120

6 Steps to Christ (1892) Ellen G. White / 60

7 The Common Sense Book of Baby and Child Care (1946) Dr. Benjamin Spock / 50

8 The Hite Report (1976) Shere Hite / 48

9 You Can Heal Your Life (1984) Louise Hay / 35

10 The Diary of Anne Frank (1947) Anne Frank / 30

11 In His Steps: What Would Jesus Do? Charles M. Sheldon / 30

12 The Purpose Driven Life (2002) Rick Warren / 30

13 Think and Grow Rich (1937) Napoleon Hill / 30

14 The Late Great Planet Earth (1970) Hal Lindsey & C.C. Carlson / 28

15 Who Moved My Cheese? (1998) Spencer Johnson / 26

16 The Happy Hooker: My Own Story (1971) Xaviera Hollander / 20

17 What to Expect When You're Expecting (1984) Arlene Eisenberg & Heidi Murkoff / 20

18 How to Win Friends and Influence People (1936) Dale Carnegie / 15

19 The Naked Ape (1968) Desmond Morris / 12

20 A Brief History of Time (1988) Stephen Hawking / 10

BOYS' NAMES IN THE US*

1	Jacob	20,858
2	Ethan	19,664
3	Michael	18,677
4	Alexander	18,025
5	William	17,696
6	Joshua	17,418
7	Daniel	17,336
8	Jayden	17,082
9	Noah	17,061
10	Anthony	16,139
11	Christopher	16,136
12	Aiden	15,846
13	Matthew	15,777
14	David	15,236
15	Andrew	14,675
16	Joseph	14,674
17	Logan	14,331
18	James	14,022
19	Ryan	12,986
20	Benjamin	12,944

* At time of printing.

1	Isabella	20,067
2	Emma	17,716
3	Olivia	17,246
4	Sophia	16,743
5	Ava	15,730
6	Emily	15,204
7	Madison	15,097
8	Abigail	14,232
9	Chloe	11,785
10	Mia	11,319

GIRLS' NAMES IN THE US*

11	Elizabeth	
12	Addison	
13	Alexis	10,897
14	Ella	10,567
15	Samantha	9,839
16	Natalie	9,560
17	Grace	9,551
18	Lily	9,324
19	Alyssa	8,194
20	Ashley	8,016
		7,900
		7,741

* At time of printing.

Source: Social Security Administration USA

PAS

United of Am

Did you know?

Some real names found in the US census records include Noble Butt, Bum Snoddy and Fanny Whiffer!

MOST POPULAR SURNAMES IN THE USA*

	Surname	Usage	Percentage frequency
1	SMITH	2,501,922	1.006
2	JOHNSON	2,014,470	0.81
3	WILLIAMS	1,738,413	0.699
4	JONES	1,544,427	0.621
5	BROWN	1,544,427	0.621
6	DAVIS	1,193,760	0.48
7	MILLER	1,054,488	0.424
8	WILSON	843,093	0.339
9	MOORE	775,944	0.312
10	TAYLOR	773,457	0.311
11	ANDERSON	773,457	0.311
12	THOMAS	773,457	0.311
13	JACKSON	770,970	0.31
14	WHITE	693,873	0.279
15	HARRIS	683,925	0.275
16	MARTIN	678,951	0.273
17	THOMPSON	669,003	0.269
18	GARCIA	631,698	0.254
19	MARTINEZ	581,958	0.234
20	ROBINSON	579,471	0.233

* According to the 1990 census.

HIGHEST SCORES IN INTERNATIONAL RUGBY UNION

Match / Match result (Year played)

1	Hong Kong v Singapore	164–13 (1994)
2	Japan v Chinese Taipei	155–3 (2002)
3	Argentina v Paraguay	152–0 (2002)
4	Argentina v Venezuela	147–7 (2004)
5	New Zealand v Japan	145–17 (1995)
6	Argentina v Paraguay	144–0 (2003)
7	Australia v Namibia	142–0 (2003)
8	Japan v Chinese Taipei	134–6 (1998)
9	South Africa v Uruguay	134–3 (2005)
10	England v Romania	134–0 (2001)
11	Zimbabwe v Botswana	130–10 (1996)
12	Japan v Sri Lanka	129–6 (2002)
13	Fiji v Niue	124–4 (1983)
14	Japan v Chinese Taipei	120–3 (2002)
15	Korea v Chinese Taipei	119–7 (2002)
16	Tonga v Korea	119–0 (2003)
17	Sweden v Luxembourg	116–3 (2001)
18	Namibia v Madagascar	116–0 (2002)
19	Samoa v Papua New Guinea	115–7 (2009)
20	Japan v Arabian Gulf	114–6 (2008)

Source: RugbyData.com

MOST POINTS SCORED IN TOTAL AT IRB WORLD CUP

Name / Points scored

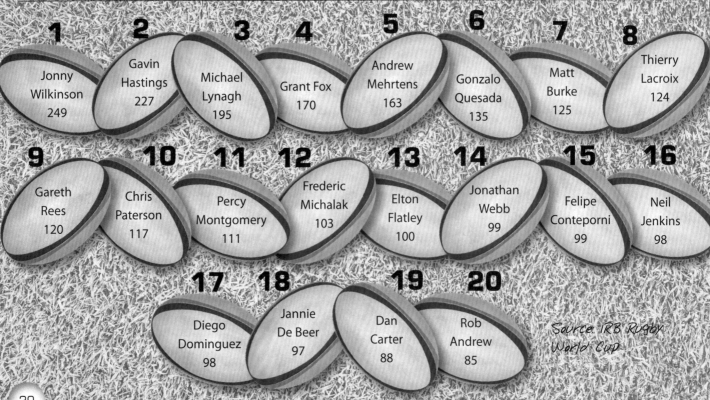

1. Jonny Wilkinson 249
2. Gavin Hastings 227
3. Michael Lynagh 195
4. Grant Fox 170
5. Andrew Mehrtens 163
6. Gonzalo Quesada 135
7. Matt Burke 125
8. Thierry Lacroix 124
9. Gareth Rees 120
10. Chris Paterson 117
11. Percy Montgomery 111
12. Frederic Michalak 103
13. Elton Flatley 100
14. Jonathan Webb 99
15. Felipe Conteporni 99
16. Neil Jenkins 98
17. Diego Dominguez 98
18. Jannie De Beer 97
19. Dan Carter 88
20. Rob Andrew 85

Source: IRB Rugby World Cup

MOST POINTS SCORED AT IRB WORLD CUP

Name / Team / Points scored (Year scored)

1 Grant Fox / New Zealand / 126 (1987)

2 Jonny Wilkinson / England / 113 (2003)

3 Thierry Lacroix / France / 112 (1995)

4 Percy Montgomery / South Africa / 105 (2007)

5 Gavin Hastings / Scotland / 104 (1995)

6 Gonzalo Quesada / Argentina / 102 (1999)

7 Matt Burke / Australia / 101 (1995)

8 Frederic Michalak / France / 101 (2003)

9 Elton Flatley / Australia / 100 (2003)

10 Jannie De Beer / South Africa / 97 (1999)

11 Felipe Conteporni / Argentina / 91 (2007)

12 Andrew Mehrtens / New Zealand / 84 (1995)

13 Michael Lynagh / Australia / 82 (1987)

14 Andrew Mehrtens / New Zealand / 79 (1999)

15 Rob Andrew / England / 79 (1995)

16 Leon MacDonald / New Zealand / 75 (2003)

17 Chris Paterson / Scotland / 71 (2003)

18 Jonny Wilkinson / England / 69 (1999)

19 Ralph Keyes / Ireland / 68 (1991)

20 Jonny Wilkinson / England / 67 (2007)

Source: IRB Rugby World Cup

Did you know?
Rugby is named after the private school in the town of Rugby, England, where the rules of the game were first laid down in 1848 by some of its senior pupils.

Source: insure.com

MOST EXPENSIVE CARS TO INSURE IN THE US

Car model / Annual cost of insurance

1	Mercedes SL65 AMG Convertible	$3,543.81	11	Mercedes CL65 AMG Coupe	$3,063.73
2	BMW 750i	$3,280.70	12	Mercedes CL63 AMG Coupe	$3,058.69
3	BMW 750Li	$3,280.70	13	Porsche 911 Carrera 4S	$3,046.87
4	Mercedes SL63 AMG Convertible	$3,263.46	14	Mercedes SL550 Convertible	$2,942.97
5	Mercedes S65 AMG Turbo	$3,220.86	15	Jaguar XJ L Supercharged	$2,940.94
6	Aston Martin DB9	$3,120.45	16	Jaguar XJ L Supersport	$2,940.94
7	Mercedes CL600	$3,114.28	17	Porsche 911 Carrera 4	$2,921.61
8	Porsche 911 Carrera GT2	$3,092.31	18	Porsche 911 Carrera S	$2,919.90
9	Aston Martin DB9 Volante	$3,088.96	19	Mercedes S63 AMG	$2,898.30
10	Mercedes G55 AMG	$3,086.49	20	Jaguar XJ Supercharged	$2,853.24

COUNTRIES THAT PRODUCE THE MOST VEHICLES

Country / Number of vehicles produced in one year

1	China	13,790,994	11	Canada	1,490,632
2	Japan	7,934,516	12	Iran	1,395,421
3	United States	5,708,852	13	UK	1,090,139
4	Germany	5,209,857	14	Thailand	999,378
5	South Korea	3,512,926	15	Czech Republic	974,569
6	Brazil	3,182,617	16	Poland	884,133
7	India	2,632,694	17	Turkey	869,605
8	Spain	2,170,078	18	Italy	843,239
9	France	2,047,658	19	Russia	722,431
10	Mexico	1,561,052	20	Belgium	537,354

MOST POWERFUL CARS

Car / Year / Maximum horsepower

#	Car	Year	Maximum horsepower
1	Bugatti Veyron16.4 Super Sports	2011	1200 hp
2	Bugatti Veyron Super Sport	2011	1183 hp
3	Zenvo ST1	2010	1104 hp
4	Bugatti Veyron Grand Sport	2009	1001 hp
5	Koenigsegg Agera	2011	910 hp
6	Brabus Mercedes–Benz SL65 AMG Black Series	2010	800 hp
7	Brabus Mercedes–Benz E V12 Coupe	2010	800 hp
8	Brabus Mercedes–Benz E V12	2010	800 hp
9	Ferrari 599 GTO	2011	670 hp
10	Lamborghini Murcielago LP670–4 SuperVeloce	2010	670 hp
11	Lamborghini Reventon Roadster	2010	670 hp
12	Pagani Zonda Tricolore	2011	670 hp
13	Mercedes-Benz SL65 AMG Black Series	2009	670 hp
14	Lamborghini Murcielago LP650–4	2010	650 hp
15	Mercedes-Benz SLR McLaren 722 S	2009	650 hp
16	Devon GTX	2010	650 hp
17	Bentley Continental Supersports	2010	630 hp
18	Maybach 62 S	2011	630 hp
19	Mercedes-Benz CL65 AMG	2011	621 hp
20	Porsche 911 GT2 RS	2011	620 hp

HIGHEST-EARNING FILMS

Title / Worldwide (million US$) / Year

1 *Avatar* $2,782.2 2009	**2.** *Titanic* $1,843.2 1997	**3.** *The Lord of the Rings: Return of the King* $1,119.1 2003	**4.** *Pirates of the Caribbean: Dead Man's Chest* $1,066.2 2006	**5.** *Toy Story 3* $1,063.2 2010
6. *Alice in Wonderland* $1,024.3 2010	**7.** *The Dark Knight* $1,001.9 2008	**8.** *Harry Potter and the Sorcerer's Stone* $974.7 2001	**9.** *Pirates of the Caribbean: At World's End* $961 2007	**10.** *Harry Potter and the Deathly Hallows Part 1* $948.9 2010
11. *Harry Potter and the Order of the Phoenix* $938.2 2007	**12.** *Harry Potter and the Half-Blood Prince* $934 2009	**13.** *The Lord of the Rings: The Two Towers* $925.3 2002	**14.** *Star Wars: Episode I – The Phantom Menace* $924.3 1999	**15.** *Shrek 2* $919.8 2004
16. *Jurassic Park* $914.7 1993	**17.** *Harry Potter and the Goblet of Fire* $895.9 2005	**18.** *Spider-Man 3* $890.9 2007	**19.** *Ice Age: Dawn of the Dinosaurs* $886.7 2009	**20.** *Harry Potter and the Chamber of Secrets* $878.6 2002

Source: Box Office Mojo

BIGGEST FILM FLOPS

Title / Total Cost (million US$) /
Net loss (inflation-adjusted million) / Year

	Title	Total Cost	Net loss	Year
1.	Cutthroat Island	$115	$146.947	1995
2.	The Alamo	$145	$134.784	2004
3.	Adventures of Pluto Nash	$120	$134.396	2002
4.	Sahara	$241	$133.141	2005
5.	13th Warrior	$160	$125.887	1999
6.	Town & Country	$105	$115.352	2001
7.	Speed Racer	$200	$106.054	2008
8.	Heaven's Gate	$44	$104.542	1980
9.	Final Fantasy: The Spirits Within	$167	$99.798	2001
10.	Inchon	$46	$89.870	1982
11.	The Nutcracker in 3D	$90	$89.765	2010
12.	Treasure Planet	$180	$83.833	2002
13.	The Postman	$80	$83.346	1997
14.	Red Planet	$100	$82.406	2000
15.	Soldier	$75	$78.912	1998
16.	Gigli	$74	$77.961	2003
17.	How Do You Know?	$120	$77.138	2010
18.	Around the World in 80 Days	$140	$76.700	2004
19.	Ishtar	$55	$76.015	1987
20.	A Sound of Thunder	$80	$74.740	2005

Source: Box Office Mojo

Top 20 SPORT

FASTEST MALE MARATHON RUNNERS

Speed / Name / Country of origin / Year

`2:03:59`	Haile Gebrselassie, Ethiopia / 2008
`2:04:27`	Duncan Kipkemboi Kibet, Kenya / 2009
`2:04:27`	Emmanuel Mutai, Kenya / 2011
`2:04:40`	James Kipsang Kwambai, Kenya / 2009
`2:04:48`	Patrick Makau, Kenya / 2010
`2:04:55`	Paul Tergat, Kenya / 2003
`2:04:55`	Geoffrey Mutai, Kenya / 2010
`2:04:56`	Sammy Korir, Kenya / 2003

Source: IAAF

`2:04:57`	Wilson Kipsang Kiprotich, Kenya / 2010
`2:05:04`	Abel Kirui, Kenya / 2009
`2:05:10`	Samuel Wanjiru, Kenya / 2009
`2:05:13`	Vincent Kipruto, Kenya / 2010
`2:05:15`	Martin Lel, Kenya / 2008
`2:05:18`	Tsegay Kebede, Ethiopia / 2009
`2:05:23`	Lelisa Gemechu Feyisa, Ethiopia / 2010
`2:05:25`	Bado Worku, Ethiopia / 2010
`2:05:27`	Jaouad Gharib, Morocco / 2009
`2:05:30`	Abderrahim Goumri, Morocco / 2008
`2:05:38`	Khalid Khannouchi, USA / 2002
`2:05:39`	Eliud Kiptanui, Kenya / 2010

FASTEST FEMALE MARATHON RUNNERS

Name / Country of origin / Year / Speed

Paula Radcliffe, UK / 2003	`2:15:25`
Catherine N'dereba, Kenya / 2001	`2:18:47`
Mizuki Noguchi, Japan / 2005	`2:19:12`
Mary Keitany, kenya / 2011	`2:19:19`
Irina Mikitenko, Germany / 2008	`2:19:19`
Deena Kastor, USA / 2006	`2:19:36`
Sun Yingjie, China / 2003	`2:19:39`
Yoko Shibui, Japan / 2004	`2:19:41`
Naoko Takahashi, Japan / 2001	`2:19:46`

Zhou Chunxiu, Chiana / 2006	`2:19:51`
Liliya Shobukhova, Russia / 2010	`2:20:25`
Berhane Adere, Ethiopia / 2006	`2:20:42`
Margaret Okayo, Kenya / 2002	`2:20:43`
Tegla Loroupe, Kenya / 1998	`2:20:47`
Galina Bogomalova, Russia / 2006	`2:20:47`
Ingrid Kristiansen, Norway / 1985	`2:21:06`
Joan Benoit, USA / 1985	`2:21:21`
Lyudmila Petrova, Russia / 2006	`2:21:29`
Constantina Dita, Rumania / 2005	`2:21:30`
Svetlana Zakharova, Russia / 2005	`2:21:31`

MOST SNOOKER TITLES

Name / Number of titles won

1 Stephen Hendry 36

2 Steve Davis 28

3 John Higgins 23

4 Ronnie O'Sullivan 22

5 Mark Williams 18

6 Jimmy White 10

7 John Parrot 9

8 Peter Ebdon 8

9 Ken Doherty 6

10 Neil Robertson 6

11 Ray Reardon 5

12 Ding Junhui 4

13 Stephen Lee 4

14 Stephen Maguire 4

15 Paul Hunter 3

16 Shaun Murphy 3

17 James Wattana 3

20 Cliff Thorburn 2*

18 Dominic Hale 2

19 Graeme Dott 2

Source: Snooker.org

* Tony Knowles, Alan McManus, Doug Mountjoy, Dennis Taylor and Ali Carter have also won two titles.

Stephen Hendry (pictured) was the youngest ever snooker world champion at the age of 21.

Canadian Cliff Thorburn won the Snooker World Championship in 1980.

Did you know?

It is believed that 80 percent of the world's gold lies undiscovered under the ground! Of all the gold in use today, 75 percent has been extracted over the last 100 years.

GOLD PRODUCERS

Country	Tons (short/metric)
1. China	346 / 314
2. Australia	250 / 227
3. USA	238 / 216
4. South Africa	226 / 205
5. Russia	204 / 185
6. Peru	198 / 180
7. Canada	105 / 95
8. Ghana	99 / 90
9. Indonesia	99 / 90
10. Uzbekistan	88 / 80
11. Mexico	78 / 71
12. Papua	71 / 64
13. Argentina	64 / 58
14. Mali	55 / 50
15. Colombia	46 / 42
16. Chile	43 / 39
17. Tanzania	40 / 36
18. Philippines	40 / 36
19. Bolivia	17 / 15
20. Kazakhstan	11 / 10

Did you know?

The San Francisco 49ers football team were named after the 1849 Gold Rush miners in California.

SILVER PRODUCERS

Country / millions of ounces/grams

1. Mexico 128.6 / 3,629 **2. Peru** 116.1 / 3,291 **3. China** 99.2 / 2,812 **4. Australia** 59.9 / 1,698 **5. Bolivia** 41.0 / 1,162

6. Chile 41.0 / 1,162 **7. USA** 38.6 / 1,094 **8. Poland** 37.7 / 1,069 **9. Russia** 36.8 / 1,043 **10. Argentina** 20.6 / 584

11. Canada 18.0 / 510 **12. Kazakhstan** 17.6 / 499 **13. Turkey** 12.3 / 349 **14. Morocco** 9.7 / 247 **15. India** 9.7 / 275

16. Sweden 9.2 / 260 **17. Indonesia** 6.9 / 196

18. Guatamala 6.3 / 179 **19. Iran** 3.4 / 96

20. South Africa 2.8 / 79

COPPER PRODUCERS

Country	Tons (short/metric)
1. Chile	5,875,649 / 5,330,300
2. USA	1,444,028 / 1,310,000
3. Peru	1,397,584 / 1,267,867
4. China	1,058,218 / 960,000
5. Australia	976 647 / 886,000
6. Russia	826 733 / 750,000
7. Indonesia	697 322 / 632,600
8. Canada	669 103 / 607,000
9. Zambia	601,861 / 546,000
10. Poland	472,891 / 429,000
11. Kazakhstan	462,971 / 420,000
12. Iran	274,475 / 249,000
13. Mexico	271,822 / 246,593
14. Congo	259,043 / 235,000
15. Brazil	227,076 / 206,000
16. Argentina	172,953 / 156,900
17. Mongolia	142 749 / 129,500
18. South Africa	120,152 / 109,000
19. Bulgaria	115,743 / 105,000
20. Uzbekistan	104 720 / 95,000

Source: United States Geological Survey Mineral Resources Program

Did you know?
The Great Pyramid of Giza, dating back to around 2470 BC, had a water supply system that was constructed partly of copper.

RICHEST DEAD CELEBRITIES*

Celebrity / Year died / How much made in their most lucrative year (in millions $/£)

	Celebrity	Year died	Amount
1	Yves Saint Laurent (fashion designer)	2008	$350 (£215)
2	Michael Jackson (singer)	2009	$275 (£169)
3	Richard Rodgers (songwriter) and	1979	
	Oscar Hammerstein (songwriter)	1960	$235 (£145)
4	Elvis Presley (singer)	1977	$60 (£37)
5	J.R.R. Tolkien (author)	1973	$50 (£31)
6	Charles M. Schultz (cartoonist)	2000	$35 (£22)
7	Heath Ledger (actor)	2008	$20 (£12)
8	Albert Einstein (physicist)	1955	$18 (£11)
9	John Lennon (singer/songwriter)	1980	$17 (£11)
10	Aaron Spelling (TV and film producer)	2006	$15 (£9)
11	Stieg Larsson (author)	2004	$15 (£9)
12	Theodor (Dr.) Seuss (writer/cartoonist)	1991	$15 (£9)
13	Andy Warhol (artist)	1987	$9 (£5.5)
14	Michael Crichton (author)	2008	$9 (£5.5)
15	Jimi Hendrix (singer/musician)	1970	$8 (£5)
16	Marilyn Monroe (actress)	1962	$6.5 (£4)
17	Steve McQueen (actor)	1980	$6 (£3.7)
18	Paul Newman (actor)	2008	$5 (£3)
19	James Dean (actor)	1955	$5 (£3)
20	Marvin Gaye (singer)	1984	$3.5 (£2.2)

* Based on the most financially successful year of their respective careers.

From left to right:
Sharon Osbourne,
Sean Connery and
Russell Crowe.

Sources:
Technorati.com,
Guardian Media

PREMATURE OBITUARIES OF THE LAST 20 YEARS

Name / Profession / Where reported

1 Gabrielle Giffords / Politician / CNN, Fox News

2 Russell Crowe / Actor / Radio

3 Jeff Goldblum / Actor / TV in Australia

4 Steve Jobs / Entrepreneur / Bloomberg

5 Donald Trautman / Catholic bishop / Vatican newspaper

6 Will Ferrell / Comedian / iNewswire

7 George Kaye / Musician / *Daily Mirror*

8 Sharon Osbourne / TV celebrity / ABC News

9 Katharine Sergava / Actress and dancer / *Daily Telegraph*

10 John Darwin / Prison officer / *Hartlepool Mail*

11 Dorothy Fay / Actress / *Daily Telegraph*

12 Arthur C. Clarke / Writer / Newsletter

13 Gabriel Garcia Marquez / Writer / *La Republica*

14 Dave Swarbrick / Musician / *Daily Telegraph*

15 Maureen O'Hara / Actress / Internet Movie Database

16 Lonnie Mack / Rock guitarist / Foreword to a book

17 Adam Rich / Actor / *Might* magazine

18 Humphrey / Downing Street Cat / Government press officer

19 Jimmy Savile / Broadcaster / BBC Radio 1

20 Sean Connery / Actor / Widespread rumor

Top Twenty

BIGGEST-SELLING DAILY NEWSPAPERS IN THE WORLD

Foreign Title (English Title)	Country	Sales (millions)
1 *Yomiuri Shimbun* (*Free Press Daily*)	Japan	13.7
2 *Asahi Shimbun* (*Morning Sun News*)	Japan	12.1
3 *Mainichi Shimbun* (*Daily News*)	Japan	5.6
4 *Nihon Keizai Shimbun* (*Japan Economic Times*)	Japan	4.6
5 *Chunichi Shimbun* (*Chunichi News*)	Japan	4.5
6 *The Times of India*	India	4.2
7 *Bild* (*Picture*)	Germany	3.6
8 *Canako Xiaoxi* (*Reference News*)	China	3.2
9 *The Sun*	UK	3
10 *Renmin Ribao* (*People's Daily*)	China	2.8
11 *Daily Mail*	UK	2.3
12 *Chosan Ilbo* (*Korea Daily*)	South Korea	2.3
13 *USA Today*	USA	2.3
14 *Tokyo Sports*	Japan	2.2
15 *Sankei Shimbun* (*Industrial and Economic Newspaper*)	Japan	2.2
16 *JoongAng Ilbo* (*JoongAng Daily*)	South Korea	2.2
17 *Dainik Jagran*	India	2.2
18 *Dong-a Ilbo* (*East Asia Daily*)	South Korea	2.1
19 *The Wall Street Journal*	USA	2
20 *Nikkan Sports*	Japan	1.9

The Yomiuri Shimbun is printed twice every day and is one of five daily papers in Japan.

The Boston Newsletter, published in 1704 was one of the first newspapers printed in the US.

Massive Fire Blazes Downtown

FOUR DEAD, 12 INJURED

Sleeping Smoker to Blame, says Fire Commisioner

April 15-- Ullamcorper veniam aliquip duis, consequat vero illum in dolor magna dolore suscipit delenit vel augue, dolore. Eros iusto, commodo eum cu wisi nulla nostrud minim nulla facilisis, aliquip dolore nisl feugait volutpat dignissim. Odio nulla amet ex veniam erat su...

THOUSANDS OF DOLLARS IN DAMAGES

Nulla lorem nonummy dignissim molestic, vero te et dignissim iusto. Autem laoreet nostrud diam vel in iriure lobortis vel cum sit, ea tation duis facilisi, aliquam feugait, hendrerit facilisis autem iusto nulla eu dolor illum. Ut, aliquip, qui vel nostrud lobortis zzril ullamcorper, facilisis zzril vel aliquam illum sed te adipiscing quis, vulputate ut delenit facilisis et minim eros euismod minim. Eu, velit elit accumsan tation commodo consequat lorem nisl. Nisl luptatum, duis eu augue odio eu vero, et, consequat dolore vel esse praesent lobortis et consequat ad, luptatum qui.

Erat wisi elit, vulputate commodo suscipit lorem te delenit molestic nostrud blandit elit molestie, zzril vero eum, luptatum volutpat nonummy feugait aliquip amet ipsum illum dolore. Commodo zzril nonummy dolore dolore wisi hendrerit duis vero, tincidunt wisi, duis sed, consectetuer nulla dolore zzril ut ut facilisis facilisi veniam, velit feugait, accumsan. Eros et nulla vulputate in erat volutpat duis ea dolore consequat.

Tation quis dolore qui velit augue sed et illum, et, sit dolor. Autem esse ex vel ut consequat qui ut eros quis accumsan aliquam adipiscing, laoreet aliquip feugiat tation sit dignissim, delenit nisl praesent ut...

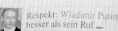

COUNTRIES BY NEWSPAPER CIRCULATION

Country / Daily circulation (millions)

1 China 96.7

2 Japan 71.7

3 India 62.4

4 USA 55.6

5 Germany 24.8

6 UK 18

7 Mexico 9.4

8 France 8.6

9 Ukraine 8.5

10 Russia 7.9

11 Brazil 7.4

12 Italy 6.1

13 Pakistan 5.8

14 Hungary 4.7

15 Spain 4.6

16 Indonesia 4.4

17 Poland 3.9

18 Sweden 3.7

19 Switzerland 2.8

20 Norway 2.7

*Source: UNESCO Institute for Statistics

ENGLISH LANGUAGE NEWSPAPERS

	Title	Country	Daily circulation
1	The Times of India	India	4.2 million
2	The Sun	UK	3 million
3	USA Today	USA	2.5 million
4	Daily Mail	UK	2.3 million
5	The Wall Street Journal	USA	2.1 million
6	The Hindu	India	1.5 million
7	Deccan Chronicle	India	1.35 million
8	Daily Mirror	UK	1.2 million
9	Hindustan Times	India	1.14 million
10	The New York Times	USA	877,000
11	Daily Star	UK	714,000
12	Daily Express	UK	640,000
13	Daily Telegraph	UK	624,000
14	The Economic Times	India	620,000
15	Los Angeles Times	USA	601,000
16	The Washington Post	USA	545,000
17	Herald Sun	Australia	515,000
18	New York Daily News	USA	512,000
19	New York Post	USA	502,000
20	The Sun-Herald	Australia	443,000

MOST POPULAR ARTISTS

1 Vincent van Gogh
2 Claude Monet

3 Jan Vermeer
4 Salvador Dalí

5 Pierre Auguste Renoir
6 Edouarde Manet

7 Diego Velázquez
8 Edgar Degas

9 J.M.W. Turner
10 Francisco Goya

11 John Constable
12 Pablo Picasso

13 Gustav Klimt
14 Caravaggio

15 Peter Paul Rubens
16 Jan van Eyck

17 Rembrandt van Rijn
18 Leonardo da Vinci

19 Andy Warhol
20 Toulouse-Lautrec

* Order produced by combining popular surveys.

BEST KNOWN ART IMAGES

1 *Mona Lisa* — Leonardo da Vinci (painting)
2 *The Creation of Adam* — Michelangelo (fresco)
3 *The Birth of Venus* — Sandro Botticelli (painting)
4 *The Last Supper* — Leonardo da Vinci (painting)
5 *David* — Michelangelo (sculpture)
6 *Blue Willow* — Thomas Minton (ceramic art)
7 *The Great Wave off Kanagawa* — Katsushika Hokusai (woodblock print)
8 *Sunflowers* — Vincent van Gogh (painting)
9 *Persistence of Memory* — Salvador Dalí (painting)
10 *The Scream* — Edvard Munch (painting)
11 *Water Lillies* — Claude Monet (painting
12 *American Gothic* — Grant Wood (painting)
13 *Raising the Flag on Iwo Jima** — Joseph John Rosenthal (photograph)
14 *The Kiss* — Auguste Rodin (sculpture)
15 *Guernica* — Pablo Picasso (painting)
16 *Campbell's Soup* — Andy Warhol (painting)
17 *Starry Night* — Vincent van Gogh (painting)
18 *Poppy Field* — Claude Monet (painting)
19 *Marilyn Diptych* — Andy Warhol (painting)
20 *Christ of St. John of the Cross* — Salvador Dali (painting)

Order based on international poll of most iconic artwork images of all time.
* This photograph was posed by the photographer and therefore regarded as art, not news.

MOST EXPENSIVE WORKS OF ART (PAINTINGS)

Title / Date / Artist / Adjusted price (millions)

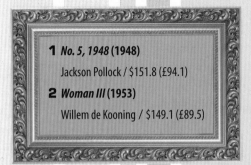

1 *No. 5, 1948* (1948)
Jackson Pollock / $151.8 (£94.1)
2 *Woman III* (1953)
Willem de Kooning / $149.1 (£89.5)

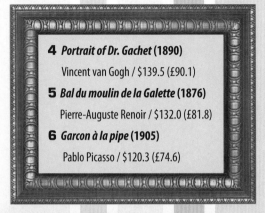

3
Portrait of Adele Bloch-Bauer I (1907)
Gustav Klimt
$145.3 (£88.6)

4 *Portrait of Dr. Gachet* (1890)
Vincent van Gogh / $139.5 (£90.1)
5 *Bal du moulin de la Galette* (1876)
Pierre-Auguste Renoir / $132.0 (£81.8)
6 *Garcon à la pipe* (1905)
Pablo Picasso / $120.3 (£74.6)

7 *Nude, Green Leaves and Bust* (1932)
Pablo Picasso
$106.6 (£66.1)
8 *Portrait of Joseph Roulin* (1889)
Vincent van Gogh
$102.7 (£63.7)

9 *Dora Maar au Chat* (1941)
Pablo Picasso
$101.7 (£63.1)
10 *Irises* (1889)
Vincent van Gogh
$102.0 (£63.2)

11 *Eight Elvises* (1963)
Andy Warhol / $100.9 (£62.6)
12 *Portrait de l'artiste sans barbe* (1889)
Vincent van Gogh
$95.3 (£59.1)

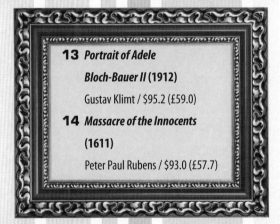

13 *Portrait of Adele Bloch-Bauer II* (1912)
Gustav Klimt / $95.2 (£59.0)
14 *Massacre of the Innocents* (1611)
Peter Paul Rubens / $93.0 (£57.7)

15 *Triptych 1976* (1976)
Francis Bacon / $87.0 (£53.9)
16 *False Start* (1959)
Jasper Johns / $86.6 (£53.7)
17 *A Wheatfield with Cypresses* (1889)
Vincent van Gogh / $86.3 (£53.50)

18 *Les Noces de Pierette* (1905)
Pablo Picasso
$85.6 (£53.1)

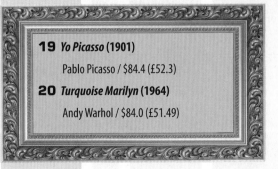

19 *Yo Picasso* (1901)
Pablo Picasso / $84.4 (£52.3)
20 *Turquoise Marilyn* (1964)
Andy Warhol / $84.0 (£51.49)

* The most copied artwork image of all time is The Queen's Head, a sculpture by Arnold Machin, which has been reproduced more than 200 billion times on British stamps.

35

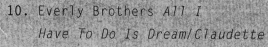

UK HITS OF THE 1950s

1. Bill Haley & His Comets *Rock Around the Clock*
2. Paul Anka *Diana*
3. Harry Belafonte *Mary's Boy Child*
4. Anton Karas *The Harry Lime Theme (The Third Man)*
5. Emile Ford & The Checkmates *What Do You Want To Make Those Eyes At Me For*
6. Elvis Presley *Jailhouse Rock*
7. Adam Faith *What Do You Want*
8. Cliff Richard & The Shadows *Living Doll*
9. Elvis Presley *All Shook Up*
10. Everly Brothers *All I Have To Do Is Dream/Claudette*
11. Frankie Laine *I Believe*
12. Al Martino *Here In My Heart*
13. Slim Whitman *Rose Marie*
14. David Whitfield *Cara Mia*
15. Eddie Calvert *Oh Mein Papa*
16. Russ Conway *Side Saddle*
17. Buddy Holly *It Doesn't Matter Anymore*
18. Elvis Presley *A Fool Such As I/I Need Your Love Tonight*
19. Russ Conway *Roulette*
20. Bobby Darin *Dream Lover*

Source: OCC

US HITS OF THE 1950s

1. Elvis Presley *Don't Be Cruel/Hound Dog*
2. Bill Haley & His Comets *Rock Around The Clock*
3. Pat Boone *Love Letters In The Sand*
4. Bobby Darin *Mack The Knife*
5. Guy Mitchell *Singing The Blues*
6. Roger Williams *Autumn Leaves*
7. Elvis Presley *Love Me Tender*
8. Elvis Presley *Heartbreak Hotel*
9. Mitch Miller *The Yellow Rose of Texas*
10. Tennessee Ernie Ford *Sixteen Tons*
11. Four Aces *Love is a Many Splendored Thing*
12. Elvis Presley *Jailhouse Rock*
13. Elvis Presley *All Shook Up*
14. Elvis Presley *Teddy Bear*
15. Johnny Horton *The Battle of New Orleans*
16. Gogi Grant *The Wayward Wind*
17. Jim Lowe *The Green Door*
18. Nelson Riddle *Lisbon Antigua*
19. Dean Martin *Memories are Made of This*
20. Danny and the Juniors *At the Hop*

Source: Rockmaven.com

UK HITS OF THE 1960s

1 The Beatles *She Loves You*

2 The Beatles *I Want To Hold Your Hand*

3 Ken Dodd *Tears*

4 The Beatles *Can't Buy Me Love*

5 The Beatles *I Feel Fine*

6 The Seekers *The Carnival Is Over*

7 The Beatles *Day Tripper/We Can Work It Out*

8 Engelbert Humperdinck *Release Me*

9 Elvis Presley *It's Now Or Never*

10 Tom Jones *Green Green Grass Of Home*

11 Engelbert Humperdinck *Last Waltz*

12 Acker Bilk *Stranger On The Shore*

13 Frank Ifield *I Remember You*

14 Cliff Richard & The Shadows *The Young Ones*

15 The Tornados *Telstar*

16 Rolf Harris *Two Little Boys*

17 The Beatles *Help*

18 Dave Clark Five *Glad All Over*

19 The Searchers *Needle And Pins*

20 The Beatles *Hey Jude*

Source: OCC

TOP US HITS OF THE 60s
Source: Billboard

1 Chubby Checker The Twist
2 The Beatles Hey Jude 3 Percy Faith A Summer Place
4 Bobby Lewis Tossin' and Turnin'
5 The beatles I want to Hold Your Hand
6 5th Dimension Aquarius/Let the Sun Shine
7 The Monkees I'm A Believer
8 Elvis Presley Are You Lonesome Tonight? 9 The Archies Sugar Sugar
10 Marvin Gaye I Heard it Through the Grapevine 11 Ray Charles I Can't Stop Loving You

12 Paul Mauriat Love is Blue 13 Everly Brothers Cathy's Clown
14 Elvis Presley It's Now or Never
15 The Rolling Stones Honky Tonk Woman
16 Jimmy Dean Big Bad John
17 Lulu To Sir With Love
18 The Rascals People Got to Be Free 19 Sly & the Family Stone Everyday People
20 The Four Seasons Big Girls Don't Cry

MOST DOWNLOADED SMARTPHONE APPS*

Blackberry / Apple

1
Blaq for Blackberry Playbook /
The Heist
2
Poynt / Keith Lemon's Mouthboard!

3
Toss It! /
Angry Birds
4
BlackBerry Messenger /
The Sims 3

5
MP3 Ringtone Creator /
Angry Birds Rio
6
Slacker Radio / Flugtap Pro

7
Photo Editor /
Touchgrind BMX
8
Ka-Glom Free /
Fifa 11 by EA Sports

9
Police Scanner Radio /
Siege Hero
10
Radio for Blackberry /
Fight Night Champion

11
Message Prevue / Fruit Ninja
12
Night Vision / Tiger Woods PGA
13
A+ Chat for Facebook /
Tiny Wings

14
Angry Farm / Battlefield: Bad Company
15
One Touch Flashlight /
Stupid Zombies

16
EasyBartender 14000 recipes /
The Sims 3 Ambitions
17
BeBuzz - LED Light Colors /
Where's Wally? in Hollywood

18
Aces Solitaire pack 2 /
Tetris

19
Jigsaw Plus /
Tunein Radio Pro

20
Doodle Jump /
Angry Birds Seasons

Sources:

Blackberry, Apple

* At time of printing

COUNTRIES WITH MOST LANDLINE TELEPHONES

Country / Number of lines (millions)

1 China 313.7	**11** Vietnam 29.6
2 USA 150.0	**12** Iran 24.8
3 Germany 48.7	**13** South Korea 21.3
4 Japan 47.6	**14** Mexico 20.7
5 Russia 44.2	**15** Spain 20.2
6 Brazil 41.5	**16** Italy 20.0
7 France 36.4	**17** Canada 18.3
8 India 35.1	**18** Turkey 17.5
9 UK 33.2	**19** Taiwan 14.3
10 Indonesia 30.4	**20** Ukraine 13.2

Source: International Telecommunication Union

Longest Phone Call

The record for the longest ever phone call, a jaw-breaking 40 hours, was set by Tony Wright of Cornwall, UK, in September 2007 on a Tesco Internet Phone, who talked to a succession of volunteers, starting with TV weather forecaster Sian Lloyd. The previous record, 39 hours 18 minutes, was set by Sandra Kobel and Stephen Hafner of Switzerland in 2005.

COUNTRIES WITH MOST MOBILE PHONES

Country / Number of phones (millions)

1 China 853.4	**2** India 771.2
3 USA 292.9	**4** Russia 213.9
5 Brazil 205.1	**6** Indonesia 168.3
7 Japan 107.5	**8** Germany 107.0
9 Pakistan 101.6	**10** Mexico 88.8
11 Italy 88.6	**12** Philippines 78.0
13 Nigeria 76.0	**14** UK 75.8
15 Turkey 66.0	
16 Bangladesh 65.1	
17 France 58.7	**18** Thailand 56.2
19 Ukraine 54.4	**20** Iran 52.0

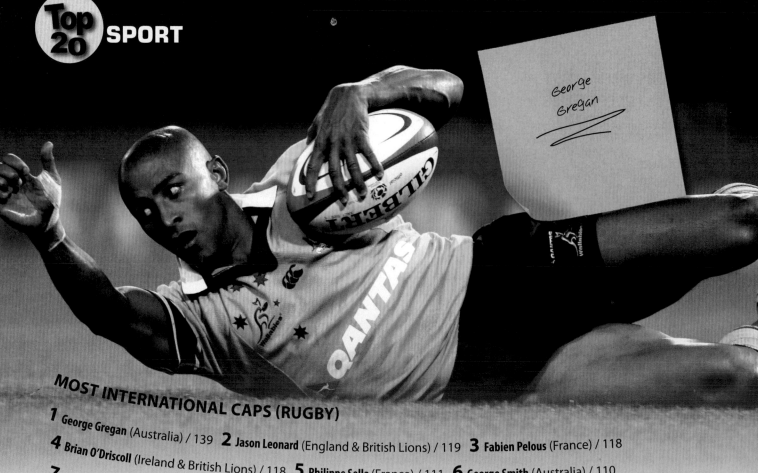

George Gregan

MOST INTERNATIONAL CAPS (RUGBY)

1 George Gregan (Australia) / 139 **2** Jason Leonard (England & British Lions) / 119 **3** Fabien Pelous (France) / 118

4 Brian O'Driscoll (Ireland & British Lions) / 118 **5** Philippe Sella (France) / 111 **6** George Smith (Australia) / 110

7 Ronan O'Gara (Ireland & British Lions) / 110 **8** John Hayes (Ireland & British Lions) / 106 **9** Victor Matfield (South Africa) / 105

10 Stephen Jones (Wales & British Lions) / 105 **11** Chris Paterson (Scotland) / 104 **12** Gareth Thomas (Wales & British Lions) / 103

13 Percy Montgomery (South Africa) / 102 **14** John Smit (South Africa) / 102 **15** Martyn Williams (Wales & British Lions) / 102

16 Stephen Larkham (Australia) / 102 **17** Alessandro Troncon (Italy) / 101 **18** David Campese (Australia) / 101

19 Raphael Ibanez (France) / 98 **20** Peter Stringer (Ireland) / 98

MOST RUGBY LEAGUE CHALLENGE CUP WINS

Team / Wins	
1 Wigan Warriors / 17	**11** Hull FC / 3
2 St. Helens / 12	**12** Oldham Roughyeds / 3
3 Leeds Rhinos / 11	**13** Featherstone Rovers / 3
4 Warrington Wolves / 7	**14** Swinton Lions / 3
5 Widnes Vikings / 7	**15** Batley Bulldogs / 3
6 Huddersfield Giants / 6	**16** Dewsbury Rams / 2
7 Halifax / 5	**17** Hunslet Hawks / 2
8 Bradford Bulls / 5	**18** Broughton Rangers / 2
9 Wakefield Trinity Wildcats / 5	**19** Leigh Centurions / 2
10 Castleford Tigers / 4	**20** Rochdale Hornets / 1

Source: Carnegiechallengecup.co.uk

MOST GRAND SLAM TENNIS TOURNAMENT WINS (MALE)

1 Roger Federer 16
2 Pete Sampras 14
3 Roy Emerson 12
4 Rod Laver 11
5 Bjorn Borg 11
6 Rafael Nadal 9
7 Ken Rosewall 8
8 Jimmy Connors 8
9 Ivan Lendl 8
10 Andre Agassi 8
11 John Newcombe 7
12 John McEnroe 7
13 Mats Wilander 7
14 Boris Becker 6
15 Stefan Edberg 6
16 Manolo Santana 4
17 Jim Courier 4
18 Guillermo Vilas 4
19 Arthur Ashe 3
20 Jan Kodes 3

Source: Sportige.com

MOST GRAND SLAM TENNIS TOURNAMENT WINS (FEMALE)

1 Margaret Court 24
2 Steffi Graf 22
3 Helen Wills Moody 19
4 Chris Evert 18
5 Martina Navratilova 18
6 Serena Williams 13
7 Billie Jean King 12
8 Monica Seles 9
9 Justine Henin 7
10 Evonne Goolagong Cawley 7
11 Venus Williams 7
12 Maria Bueno 7
13 Martina Hingis 5
14 Hana Mandlikova 4
15 Arantxa Sanchez Vicario 4
16 Kim Clijsters 4
17 Darlene Hard 3
18 Maria Sharapova 3
19 Ann Haydon Jones 3
20 Virginia Wade 3

41

UK HITS OF THE 1990s

1 Elton John

Candle In The Wind 1997/Something About The Way You Look Tonight

2 Robson & Jerome

Unchained Melody/White Cliffs Of Dover

3 Wet Wet Wet *Love Is All Around*

4 Aqua *Barbie Girl*

5 Cher *Believe*

6 Bryan Adams

(Everything I Do) I Do It For You

7 Various Artists *Perfect Day*

8 Britney Spears *Baby One More Time*

9 Puff Daddy & Faith Evans Featuring 112

I'll Be Missing You

10 Whitney Houston *I Will Always Love You*

11 Baddiel & Skinner & The Lightning Seeds

Three Lions

12 Celine Dion *My Heart Will Go On*

13 Coolio Featuring LV

Gangsta's Paradise

14 The Fugees *Killing Me Softly*

15 Spice Girls *Wannabe*

16 All Saints *Never Ever*

17 Celine Dion *Think Twice*

18 Run DMC vs Jason Nevins

It's Like That

19 Steps *Heartbeat/Tragedy*

20 Michael Jackson *Earth Song*

Source: OCC

US HITS OF THE 1990s

1 Mariah Carey & Boyz II Men *One Sweet Day*

2 Whitney Houston *I Will Always Love You*

3 Boyz II Men *I'll Make Love To You*

4 Los Del Rio *Macarena*

5 Elton John *Candle In The Wind 1997/Something About The Way You Look Tonight*

6 Boyz II Men *End Of The Road*

7 Brandy & Monica *The Boy is Mine*

8 Santana Featuring Rob Thomas *Smooth*

9 All-4-One *I Swear*

10 Toni Braxton *Un-break My Heart*

11 Puff Daddy & Faith Evans Featuring 112 *I'll Be Missing You*

12 Kriss Kross *Jump*

13 Janet Jackson *That's The Way Love Goes*

14 Mariah Carey *Dreamlover*

15 Mariah Carey *Fantasy*

16 Bone Thugs-N-Harmony *Tha Crossroads*

17 Bryan Adams *(Everything I Do) I Do It For You*

18 Michael Jackson *Black or White*

19 Snow *Informer*

20 UB40 *Can't Help Falling In Love*

Source: Billboard

UK HITS OF THE 2000s

1 Will Young *Evergreen/Anything Is Possible*

2 Gareth Gates *Unchained Melody*

3 Tony Christie Featuring Peter Kay *(Is This The Way To) Amirillo*

4 Shaggy Featuring Rikrok *It Wasn't Me*

5 Alexandra Burke *Hallelujah*

6 Band Aid 20 *Do They Know It's Christmas?*

7 Kylie Minogue *Can't Get You Out Of My Head*

8 Hear'Say *Pure And Simple*

9 Shayne Ward *That's My Goal*

10 Bob The Builder *Can We Fix It?*

11 Leona Lewis *Bleeding Love*

12 Gnarls Barkley *Crazy*

13 Atomic Kitten *Whole Again*

14 Kings Of Leon *Sex On Fire*

15 Lady Gaga *Poker Face*

16 Leona Lewis *A Moment Like This*

17 Enrique Iglesias *Hero*

18 Black Eyed Peas *I Gotta Feeling*

19 X Factor Finalists *Hero*

20 DJ Otzi *Hey Baby*

Source: OCC

US HITS OF THE 2000s

1. Mariah Carey *We Belong Together*
2. Black Eyed Peas *I Got A Feeling*
3. Eminem *Lose Yourself*
4. Usher Featuring Lil Jon & Ludacris *Yeah!*
5. Black Eyed Peas *Boom Boom Pow*
6. Destiny's Child *Independent Women*
7. Beyoncé *Irreplaceable*
8. Flo rida Featuring T-Pain *Low*
9. Santana Featuring The Product G&B *Maria Maria*
10. Ashanti *Foolish*
11. Nelly Featuring Kelly Rowland *Dilemma*
12. Kanye West Featuring Jamie Foxx *Gold Digger*
13. 50 Cent *In Da Club*
14. Beyonce Featuring Sean Paul *Baby Boy*
15. Outkast *Hey Ya!*
16. Mario *Let Me Love You*
17. 50 Cent Featuring Olivia *Candy Shop*
18. Beyonce Featuring Jay-Z *Crazy In Love*
19. Usher *Burn*
20. Nelly *Hot In Herre*

Source: Billboard

BUSIEST LONDON UNDERGROUND STATIONS

Station / Number of users per year (millions)

	Station	Users		Station	Users
1	Victoria	77.4	11	Bond Street	36.9
2	Waterloo	76.0	12	Leicester Square	35.6
3	Oxford Circus	74.0	13	Tottenham Court Road	34.9
4	King's Cross St. Pancras	66.2	14	Holborn	30.1
5	London Bridge	61.5	15	Green Park	28.3
6	Liverpool Street	60.9	16	South Kensington	28.2
7	Paddington	42.0	17	Euston	28.1
8	Bank & Monument	40.7	18	Hammersmith	27.4
9	Canary Wharf	39.6	19	Stratford	27.0
10	Piccadilly Circus	38.6	20	Finsbury Park	26.3

Source: Transport for London

Liverpool Street Station in London

BIGGEST UNDERGROUND RAIL SYSTEMS

City / Number of stations

#	City	Stations	#	City	Stations	#	City	Stations	#	City	Stations
1	New York	423	6	Madrid	232	11	Moscow	146	16	Osaka	104
2	Paris	300	7	Tokyo	205	12	Chicago	144	17	Santiago	100
3	Seoul	298	8	Berlin	173	13	Barcelona	135	18	Stockholm	100
4	London	268	9	Beijing	172	14	Delhi	133	19	Munich	96
5	Shanghai	235	10	Mexico City	147	15	Guangzhou	132	20	Vienna	90

BUSIEST UNDERGROUND SYSTEMS

City / Number of daily riders (millions)

#	City	Daily riders
1	Tokyo	8.7
2	Moscow	6.6
3	Seoul	5.6
4	New York	4.3
5	Paris	4.1
6	Beijing	4.0
7	Mexico City	3.9
8	Hong Kong	3.6
9	Shanghai	3.6
10	London	3.0
11	Osaka	2.4
12	St. Petersburg	2.3
13	Sao Paolo	2.0
14	Cairo	1.9
15	Guangzhou	1.9
16	Singapore	1.8
17	Madrid	1.8
18	Kiev	1.8
19	Santiago	1.7
20	Prague	1.6

IVOR NOVELLO AWARD WINNERS

Winner / Number of awards

1.	Paul McCartney	18
2.	John Lennon	15
3.	Lord Andrew Lloyd-Webber	14
4.	Tim Rice	12
5.	Elton John	12
6.	Robin Gibb	11
7.	Barry Gibb	11
8.	Maurice Gibb	10
9.	Tony Macauley	8
10.	Sting	8
11.	Mike Stock	8
12.	Bernie Taupin	8
13.	Pete Waterman	8
14.	Matt Aitken	8
15.	Lionel Bart	7
16.	Leslie Bricusse	7
17.	Phil Collins	7
18.	George Fenton	6
19.	George Michael	6
20.	Michael Kamen	6

Source: BASCA (British Academy of Songwriters, Composers and Authors)

MOST MTV AWARDS

Artist / Number of awards — Source: MTV

1.	Madonna	20	11.	Michael Jackson	8
2.	Peter Gabriel	13	12.	A-ha	7
3.	R.E.M.	12	13.	En Vogue	7
4.	Eminem	12	14.	*N Sync	7
5.	Green Day	11	15.	Justin Timberlake	7
6.	Aerosmith	11	16.	Red Hot Chili Peppers	7
7.	Lady Gaga	11	17.	The Smashing Pumpkins	7
8.	Beyoncé	10	18.	Beck	6
9.	Fatboy Slim	9	19.	U2	6
10.	Janet Jackson	9	20.	Don Henley*	5

*Gnarls Barkley, Herbie Hancock, Jay-Z, INXS, Missy Elliott, Nirvana, No Doubt, Outkast, P!nk, Ricky Martin and TLC all have five awards.

MERCURY PRIZE WINNERS

1992
Primal Scream *Screamadelica*

1993
Suede *Suede*

1994
M People *Elegant Slumming*

1995
Portishead *Dummy*

1996
Pulp *Different Class*

1997
Roni Size & Reprazent *New Forms*

1998
Gomez *Bring It On*

1999
Talvin Singh *OK*

2000
Badly Drawn Boy
The Hour Of Bewilderbeast

2001
P.J. Harvey
Stories From The City, Stories From The Sea

2002
Ms Dynamite *A Little Deeper*

2003
Dizzee Rascal *Boy In Da Corner*

2004
Franz Ferdinand *Franz Ferdinand*

2005
Antony & The Johnsons *I Am A Bird Now*

2006
Arctic Monkeys
Whatever People Say I Am, That's What I'm Not

2007
Klaxons *Myths Of The Near Future*

2008
Elbow *A Seldom Seen Kid*

2009
Speech Debelle *Speech Therapy*

2010
The XX *The XX*

MOST BRIT AWARDS

Artist / Number of awards

1.	Robbie Williams	17	**8.**	Spice Girls	5	**15.**	The Beatles	4
2.	Annie Lennox	8	**9.**	Arctic Monkeys	5	**16.**	Blue	4
3.	Take That	8	**10.**	Phil Collins	5	**17.**	Dido	4
4.	U2	7	**11.**	Prince	5	**18.**	Manic Street Preachers	4
5.	Oasis	6	**12.**	George Michael	5	**19.**	Paul Weller	4
6.	Coldplay	6	**13.**	Freddie Mercury	5	**20.**	Bjork	4
7.	Michael Jackson	6	**14.**	Elton John	4			

Source: BPI

Robbie Williams' tally includes 5 awards won with Take That. George Michael's tally includes 3 with Wham! Freddie Mercury's tally includes 3 with Queen (two of the awards were won posthumously).

Did you know?

The youngest person to win a Grammy is LeAnn Rimes, who scooped the awards for Best New Artist and Best Female Country Vocal Performance at the age of 14.

MOST GRAMMY AWARDS

Artist / Number of awards

1. Georg Solti / 31
2. Quincy Jones / 27
3. Alison Krauss / 26
4. Pierre Boulez / 26
5. Vladimir Horowitz / 25
6. Stevie Wonder / 22
7. U2 / 22
8. John Williams / 21
9. Henry Mancini / 20
10. Bruce Springsteen / 20
11. Vince Gill / 20
12. Aretha Franklin / 18
13. Paul McCartney / 18
14. Pat Metheny / 18
15. Jimmy Sturr / 18
16. Ray Charles / 17
17. Eric Clapton / 17
18. Al Schmitt / 17
19. Beyoncé / 16
20. Leonard Bernstein / 16

Source: Grammy.com

Top 20

HIGHEST EARNING SPORTSMEN

Name / Sport played / Money earned in a year (millions of $)

1 Tiger Woods (Golf) — $ 90.5

2 Roger Federer (Tennis) — $ 61.8

3 Phil Mickelson (Golf) — $ 61.7

4 Floyd Merriweather Jr (Boxing) — $ 61.3

5 LeBron James (Basketball) — $ 45.8

6 Lionel Messi (Association Football) — $ 44

7 David Beckham (Association Football) — $ 40.5

8 Cristiano Ronaldo (Association Football) — $ 40

9 Manny Pacquiao (Boxing) — $ 38

10 Alex Rodriguez (Baseball) — $ 37

11 Ichiro Suzuki (Baseball) — $ 37

12 Shaquille O' Neal (Basketball) — $ 36.8

13 Valentino Rossi (Motor Racing) — $ 34.4

14 Yao Ming (Basketball) — $ 61.3

15 Kobe Bryant (Basketball) — $ 33

16 Peyton Manning (Association Football) — $ 31

17 Derek Jeter (American Football) — $ 30.8

18 Dwayne Wade (Basketball) — $ 27.8

19 Matthew Stanford (American Football) — $ 27.7

20 Rafael Nadal (Tennis) — $ 27.5

BIGGEST SPORTS STADIUMS BY CAPACITY

Stadium (location) / Capacity

1 May Day Stadium, Pyongyang (North Korea) / 150,000   **2** Salt Lake Stadium, Kolkata (India) / 120,000

3 Michigan Stadium, Ann Arbor (USA) / 109,901   **4** Beaver Stadium, Pennsylvania (USA) / 107,283

5 Estadio Azteca, Mexico City (Mexico) / 105,000   **6** Neyland Stadium, Knoxville (USA) / 102,455

7 Ohio Stadium, Columbus (USA) / 102,329   **8** Bryant-Denny Stadium, Tuscaloosa (USA) / 101,821

9 Darrell K Royal Texas Memorial Stadium, Austin (USA) / 100,119

10 Melbourne Cricket Ground, Melbourne (Australia) / 100,018   **11** Azadi Stadium, Tehran (Iran) / 100,000

12 Camp Nou, Barcelona (Spain) / 99,354   **13** FNB Stadium, Johannesburg (South Africa) / 94,700

14 Los Angeles Memorial Coliseum (USA) / 93,607   **15** Sanford Stadium, Athens (USA) / 92,746

16 Rose Bowl, Pasadena (USA) / 92,542   **17** Tiger Stadium, Baton Rouge (USA) / 92,400

18 Cotton Bowl, Dallas (USA) / 92,100   **19** Eden Gardens, Kolkata (India) / 90,000

20 Wembley Stadium, London (England) / 90,000

The fastest knock out in boxing history, including the ten second count by the referee, was the September 24 1946 clash between Aurele "Al" Coutoure and Ralph Walton, with Walton being counted out after ten and a half seconds!

Source: SIcom

Top 20 MUSIC

LONGEST RUN IN THE UK SINGLES CHART

Black Eyed Peas, Engelbert Humperdinck, and Acker Bilk have each spent more than a year in the singles chart without a break.

1 Frank Sinatra *My Way* (124 weeks)	**2** Snow Patrol *Chasing Cars* (98 weeks)

3 Kings Of Leon *Sex On Fire* (87 weeks)	**4** Black Eyed Peas *I Gotta Feeling* (73 weeks)	**5** Take That *Rule The World* (73 weeks)	**6** Judy Collins *Amazing Grace* (67 weeks)	**7** Lady Gaga *Poker Face* (66 weeks)
8 Journey *Don't Stop Believin'* (63 weeks)	**9** Kings Of Leon *Use Somebody* (62 weeks)	**10** Engelbert Humperdinck *Release Me* (56 weeks)	**11** Jason Mraz *I'm Yours* (56 weeks)	**12** Amy Winehouse *Rehab* (56 weeks)
13 Acker Bilk *Stranger On The Shore* (55 weeks)	**14** Frankie Goes To Hollywood *Relax* (52 weeks)	**15** Oasis *Whatever* (51 weeks)	**16** Rihanna Featuring Jay-Z *Umbrella* (51 weeks)	Nickelback *Rockstar* (50 weeks)
18 Tinie Tempah *Pass Out* (50 weeks)	**19** Flo Rida Featuring T-Pain *Low* (48 weeks)	**20** Lady Gaga *Bad Romance* (47 weeks)		

Source: OCC

LONGEST RUN IN THE US SINGLES CHART

Artist or band / Single / Number of weeks in the chart

1. Jason Mraz *I'm Yours* (76 weeks)
2. LeAnn Rimes *How Do I Live* (69 weeks)
3. Jewel *You Were Meant For Me* (65 weeks)
4. Carrie Underwood *Before He Cheats* (64 weeks)
5. Lifehouse *You And Me* (62 weeks)
6. Los Del Rio *Macarena* (60 weeks)
7. Lady Antebellum *Need You Now* (60 weeks)
8. Santana Featuring Rob Thomas *Smooth* (58 weeks)
9. The Fray *How To Save A Life* (58 weeks)
10. Creed *Higher* (57 weeks)
11. Kings Of Leon *Use Somebody* (57 weeks)
12. Paula Cole *I Don't Want To Wait* (56 weeks)
13. Faith Hill *The Way You Love Me* (56 weeks)
14. Black Eyed Peas *I Gotta Feeling* (56 weeks)
15. Everything But The Girl *Missing* (55 weeks)
16. Duncan Sheik *Barely Breathing* (55 weeks)
17. Lonestar *Amazed* (55 weeks)
18. Four Seasons *December '63 (Oh What A Night)* (54 weeks)
19. Lifehouse *Hanging By A Moment* (54 weeks)
20. Matchbox Twenty *Unwell* (54 weeks)

Source: Billboard

LONGEST RUN IN THE US ALBUMS CHART

Artist or band / Album / Number of weeks in the chart

1.	Pink Floyd *Dark Side Of The Moon*	741
2.	Johnny Mathis *Johnny's Greatest Hits*	490
3.	Original Cast Album *My Fair Lady*	482
4.	Original Cast Album *Highlights From Phantom Of The Opera*	331
5.	Carole King *Tapestry*	304
6.	Johnny Mathis *Heavenly*	295
7.	Film Soundtrack *Oklahoma!*	283
8.	Enigma *MCMXC AD*	282
9.	Metallica *Metallica*	281
10.	Film Soundtrack *The King And I*	277
11.	Tennessee Ernie Ford *Hymns*	277
12.	Original Cast Album *The Sound Of Music*	276
13.	Original Cast Album *Camelot*	265
14.	Film Soundtrack *South Pacific*	262
15.	Led Zeppelin *Led Zeppelin IV*	259
16.	Original Cast Album *The Phantom Of The Opera*	255
17.	Nirvana *Nevermind*	252
18.	Pearl Jam *Ten*	250
19.	Original Cast Album *The Music Man*	245
20.	Rolling Stones *Hot Rocks 1964–1971*	243

Source: Billboard

LONGEST RUN IN THE UK ALBUMS CHART

Artist or band / Album / Number of weeks in the chart

1.	Fleetwood Mac *Rumours* 477
2.	Queen *Queen's Greatest Hits* 475
3.	Meat Loaf *Bat Out Of Hell* 474
4.	ABBA *Gold Greatest Hits* 439
5.	Film Soundtrack *The Sound Of Music* 381
6.	Pink Floyd *Dark Side Of The Moon* 351
7.	Bob Marley & The Wailers *Legend: The Best Of Bob Marley & The Wailers* 340
8.	Film Soundtrack *South Pacific* 313
9.	Simon & Garfunkel *Bridge Over Troubled Water* 307
10.	Simon & Garfunkel *Greatest Hits* 283
11.	Mike Oldfield *Tubular Bells* 278
12.	Phil Collins *Face Value* 274
13.	Dire Straits *Making Movies* 251
14.	Madonna *The Immaculate Collection* 242
15.	Jeff Wayne *War Of The Worlds* 235
16.	Dire Straits *Brothers In Arms* 228
17.	Michael Jackson *Thriller* 223
18.	U2 *Under A Blood Red Sky* 203
19.	Michael Jackson *Off The Wall* 202
20.	Film Soundtrack *The King And I* 200

Source: OCC

LANGUAGE AND LITERATURE

MOST WIDELY-SPOKEN LANGUAGES

Language / Country or region of origin / Speakers (millions)

1 Mandarin Chinese / China / 845
2 Spanish / Spain / 329
3 English / UK / 328
4 Arabic / Middle East / 221

5 Hindi / India / 182
6 Bengali / India, Bangladesh / 181
7 Portuguese / Portugal / 178
8 Russian / Russia / 144

9 Japanese / Japan / 122
10 German / Germany / 90.3
11 Javanese / Java / 84.6

12 Punjabi / India / 78.3
13 Wu / Northern China, Tibet / 77.2
14 Telugu / India / 69.8
15 Vietnamese / Vietnam / 68.6
16 Marathi / India / 68.0

17 French / France / 67.8
18 Korean / Korea / 66.3
19 Tamil / India, Sri Lanka / 65.7
20 Italian / Italy / 61.7

Did you know?
The most spoken language, mandarin, is actually a collection of Chinese dialects that is spoken across most of China.

Most Widely-Written Languages

1.	English	11.	Punjabi
2.	Spanish	12.	French
3.	Mandarin Chinese	13.	Italian
4.	Arabic	14.	Urdu
5.	Bengali	15.	Javanese
6.	Hindi	16.	Wu (Chinese)
7.	Russian	17.	Tamil
8.	Portuguese	18.	Korean
9.	Japanese	19.	Latin
10.	German	20.	Greek

* Based on literacy rates educational status;
source: UNESCO

LEAST-SPOKEN LANGUAGES

	Language	Country of origin	Speaker(s)
1.	Yaghan	Chile	1
2.	Ter Sami	Russia	2
3.	Hiren	Peru	6
4.	Kayardild	Australia	fewer than 10
5.	Votic	Russia	20
6.	Ume Sami	Northern Scandinavia	20
7.	Pite Sami	Northern Scandinavia	20
8.	Kawésqar	Chile	fewer than 22
9.	Manchu	Northern China	60
10.	Pitkern	Pitcairn Island	70
11.	Enets	Russia	70
12.	Tobian	Palau	100
13.	Livonian	Latvia	150
14.	Hinukh	Russia	200
15.	Comanche	USA	200
16.	Halkomelem	Canada/USA	225
17.	Washo	USA	252
18.	Piraha	Brazil	300
19.	Ingrian	Russia	300
20.	Mlabri	Thailand/Laos	400

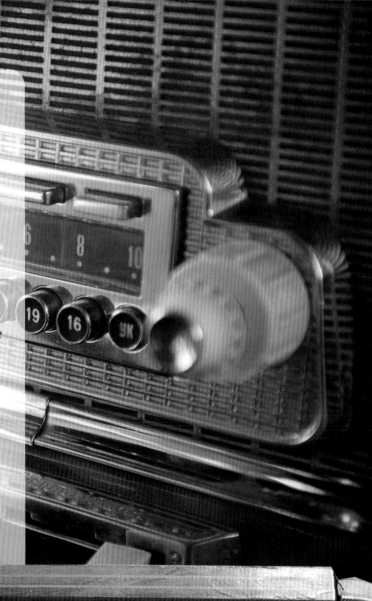

MOST PLAYED SONGS IN THE US

1 Righteous Brothers *You've Lost That Lovin' Feelin'*
2 The Association *Never My Love*
3 The Beatles *Yesterday*
4 Ben E King *Stand By Me*
5. Otis Redding *Dock Of The Bay*
6 Simon & Garfunkel *Mrs Robinson*
7 Johnny Rivers *Baby, I Need Your Loving*
8 Ray Charles *Georgia On My Mind*
9 The Police *Every Breath You Take*
10 Roy Orbison *Pretty Woman*
11 Gladys Knight & The Pips *I Heard It Through The Grapevine*
12 Everly Brothers *All I Have To Do Is Dream*
13 The Platters *Only You*
14 The Chi-Lites *Oh Girl*
15 Elton John *Your Song*
16 James Taylor *How Sweet It Is*
17 Rita Coolidge *Higher And Higher*
18 Ray Charles *I Can't Stop Loving You*
19 Bette Midler *Wind Beneath My Wings*
20 Fifth Dimension *Up, Up And Away*

Source: ASCAP

MOST PLAYED SONGS IN THE UK

1 Procol Harum *A Whiter Shade Of Pale*
2 Everly Brothers *All I Have To Do Is Dream*
3 Wet Wet Wet *Love Is All Around*
4 Bryan Adams *(Everything I Do) I Do It For You*
5 Robbie Williams *Angels*
6 Elvis Presley *All Shook Up*
7 ABBA *Dancing Queen*
8 Perry Como *Magic Moments*
9 Bing Crosby *White Christmas*
10 Rod Stewart *Maggie May*

11 All Saints *Pure Shores*
12 Robbie Williams *Rock DJ*
13 Whitney Houston *I Will Always Love You*
14 George Harrison *My Sweet Lord*
15 The Rolling Stones *Honky Tonk Woman*
16 Sinead O'Connor *Nothing Compares 2 U*
17 The Verve *Bitter Sweet Symphony*
18 Natalie Imbruglia *Torn*
19 Elton John & Kiki Dee *Don't Go Breaking My Heart*
20 T. Rex *Hot Love*

Source: PRS

MOST NUMBER ONE ALBUMS IN THE UK

1 The Beatles / 15   **2** Elvis Presley / 11   **3** Madonna / 11

4 The Rolling Stones / 11   **5** U2 / 10   **6** Abba / 9

7 Michael Jackson / 9   **8** Queen / 9   **9** Robbie Williams / 9

10 David Bowie / 8   **11** Led Zeppelin / 8   **12** Oasis / 8

13 R.E.M. / 8   **14** Bruce Springsteen / 8   **15** Bob Dylan / 7

16 Paul McCartney/Wings / 7   **17** Cliff Richard* / 7

18 The Shadows** / 7   **19** Rod Stewart / 7   **20** Westlife / 7

* Cliff Richard's tally includes three with The Shadows
** The Shadows' tally includes three with Cliff Richard

Source: OCC

MOST NUMBER ONE ALBUMS IN THE US

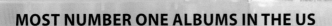

1 The Beatles / 19

2 Jay-Z / 11

3 Elvis Presley / 10

4 Bruce Springsteen / 9

5 The Rolling Stones / 9

6 Barbra Streisand / 9

7 Garth Brooks / 8

8 Elton John / 7

9 Led Zeppelin / 7

10 Madonna / 7

11 U2 / 7

12 Paul McCartney/Wings / 7

13 Frank Sinatra / 6

14 The Eagles / 6

15 Mariah Carey / 6

16 Michael Jackson / 6

17 Eminem / 6

18 Kenny Chesney / 6

19 R Kelly / 6

20 Kingston Trio / 5

Frank Sinatra also scored a number one hit in 1946 with his album *The Voice Of Frank Sinatra*, but most achievement lists start in 1955.

Source: Billboard

TV-OWNING COUNTRIES

Country / TVs per 1000 of population

Source: Encyclopedia of Television

Rank	Country	TVs per 1000
1	Bermuda	1,009.71
2	Monaco	771.391
3	United States	740.53
4	Malta	702.53
5	Japan	678.873
6	Canada	655.388
7	Guam	628.841
8	Virgin Islands	625.529
9	Germany	623.552
10	Finland	612.675
11	Luxembourg	608.232
12	Denmark	574.558
13	France	572.727
14	Saint Pierre	570.451
15	Georgia	549.498
16	Brunei	542.498
17	Palau	541.792
18	Oman	532.978
19	Latvia	532.751
20	Greenland	532.151

LONGEST-RUNNING STAGE SHOWS

Title / First performance (city) / Number of performances

1
The Mousetrap
1952 (London)
More than 24,000

2
Les Miserables
1980 (Paris)
More than 20,000

3
The Phantom of the Opera
1986 (London)
More than 19,500

4
Cats
1981 (London)
More than 17,000

5
Mamma Mia!
1999 (London)
More than 12,000

6
Chicago
1996 (New York)
More than 11,000

7
Blood Brothers
1983 (London)
More than 10,000

8
The Woman in Black
1989 (London)
More than 9,000

9
Starlight Express
1984 (London)
More than 9,000

10
Oh! Calcutta!
1976 (London)
More than 8,300

11
Black and White Minstrels
1960 (London)
More than 6,477

12
A Chorus Line
1975 (New York)
More than 6,137

13
Beauty and the Beast
1994 (New York)
More than 5,500

14
The Lion King
1994 (New York)
More than 5,500

15
42nd Street
1980 (New York)
More than 5,300

16
Buddy
1995 (London)
More than 5,100

17
Rent
1996 (New York)
More than 5,100

18
Miss Saigon
1989 (London)
More than 4,500

19
No Sex Please, We're British
1971 (London)
More than 4,000

20
Jesus Christ Superstar
1971 (New York)
More than 4,000

ENERGY AND RESOURCES

COAL PRODUCERS

Country / Short tons annually

| 1 China 2,620,500,000 | 2 USA 1,162,750,000 | 3 India 498,860,000 |

| 4 Australia 419,580,000 | 5 North Korea 390,140,000 |

| 6 Russia 228,200,000 | 7 South Africa 269,370,000 | 8 Germany 220,550,000 |

| 9 Indonesia 213,170,000 | 10 Poland 171,120,000 |

| 11 Kazakhstan 106,170,000 | 12 Canada 72,750,000 | 13 Greece 72,370,000 |

| 14 Turkey 71,510,000 | 15 Colombia 70,220,000 |

| 16 Czech Republic 69,740,000 | 17 Ukraine 68,030,000 | 18 Vietnam 45,060,000 |

| 19 Former Serbia & Montenegro 42,970,000 | 20 Bulgaria 8,090,000 |

GAS PRODUCERS

Country / Billion cubic feet / meters / Percentage share of world total

	Country	Billion cubic feet / meters	Percentage share of world total
1.	USA	20,900 / 593	20.1
2.	Russia	18,600 / 528	17.6
3.	Canada	5,700 / 161	5.4
4.	Iran	4,600 / 131	4.4
5.	Norway	3,700 / 104	3.5
6.	Qatar	3,200 / 90	3.0
7.	China	3,000 / 86	2.8
8.	Algeria	2,860 / 81	2.7
9.	Saudi Arabia	2,800 / 78	2.6
10.	Indonesia	2,500 / 72	2.4
11.	Uzbekistan	2,300 / 64	2.2
12.	Netherlands	2,225 / 63	2.1
13.	Egypt	2,225 / 63	2.1
14.	Malaysia	2,225 / 63	2.1
15.	UK	2,100 / 60	2.0
16.	Mexico	2,000 / 58	1.9
17.	United Arab Emirates	1,730 / 49	1.6
18.	Australia	1,500 / 42	1.4
19.	Argentina	1,450 / 41	1.4
20.	Trinidad & Tobago	1,450 / 41	1.4

Source: BP Statistical Review of World Energy

LEADERS IN ENVIRONMENTAL PERFORMANCE

Country/EPI rating

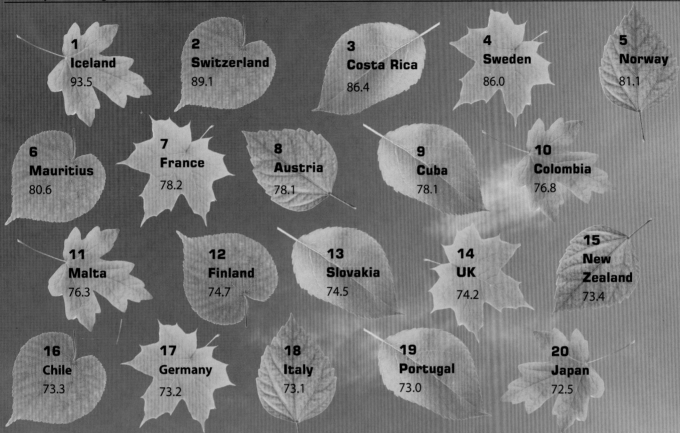

1 Iceland 93.5

2 Switzerland 89.1

3 Costa Rica 86.4

4 Sweden 86.0

5 Norway 81.1

6 Mauritius 80.6

7 France 78.2

8 Austria 78.1

9 Cuba 78.1

10 Colombia 76.8

11 Malta 76.3

12 Finland 74.7

13 Slovakia 74.5

14 UK 74.2

15 New Zealand 73.4

16 Chile 73.3

17 Germany 73.2

18 Italy 73.1

19 Portugal 73.0

20 Japan 72.5

Source: Environmental Performance Index (EPI)

WORST ENVIRONMENTAL PERFORMANCE

Country	EPI rating	Country	EPI rating
1. Sierra Leone	32.1	12. United Arab Emirates	40.7
2. Central African Republic	33.3	13. Chad	40.8
3. Mauritania	33.7	14. Iraq	41.0
4. Angola	36.3	15. Botswana	41.3
5. Togo	36.4	16. Cambodia	41.7
6. Niger	37.6	17. North Korea	41.8
7. Turkmenistan	38.4	18. Equatorial Guinea	41.9
8. Mali	39.4	19. Bahrain	42.0
9. Haiti	39.5	20. Uzbekistan	42.3
10. Benin	39.6		
11. Nigeria	40.2		

Source: Environmental Performance Index (EPI)

HIGHEST-EARNING BOND FILMS

	Title	Box office gross	Year
1.	Casino Royale	$596,365,000	2006
2.	Quantum of Solace	$576,368,427	2008
3.	Die Another Day	$431,942,139	2002
4.	The World Is Not Enough	$361,730,660	1999
5.	GoldenEye	$356,429,941	1995
6.	Tomorrow Never Dies	$339,504,276	1997
7.	Moonraker	$210,300,000	1979
8.	For Your Eyes Only	$195,300,000	1981
9.	The Living Daylights	$191,200,000	1987
10.	Octopussy	$187,500,000	1983
11.	The Spy Who Loved Me	$185,400,000	1977
12.	Live and Let Die	$161,800,000	1973
13.	Never Say Never Again	$160,000,000	1983
14.	Licence to Kill	$156,167,015	1989
15.	A View to A Kill	$152,627,960	1985
16.	Thunderball	$141,200,000	1965
17.	Goldfinger	$124,900,000	1964
18.	Diamonds Are Forever	$116,000,000	1971
19.	You Only Live Twice	$111,600,000	1967
20.	The Man with the Golden Gun	$ 97,600,000	1974

Source: Movie Information Database

FILMS WINNING MOST OSCARS

	Title	Year	Wins	Nominations
1.	Titanic	1997	11	14
2.	Ben-Hur	1959	11	12
3.	The Lord of the Rings: The Return of the King	2003	11	11
4.	West Side Story	1961	10	11
5.	The English Patient	1996	9	12
6.	Gigi	1958	9	9
7.	The Last Emperor	1987	9	9
8.	Gone With The Wind	1939	8	13
9.	From Here to Eternity	1953	8	13
10.	Schindler's List	1993	8	12
11.	On the Waterfront	1954	8	12
12.	My Fair Lady	1964	8	12
13.	Gandhi	1982	8	11
14.	Dances with Wolves	1984	8	11
15.	Out of Africa	1985	8	10
16.	Going My Way	1944	7	13
17.	Lawrence of Arabia	1962	7	12
18.	Patton	1970	7	12
19.	The Sting	1973	7	11
20.	The Best Years of Our Lives	1946	7	10

Source: The Academy Awards archive

HIGHEST-EARNING COMEDY FILMS

	Title	Box office gross	Year
1.	Shrek 2	$441,226,247	2004
2.	Toy Story 3	$415,004,880	2010
3.	Finding Nemo	$339,714,978	2003
4.	Shrek the Third	$322,719,944	2007
5.	Up	$293,004,164	2009
6.	Home Alone	$285,761,243	1990
7.	Meet the Fockers	$279,261,160	2004
8.	The Hangover	$277,322,503	2009
9.	Shrek	$267,665,011	2001
10.	The Incredibles	$261,441,092	2004
11.	How the Grinch Stole Christmas	$260,044,825	2000
12.	Monsters, Inc	$255,873,250	2001
13.	Despicable Me	$251,513,985	2010
14.	Men in Black	$250,690,539	1997
15.	Toy Story 2	$245,852,179	1999
16.	Cars	$244,082,982	2006
17.	Bruce Almighty	$242,374,454	2003
18.	My Big Fat Greek Wedding	$241,438,208	2002
19.	Shrek Forever After	$238,736,787	2010
20.	Ghostbusters	$238,632,124	1984

HIGHEST-EARNING HORROR FILMS

Title / Box office gross / Year

1
The Sixth Sense
$293,506,292
1999

2
Jaws
$260,000,000
1975

3
Signs
$258,157,400
2002

4
The Amityville Horror
$226,568,300
1979

5
The Exorcist
$193,000,000
1973

6
What Lies Beneath
$155,464,351
2000

7
The Blair Witch Project
$140,539,099
1999

8
The Silence of the Lambs
$130,742,922
1991

9
The Ring
$129,128,133
2002

10
Shutter Island
$128,012,934
2010

11
Van Helsing
$120,177,084
2004

12
The Village
$114,197,520
2004

13
The Grudge
$110,359,362
2004

14
Paranormal Activity
$107,918,810
2009

15
Interview with the Vampire
$105,264,608
1994

16
Scream
$103,046,663
1996

17
Scream 2
$101,363,301
1997

18
Sleepy Hollow
$101,071,502
1999

19
The Others
$96,522,687
2001

20
The Haunting
$91,411,151
1999

Source: Box Office Mojo

OLYMPIANS WITH MOST MEDALS (WINTER GAMES)

Name (country of origin) / Sport / Number of medals won

1 Bjorn Daehlie (Norway) / Cross Country Skiing / 12
2 Ole Einar Bjørndalen (Norway) / Biathlon / 11
3 Raisa Smetanina (Soviet Union) / Cross Country Skiing / 10
4 Lyubov Yegorova (Russia) / Cross Country Skiing / 9
5 Claudia Pechstein (Germany) / Speed Skating / 9
6 Sixten Jernberg (Sweden) / Cross Country Skiing / 9
7 Ricco Gross (Germany) / Biathlon / 8
8 Kjetil André Aamodt (Norway) / Alpine Skiing / 8
9 Sven Fischer (Germany) / Biathlon / 8
10 Galina Kulakova (Soviet Union) / Cross Country Skiing / 8
11 Karin Enke (Germany) / Speed Skating / 8
12 Gunda Neimann-Stirnemann (Germany) / Speed Skating / 8
13 Apolo Ohno (United States) / Short Track / 8
14 Larisa Lazutina (Russia) / Cross Country Skiing / 7
15 Clas Thunberg (Finland) / Speed Skating / 7
16 Ivar Ballangrud (Norway) / Speed Skating / 7
17 Veikko Hakulinen (Finland) / Cross Country Skiing / 7
18 Marit Bjorgen (Norway) / Cross Country Skiing / 7
19 Eero Mantyranta (Finland) / Cross Country Skiing / 7
20 Marja-Liisa Kirvesniemi (Finland) / Cross Country Skiing / 7

Source: IOC

OLYMPIC SWIMMING GOLD MEDALS

Country / Number of medals won

1	**2**	**3**	**4**
USA	Australia	East Germany	Hungary
214	56	38	23

5	**6**	**7**	**8**	**9**	**10**	**11**	**12**
Japan	Netherlands	Great Britain	Germany	Soviet Union	Sweden	China	Canada
20	17	15	13	12	8	7	7

13	**14**	**15**	**16**	**17**	**18**	**19**	**20**
Unified Team	Russia	France	Ukraine	Italy	South Africa	West Germany	Romania
6	5	4	4	4	4	3	3

OLYMPIC GYMNASTICS GOLD MEDALS

1 Soviet Union 72 2 USA 30 3 Japan 28 4 Romania 24 5 China 24
6 Switzerland 16 7 Hungary 14 8 Italy 14 9 Czechoslovakia 12
10 Germany 12 11 Unified Team 9 12 Russia 9 13 Finland 8
14 East Germany 6 15 Yugoslavia 5 16 Sweden 5 17 Greece 4
18 Ukraine 4 19 France 3 20 Bulgaria 2

OLYMPIC FIGURE SKATING GOLD MEDALS

Country / Number of medals won

1 USA 14
2 Russia 12
3 Soviet Union 10
4 Austria 7
5 Great Britain 5
6 Sweden 5
7 Canada 4
8 East Germany 3
9 France 3
10 Norway 3
11 Unified Team 3
12 Germany 2
13 China 1
14 Japan 1
15 Germany UEA 1
16 Netherlands 1
17 Czechoslovakia 1
18 Finland 1
19 West Germany 1
20 Belgium 1

Did you know?

Former Soviet gymnast Larissa Semyonovna Latynin is the only female athlete to win nine Olympic gold medals. She holds 18 medals in total, more Olympic medals than any other competitor in any sport and was responsible for establishing the Soviet Union as the dominant force in gymnastics.

Source: IOC

MOST BORROWED BOOKS FROM LIBRARIES*

1	Sail (2008)	James Patterson
2	No Time for Goodbye (2008)	Linwood Barclay
3	7th Heaven (2008)	James Patterson with Maxine Paetro
4	You've Been Warned (2007)	James Patterson and Howard Roughan
5	The Outcast (2008)	Sadie Jones
6	Nothing to Lose (2008)	Lee Child
7	The Front (2008)	Patricia Cornwell
8	Hold Tight (2008)	Harlan Coben
9	The Appeal (2008)	John Grisham
10	Friday Nights (2008)	Joanna Trollope
11	The House at Riverton (2007)	Kate Morton
12	Horrid Henry & the Football Fiend (2006)	Francesca Simon Illustrated by Tony Ross
13	Exit Music (2007)	Ian Rankin
14	The Quickie (2007)	James Patterson & Michael Ledwidge
15	Doors Open (2008)	Ian Rankin
16	Rogue (2008)	Danielle Steel
17	Devil Bones (2008)	Kathy Reichs
18	The Pirate's Daughter (2008)	Margaret Cezair-Thompson
19	East of The Sun (2008)	Julia Gregson
20	A Thousand Splendid Suns (2007)	Khaled Hosseini

* From UK libraries

LARGEST LIBRARIES IN THE WORLD*

Library / Location / Volumes (millions)

1 **Library of Congress** / Washington, DC, USA / **33**

2 **National Library of China** / Beijing, China / **24**

3 **German National Library** / Frankfurt, Germany / **22**

5 **Library of the Russian Academy of Sciences** / St. Petersburg, Russia / **20.5**

4 **New York Public Library** / New York, USA / **20.4**

6 **National Library of Canada** / Ottawa, Canada / **18.5**

7 **Harvard University Library** / Cambridge, MA, USA / **15.8**

8 **British Library** / London, UK / **14**

9 **Russian State Library** / Moscow, Russia / **14**

10 **Bibliothèque Nationale de France** / Paris, France / **14**

11 **Yale University Library** / New Haven, Conn., USA / **13**

12 **Toronto Public Library** / Toronto, Canada / **11**

13 **Bodleian Library** / Oxford, UK / **11**

14 **Chicago Public Library** / Chicago, USA / **10.8**

15 **Bavarian State Library** / Munich, Germany / **9.4**

16 **National Central Library** / Rome, Italy / **7**

17 **Los Angeles Public Library** / Los Angeles, USA / **6.4**

18 **Boston Public Library** / Boston, USA / **6.1**

19 **Royal Danish Library** / Copenhagen, Denmark / **6**

20 **Carnegie Library of Pittsburgh** / Pittsburgh, USA / **5.2**

* Based on number of volumes.

PAID-FOR MAGAZINES BY CIRCULATION

Title / Location / Monthly sales (millions)

1 Reader's Digest */ USA / 17

2 National Geographic / USA / 8.9

3 Better Homes and Gardens / USA / 7.6

4 TIME **/ USA / 5.2

5 Good Housekeeping / USA / 4.7

6 Family Circle / USA / 3.9

7 Woman's Day / USA / 3.8

8 Ladies' Home Journal / USA / 3.8

9 People / USA / 3.8

10 Game Informer / USA / 3.5

11 Taste of Home / USA / 3.2

12 Sports Illustrated / USA / 3.0

13 Cosmopolitan / USA / 3.0

14 Playboy / USA / 3.0

15 Prevention / USA / 2.9

16 Southern Living / USA / 2.8

17 Maxim / USA / 2.5

18 O: The Oprah Magazine / USA / 2.5

19 TV Guide / USA / 2.4

20 Parenting / USA / 2.2

* Reader's Digest is the biggest selling magazine in the world.

** TIME is the biggest selling news magazine in the world.

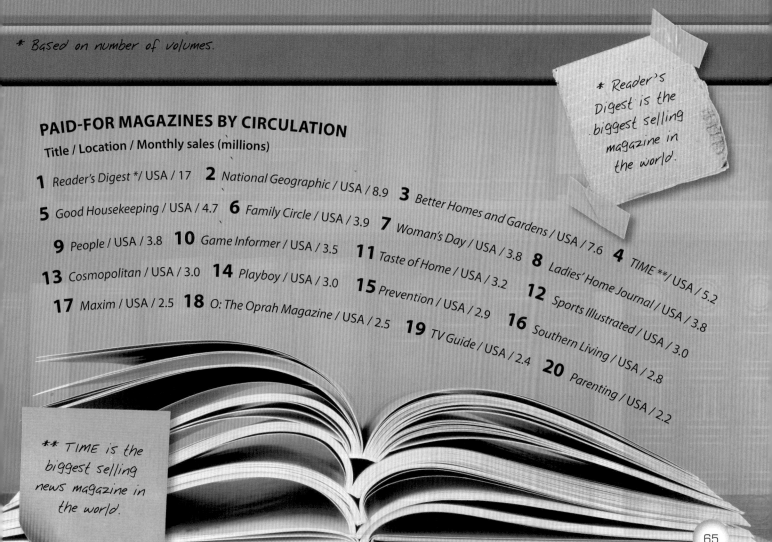

BIGGEST LANDFILL SITES

Name	Location	Country	Tons per day (short / metric)
1. Sudokwon	Incheon	South Korea	22,046 / 20,000
2. Bordo Poniente	Mexico City	Mexico	13,227 / 12,000
3. Apex	Las Vegas	USA	11,574 / 10,500
4. Puente Hills	Los Angeles	USA	11,354 / 10,300
5. Laogang	Shanghai	China	10,031 / 9,100
6. Lagos landfill	Lagos	Nigeria	9,201 / 9,000
7. Newton County	Brook, Indiana	USA	8,818 / 8,000
8. Okeechobee	Okeechobee, Florida	USA	7,937 / 7,200
9. Xingfeng	Guangzhou	China	7,937 / 7,200
10. São João	São Paulo	Brazil	7,716 / 7,000
11. Atlantic Waste	Waverly, Virginia	USA	7,000 / 6,350
12. West New Territories	Hong Kong	China	6,906 / 6,265
13. Deonar	Mumbai	India	6,614 / 6,000
14. Rumpke Sanitary	Colerain, Ohio	USA	6,558 / 5,950
15. Pine Tree Acres	Lenox, Michigan	USA	6,393 / 5,800
16. El Sobrante	Corona, California	USA	6,283 / 5,700
17. Veolia Orchard Hills	Davis, Illinois	USA	6,283 / 5,700
18. Denver Arapahoe Site	Denver	USA	5,842 / 5,300
19. Guiyu E-waste	Guangdong	China	4,519 / 4,100
20. Malagrotta	Lazio, Rome	Italy	4,519 / 4,000

BIGGEST RUBBISH PRODUCERS

Country	Average per person, per year (lb / kg)
1. Russia	3,000 / 1,342
2. USA	1,700 / 760
3. Australia	1,520 / 690
4. Denmark	1,500 / 660
5. Switzerland	1,430 / 650
6. Canada	1,400 / 640
7. Norway	1,370 / 620
8. Netherlands	1,340 / 610
9. Spain	1,280 / 580
10. Austria	1,230 / 560
11. UK	1,230 / 560
12. Ireland	1,230 / 560
13. Belgium	1,200 / 550
14. Germany	1,190 / 540
15. France	1,120 / 510
16. Italy	1,100 / 500
17. Finland	1,000 / 460
18. Sweden	990 / 450
19. Japan	900 / 410
20. Turkey	770 / 350

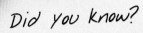

Did you know?
Hydropower provides about 20 percent of the world's electricity and is the main energy source for more than 30 countries.

HYDRO-ELECTRICITY CONSUMERS

Country	Million tons oil equivalent	Percentage of world total
1. China	139.3	18.8
2. Canada	90.2	12.2
3. Brazil	88.5	12.0
4. USA	62.2	8.4
5. Russian Federation	39.8	5.4
6. Norway	28.8	3.9
7. India	24.0	3.2
8. Venezuela	19.5	2.6
9. Japan	16.7	2.3
10. Sweden	14.9	2.0
11. France	13.1	1.8
12. Italy	10.5	1.4
13. Colombia	9.3	1.3
14. Argentina	9.2	1.2
15. Austria	8.3	1.1
16. Turkey	8.1	1.1
17. Switzerland	8.1	1.1
18. Pakistan	6.2	0.8
19. Spain	6.1	0.8
20. Mexico	6.0	0.8

PRODUCERS OF NUCLEAR POWER

Country	Megawatts
1. USA	97,603
2. France	61,443
3. Japan	43,692
4. Germany	20,844
5. Russia	19,897
6. Ukraine	13,045
7. UK	12,728
8. South Korea	10,733
9. Canada	10,306
10. Sweden	10,002
11. Spain	7,085
12. Belgium	5,712
13. Taiwan	4,884
14. India	4,780
15. Czech Republic	3,830
16. Bulgaria	3,420
17. Switzerland	2,985
18. Lithuania	2,760
19. Finland	2,520
20. China	2,100

Source: World Nuclear Industry Status Report

HIGHEST-PAID ACTORS

	Actor	Average annual earnings			Actor	Average annual earnings
1.	Harrison Ford	$65 million		6.	Tom Hanks	$35 million
2.	Adam Sandler	$55 million		7.	Tom Cruise	$30 million
3.	Will Smith	$45 million		8.	Jim Carey	$28 million
4.	Eddie Murphey	$40 million		9.	Brad Pitt	$28 million
5.	Nicolas Cage	$40 million		10.	Johnny Depp	$27 million

HIGHEST-EARNING DOCUMENTARY FILMS

	Title	Box office gross	Year		Rank	Title	Box office gross	Year
1.	Fahrenheit 9/11	$119,194,771	2004		17.	Tupac: Resurrection	$7,718,961	2003
2.	March of the Penguins	$77,437,223	2005		18.	Babies	$7,320,323	2010
3.	Justin Bieber: Never Say Never	$62,963,741	2011		19.	Roger and Me	$6,706,368	1989
4.	Earth	$32,011,576	2009		20.	Waiting for Superman	$6,417,135	2010
5.	Sicko	$24,540,079	2007					
6.	An Inconvenient Truth	$24,146,161	2006					
7.	Bowling for Columbine	$21,576,018	2002					
8.	Oceans	$19,422,319	2010					
9.	Madonna: Truth or Dare	$15,012,935	1991					
10.	Capitalism: A Love Story	$14,363,397	2009					
11.	Religulous	$13,011,160	2008					
12.	Winged Migration	$11,689,053	2003					
13.	Super Size Me	$11,536,423	2004					
14.	Mad Hot Ballroom	$8,117,961	2005					
15.	Hoop Dreams	$7,830,611	1994					
16.	Expelled: No Intelligence Allowed	$7,720,487	2008					

Source: Box Office Mojo

	Actor	Average annual earnings		Actor	Average annual earnings
11.	Geroge Clooney	$25 million	16.	Ben Stiller	$14 million
12.	Russel Crowe	$20 million	17.	Seth Rogan	$12 million
13.	Robert Downey Jr.	$20 million	18.	Matt Damon	$11 million
14.	Denzel Washington	$20 million	19.	Christian Bale	$10 million
15.	Vince Vaughn	$14 million	20.	Will Ferrell	$10 million

Source: Forbes

HIGHEST-PAID ACTRESSES

	Actress	Average annual earnings
1.	Sandra Bullock	$56 million
2.	Reese Witherspoon	$32 million
3.	Cameron Diaz	$32 million
4.	Jennifer Aniston	$27 million
5.	Sarah Jessica Parker	$25 million
6.	Julia Roberts	$20 million
7.	Angelina Jolie	$20 million
8.	Emma Watson	$20 million
9.	Drew Barrymore	$15 million
10.	Meryl Streep	$13 million
11.	Halle Berry	$12 million
12.	Kristen Stewart	$12 million
13.	Eva Longoria Parker	$12 million
14.	Kate Hudson	$11 million
15.	Charlize Theron	$10 million
16.	Jennifer Love Hewitt	$6.5 million
17.	Katherine Heigl	$6 million
18.	Anne Hathaway	$5 million
19.	Nicole Kidman	$5 million
20.	Kate Winslet	$2 million

Source: Rolling Stone magazine, based on a poll of 172 music critics and artists.

MOST POPULAR POP SONGS

Song / Recording artist

1 **Like A Rolling Stone** / Bob Dylan
2 **Satisfaction** / The Rolling Stones
3 **Imagine** / John Lennon
4 **What's Going On** / Marvin Gaye
5 **Respect** / Aretha Franklin
6 **Good Vibrations** / The Beach Boys
7 **Johnny B. Goode** / Chuck Berry
8 **Hey Jude** / The Beatles
9 **Smells Like Teen Spirit** / Nirvana
10 **What'd I Say (Live Berlin) 1962** / Ray Charles
11 **My Generation** / The Who
12 **A Change Is Gonna Come** / Sam Cooke
13 **Yesterday** / The Beatles
14 **Blowin' in The Wind** / Bob Dylan
15 **London Calling** / The Clash
16 **I Want To Hold Your Hand** / The Beatles
17 **Purple Haze** / Jimi Hendrix
18 **Maybellene** / Chuck Berry
19 **Hound Dog** / Elvis Presley
20 **Let It Be** / The Beatles

Did you know? Elvis was a black belt in karate and over one two-year period he ate nothing but meatloaf, mashed potatoes and tomatoes.

COUNTRIES WITH THE HIGHEST SCOUT AND GUIDE MEMBERSHIPS

Country / Membership

1 Indonesia 17,100,000　**2** USA 7,500,000　**3** India 4,150,000　**6** Bangladesh 1,050,000

7 UK 1,000,000　**4** Philippines 2,150,000　**5** Thailand 1,300,000　**12** Uganda 230,000

8 Pakistan 575,000　**9** Kenya 480,000

10 South Korea 270,000　**11** Germany 250,000　**15** Japan 200,000　**18** Poland 160,000

13 Italy 220,000　**14** Canada 220,000

16 France 200,000　**17** Belgium 170,000　**19** Nigeria 160,000　**20** Hong Kong 160,000

BOY SCOUTS OF AMERICA
U.S. POSTAGE 4¢
1910 · 1960

BOY SCOUTS
THE FLAG
TENDERFOOT TEST

Did you know?

There are over 30 million Scouts in 161 countries around the world. Famous members of the movement have included Bill Gates, George Michael, Steven Spielberg and King Juan Carlos of Spain.

During the Scout Jamboree in 1971 16,000 Scouts had to be evacuated due to a typhoon hitting Japan, where the event was being held.

ISRAEL SCOUT ASSOCIATION — NATIONAL JAM

ISRAEL
10 ISRAEL

הסתדרות הצופים העברים בישראל

LARGEST SAILING VESSELS

	Name / Date and type of vessel	Length of vessel (feet/meters)
1	Wind Surf Club Med 1 / 1990 cruise ship	617 / 187
2	Preussen / 1902 cargo ship	482 / 147
3	France II / 1913 cargo ship	481 / 146.5
4	Thomas W. Lawson / 1902 cargo ship	475 / 145
5	Wyoming / 1909 cargo ship	450 / 137
6	Wind Star / 1986 cruise ship	440 / 134
7	Royal Clipper / 2000 cruise ship	439 / 134
8	France I / 1890 cargo ship	435 / 133
9	HMS Black Prince / 1862 warship	420 / 128
10	HMS Warrior / 1860 warship	418 / 127
11	HMS Minotaur / 1867 warship	407 / 124
12	HMS Northumberland / 1868 warship	407 / 124
13	Moshulu / 904 cargo ship	396 / 121
14	Sedov / 1921 training ship	386 / 118
15	Sea Cloud II / 2001 cruise ship	384 / 117
16	Lawhill / 1892 cargo ship	382 / 116.4
17	HMS Achilles / 1864 warship	380 / 115.8
18	HMS Agincourt / 1867 warship	379 / 115.5
19	Peking / 1911 Flying P-liner	377.5 / 115.2
20	Pamir / 1905 Flying P-liner	375.6 / 114.5

BIGGEST PASSENGER SHIPS

	Ship	Country	Year	Weight in tonnes	Passengers
1	MS Oasis of the Seas	Finland	2009	225,282	7,565
2	MS Allure of the Seas	Finland	2010	225,000	6,300+
3	MS Freedom of the Seas	Finland	2006	154,407	4,994
4	RMS Queen Mary 2	France	2004	151,400	4,309
5	MS Voyager of the Seas	Finland	1999	137,376	4,319
6	MS Explorer of the Seas	Finland	1999	137,308	4,294
7	MS Grand Princess	Italy	1998	109,000	4,200
8	MS Carnival Destiny	Italy	1996	101,353	3,682
9	RMS Queen Elizabeth	UK	1940	83,673	3,283
10	SS Normandie	France	1935	79,280	3,317
11	MS Sun Princess	Italy	1995	77,499	2,890
12	SS France	France	1961/90	76,049	3,440
13	MS Sovereign of the Seas	France	1988	73,192	2,852+
14	RMS Majestic	Germany	1922	56,551	2,145
15	SS Vaterland	Germany	1914	54,282	1,165
16	SS Imperator	Germany	1913	52,117	5,414
17	RMS Olympic	UK	1912	46,439	2,435+
18	RMS Titanic	Ireland	1912	46,329	3,547
19	RMS Mauretania	UK	1907	31,938	2,967
20	RMS Lusitania	UK	1907	31,550	3,048

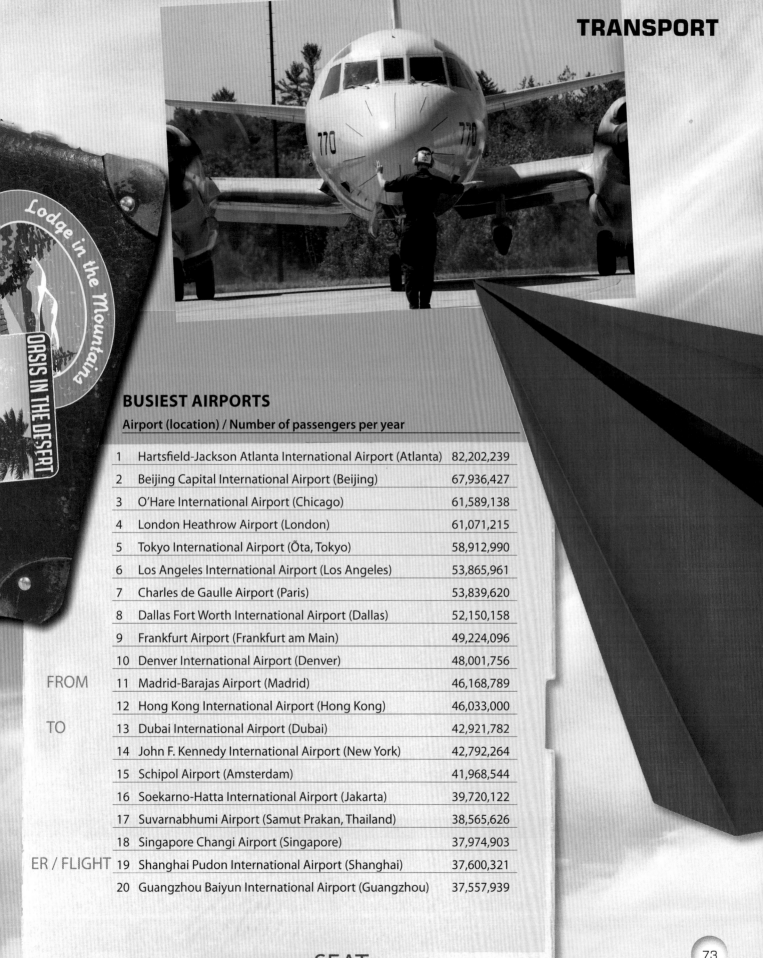

BUSIEST AIRPORTS

Airport (location) / Number of passengers per year

1	Hartsfield-Jackson Atlanta International Airport (Atlanta)	82,202,239
2	Beijing Capital International Airport (Beijing)	67,936,427
3	O'Hare International Airport (Chicago)	61,589,138
4	London Heathrow Airport (London)	61,071,215
5	Tokyo International Airport (Ōta, Tokyo)	58,912,990
6	Los Angeles International Airport (Los Angeles)	53,865,961
7	Charles de Gaulle Airport (Paris)	53,839,620
8	Dallas Fort Worth International Airport (Dallas)	52,150,158
9	Frankfurt Airport (Frankfurt am Main)	49,224,096
10	Denver International Airport (Denver)	48,001,756
11	Madrid-Barajas Airport (Madrid)	46,168,789
12	Hong Kong International Airport (Hong Kong)	46,033,000
13	Dubai International Airport (Dubai)	42,921,782
14	John F. Kennedy International Airport (New York)	42,792,264
15	Schipol Airport (Amsterdam)	41,968,544
16	Soekarno-Hatta International Airport (Jakarta)	39,720,122
17	Suvarnabhumi Airport (Samut Prakan, Thailand)	38,565,626
18	Singapore Changi Airport (Singapore)	37,974,903
19	Shanghai Pudon International Airport (Shanghai)	37,600,321
20	Guangzhou Baiyun International Airport (Guangzhou)	37,557,939

YOUTUBE VIDEOS*

Title	Views	Title	Views
1. Justin Bieber *Baby*	556,344,504	11. *Tootin' bathtub Baby Cousins*	188,550,662
2. Lady Gaga *Bad Romance*	384,348,305	12. *Hahaha*	183,425,843
3. Shakira *Waka Waka*	348,950,176	13. Pitbull *I Know You Want Me (Calle Ocho)*	181,172,551
4. Eminem *The Way You Lie*	341,688,252	14. Rihanna *What's My Name?*	176,676,891
5. *Charlie Bit my Finger – again!*	331,716,808	15. *Evolution of Dance*	173,887,357
6. Eminem *Not Afraid*	241,532,031	16. *An Experiment*	173,434,262
7. Miley Cyrus *Party in the USA*	223,112,270	17. Bruno Mars *Grenade*	167,611,137
8. Justin Beiber *Never Say Never ft. Jaden Smith*	215,971,078	18. Justin Bieber *Somebody to Love ft. Usher*	163,704,553
9. Jennifer Lopez *On The Floor ft. Pitbull*	211,902,753	19. Don Omar *Danza Kuduro*	161,618,810
10. Katy Perry *Firework*	190,910,482	20. Rihanna *Rude Boy*	154,701,962

Source: *youtube.com*

* At time of printing.

BESTSELLING FILMS ON DVD (UK)

	Title	Year		Title	Year
1.	Mamma Mia!	2008	12.	The Shawshank Redemption	1995
2.	Pirates of the Caribbean: Curse of the Black Pearl	2008	13.	Gladiator	2000
3.	The Lord of the Rings: Fellowship of the Ring	2001	14.	The Hangover	2009
4.	The Lord of the Rings: The Two Towers	2003	15.	Finding Nemo	2006
5.	The Dark Knight	2008	16.	Harry Potter and the Prisoner of Azkaban	2004
6.	The Bourne Ultimatum	2007	17.	Iron Man	2008
7.	Pirates of the Caribbean: Dead Man's Chest	2006	18.	Harry Potter and the Half Blood Prince	2009
8.	The Lord of the Rings: The Return of the King	2004	19.	Twilight	2008
9.	Transformers	2007	20.	Casino Royale	2006
10.	Shrek 2	2004			
11.	Planet Earth	2006			

Source: The Official UK Charts Company

LONGEST-RUNNING TV SHOWS

	Title	Country	Duration
1.	Meet the Press	USA	1947–now
2.	Tagesschau	Germany	1952–now
3.	Zenigata Heiji	Japan	1952–now
4.	Hockey Night in Canada	Canada	1952–now
5.	Panorama	UK	1953–now
6.	The Tonight Show	USA	1954–now
7.	Eurovision Song Contest	Europe	1956–now
8.	It Is Written	USA	1956–now
9.	The Sky at Night	UK	1957–now
10.	Blue Peter	UK	1958–now
11.	Coronation Street	UK	1960–now
12.	Hasta La Cocina	Mexico	1960–now
13.	Radio Rochela	Venezuela	1960–now
14.	Points of View	UK	1961–now
15.	The Late, Late Show	Ireland	1962–now
16.	Sabado Gigante	Chile	1962–now
17.	Timewatch	UK	1963–now
18.	Days of Our Lives	USA	1965–now
19.	The Money Programme	UK	1966–now
20.	Sazae-san	Japan	1969–now

Source: Broadcast

LARGEST ISLANDS

Name / Location / Area by square miles (km)

1 Greenland (North Atlantic) 839,800 (2,175,600)   **2** New Guinea (South West Pacific) 317,000 (821,030)

3 Borneo (South East Asia) 287,400 (744,380)   **4** Madagascar (Indian Ocean) 226,660 (587,040)

5 Baffin Island (Canada) 196,100 (508,000)   **6** Sumatra (Indonesia) 182,860 (473,600)

7 Honshu (Japan) 88,980 (230,500)   **8** Great Britain (North Atlantic) 88,700 (229,880)

9 Victoria Island (Canada) 81,900 (212,200)   **10** Ellesmere Island (Canada) 81,800 (212,000)

11 Celebes (Indonesia) 73,000 (189,000)   **12** New Zealand South Island (South West Pacific) 58,100 (150,500)

13 Java (Indonesia) 48,900 (126,700)   **14** New Zealand North Island (South West Pacific) 44,300 (114,700)

15 Cuba (Caribbean) 42,800 (110,860)   **16** Newfoundland (Canada) 42,700 (110,680)

17 Luzon (Philippines) 40,400 (104,700)   **18** Iceland (North Atlantic) 39,000 (103,000)

19 Mindanao (Philippines) 38,200 (101,500)   **20** Ireland (North Atlantic) 32,600 (84,400)

LARGEST OCEANS AND SEAS

Name / Area by square miles (km)

#	Name	Area sq miles (km)
1	Pacific Ocean	60,060,700 (155,557,000)
2	Atlantic Ocean	29,637,900 (76,762,000)
3	Indian Ocean	26,469,500 (68,556,000)
4	Southern Ocean	7,848,300 (20,327,000)
5	Arctic Ocean	5,427,000 (14,056,000)
6	Caribbean Sea	1,049,500 (2,718,200)
7	Mediterranean Sea	965,000 (2,500,000)
8	South China Sea	895,400 (2,319,000)
9	Bering Sea	884,900 (2,291,900)
10	Gulf of Mexico	615,000 (1,592,800)
11	Okhotsk Sea	613,800 (1,589,700)
12	East China Sea	482,300 (1,249,200)
13	Hudson Bay	475,800 (1,232,300)
14	Japan Sea	389,100 (1,007,800)
15	Andaman Sea	308,000 (797,700)
16	North Sea	222,100 (575,200)
17	Red Sea	169,100 (438,000)
18	Black Sea	168,500 (436,400)
19	Baltic Sea	163,000 (422,200)
20	Caspian Sea	143,200 (371,000)

LARGEST LAKES

Name / Location / Area by square miles (km)

1 Lake Superior, Canada, USA
31,800 (82,350)

2 Lake Victoria, Uganda, Kenya
26,000 (68,000)

3 Lake Huron, Canada, USA
23,010 (59,600)

4 Lake Michigan, United States
22,400 (58,000)

5 Lake Tanganyika , Burundi, Congo, Tanzania, Zambia
13,000 (33,000)

6 Great Bear Lake, Canada
12,280 (31,800)

7 Lake Baikal, Russia
11,780 (30,500)

8 Lake Malawi, Malawi, Mozambique, Tanzania
11,430 (29,600)

9 Great Slave Lake, Canada
11,000 (28,500)

10 Lake Erie, Canada, USA
9,900 (5,700)

11 Lake Chad, Nigeria, Chad, Cameroon, Niger
9,700 (25,000)

12 Lake Winnipeg, Canada
9,400 (24,400)

13 Tonlé Sap, Cambodia
7,700 (20,000)

14 Lake Ontario, Canada, USA
7,500 (19,500)

15 Lake Balkhash, Kazakhstan
7,100 (18,500)

16 Lake Ladoga, Russia
6,800 (17,700)

17 Dongting Hu, China
4,600 (12,000)

18 Lake Onega, Russia
3,700 (9,700)

19 Lake Titicaca, Peru, Bolivia
3,141 (8,135)

20 Lake Nicaragua, Nicaragua
3,089 (8,001)

Did you know?

Lake Superior contains ten percent of the world's fresh surface water. In the summer, the sun sets more than 35 minutes later on the western shore of Lake Superior than at its southeastern edge.

CHEESE-CONSUMING COUNTRIES

Country / Amount of cheese consumed per person per year (lb/kg)

1 Germany 68.5 / 31.1
2 Finland 57.5 / 26.1
3 Iceland 55.9 / 25.4
4 France 49.8 / 22.6
5 Switzerland 47.2 / 21.4
6 Italy 46.2 / 21.0
7 Turkey 42.7 / 19.4
8 Sweden 41.6lb / 18.9
9 Austria 38.3 / 17.4
10 Czech Republic 36.8 / 16.7
11 Israel 36.1 / 16.4
12 Norway 33.7 / 15.3
13 United States 32.6 / 14.8
14 Canada 27.1 / 12.3
15 Australia 26.4 / 12.0
16 Argentina 24.9 / 11.3
17 Greece 24.2 / 11.0
18 UK 24.03 / 10.9
19 Netherlands 23.8 / 10.8
20 Japan 3.75 / 1.7

MILK-CONSUMING COUNTRIES

Country / Amount of milk consumed per person per year (pints/liters)

1 Finland 323.6 / 183.9
2 Sweden 256 / 145.5
3 Ireland 228 / 129.8
4 Netherlands 216 / 122.9
5 Spain 209.6 / 119.1
6 Norway 205 / 116.7
7 Switzerland 198 / 112.5
8 UK 195.6 / 111.2
9 Australia 187 / 106.3
10 Canada 166.7 / 94.7
11 Germany 162 / 92.3
12 France 162 / 92.2
13 New Zealand 158 / 90.0
14 USA 147.6 / 83.9
15 Austria 141 / 80.2
16 Greece 121 / 69.0lt
17 Argentina 115.8 / 65.8
18 Italy 100.8 / 57.3
19 Mexico 71.6 / 40.7
20 China 15.4 / 8.8

ALCOHOL-CONSUMING COUNTRIES

Country / Consumption of pints / liters per person per year*

1 Moldova 32 / 18.22
2 Czech Republic 28.9 / 16.45
3 Hungary 28.6 / 16.27
4 Russia 27.7 / 15.76
5 Ukraine 27.4 / 15.60
6 Estonia 27.3 / 15.57
7 Andorra 27.2 / 15.48
8 Romania 26.9 / 15.30
9 Slovenia 26.7 / 15.19
10 Belarus 26.6 / 15.13
11 Croatia 26.5 / 15.11
12 Lithuania 26.4 / 15.03
13 South Korea 26.04 / 14.80
14 Portugal 25.6 / 14.55
15 Ireland 25.3 / 14.41
16 France 24.03 / 13.66
17 UK 23.5 / 13.37
18 Denmark 23.5 / 13.37
19 Slovakia 23.4 / 13.33
20 Netherlands 23.3 / 13.25

*Combined count including beer, wine, spirits, and other forms of alcohol

McDonald's

BILLIONS AND BILLIONS SERVED

DRIVE-THRU

Source: www.nationmaster.com

COUNTRIES WITH MOST MCDONALD'S RESTAURANTS

Country / Number of restaurants

1. USA..................12,804
2. Japan................3,598
5. Germany.............1,804
3. Canada...............1,154
4. UK....................1,115
6. France...............857
7. Australia.............701
8. Taiwan...............338
9. China................326
10. Italy................290
11. Spain...............276
12. South Korea........243
13. Philippines.........235
14. Sweden.............227
15. Netherlands........205
16. Mexico.............205
17. Poland.............181
18. Hong Kong.........177
19. New Zealand........149
20. Austria............148

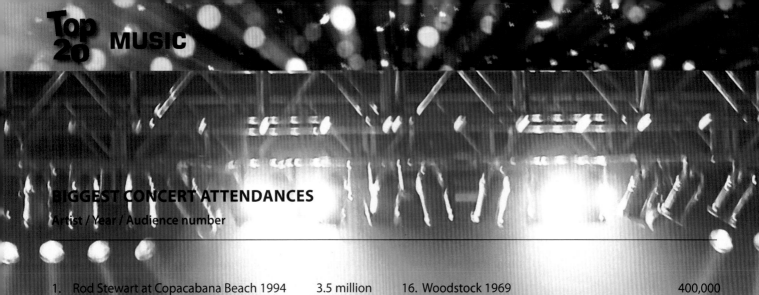

BIGGEST CONCERT ATTENDANCES

Artist / Year / Audience number

1.	Rod Stewart at Copacabana Beach 1994	3.5 million
2.	Jean Michel Jarre in Moscow 1997	3.5 million
3.	Jean Michel Jarre in Paris 1994	2.5 million
4.	AC/DC Monsters of Rock in Moscow 1991	1.6 million
5.	Rolling Stones at Copacabana Beach 2006	1.5 million
6.	Peace Without Border in Havana 2009	1.5 million
7.	New York Philharmonic in Central Park 1986	800,000
8.	Garth Brooks in Central Park 1997	750,000
9.	Steve Wozniak's 1983 US Festival	670,000
10.	Summer Jam at Watkins Glen 1973	600,000+
11.	Isle of Wight Festival 1970	600,000
12.	Simon & Garfunkel in Central Park 1981	500,000
13.	Genesis Turn It On Again in Rome 2007	500,000
14.	Toronto SARS Benefit 2003	450,000
15.	Queen & Iron Maiden Rock In Rio 1985	400,000
16.	Woodstock 1969	400,000
17.	Parkpop in Den Haag 2002	400,000
18.	Blockbuster RockFest 1997	385,000
19.	Heavy Metal Day in San Bernadino 1983	375,000
20.	Tina Turner at The Maracana Stadium, Rio De Janeiro 1988	180,000

Did you know?
Live Aid in 1985 drew a combined live and television audience of 2 billion for the seven venues that held events.

LONGEST AT THE TOP OF THE UK CHART (SINGLES)

Artist / Song / Number of weeks at number one

1 Frankie Laine / *I Believe* / 18
2 Bryan Adams / *(Everything I Do) I Do It For You* / 16
3 Wet Wet Wet / *Love Is All Around* / 15
4 Slim Whitman / *Rose Marie* / 11
5 David Whitfield / *Cara Mia* / 10
6 Whitney Houston / *I Will Always Love You* / 10
7 Rihanna Featuring Jay-Z / *Umbrella* / 10
8 Al Martino / *Here In My Heart* / 9
9 Eddie Calvert / *Oh Mein Papa* / 9
10 Doris Day / *Secret Love* / 9
11 Paul Anka / *Diana* / 9
12 Queen / *Bohemian Rhapsody* / 9
13 Wings / *Mull Of Kintyre/Girls' School* / 9
14 John Travolta & Olivia Newton John / *You're The One That I Want* / 9
15 Frankie Goes To Hollywood / *Two Tribes* / 9
16 Gnarls Barkley / *Crazy* / 9
17 Frankie Laine / *Answer Me* / 8
18 Perry Como / *Magic Moments* / 8
19 Elvis Presley / *It's Now Or Never* / 8
20 The Shadows / *Wonderful Land* / 8

Source: OCC

Frankie Laine's *I Believe* hit the top three times during its run. Bryan Adams' *(Everything I Do) I Do It For You* holds the record for the most consecutive weeks at number one with a total of 16 at the top spot.

LONGEST AT THE TOP OF THE US CHART (SINGLES)

Artist / Song / Number of weeks at number one

Source: Billboard

#	Artist / Song / Weeks
1	Mariah Carey & Boyz II Men / One Sweet Day / 16
2	Whitney Houston / I Will Always Love You / 15
3	Boyz II Men / I'll Make Love To You / 15
4	Los Del Rio / Macarena / 15
5	Elton John / Candle In The Wind 1997/Something About The Way You Look Tonight / 15
6	Mariah Carey / We Belong Together / 15
7	Black Eyes Peas / I Gotta Feeling / 14
8	Brandy & Monica / The Boy Is Mine / 13
9	Boyz II Men / End Of The Road / 13
10	Santana Featuring Rob Thomas / Smooth / 12
11	Eminem / Lose Yourself / 12
12	Usher Featuring Lil Jon & Ludacris / Yeah! / 12
13	Black Eyed Peas / Boom Boom Pow / 12
14	Elvis Presley / Hound Dog/Don't Be Cruel / 11
15	All-4-One / I Swear / 11
16	Toni Braxton / Un-break My Heart / 11
17	Puff Daddy & Faith Evans Featuring 112 / I'll Be Missing You / 11
18	Destiny's Child / Independent Woman / 11
19	McGuire Sisters / Sincerely / 10
20	Perez Prado / Cherry Pink And Apple Blossom White / 10

In February 1905, Sunderland forward, Alf Common became the first player to be transferred for £1,000 when he joined Middlesbrough.

HIGHEST TRANSFER FEES*

Name / Team change / Fee (millions $/£ unless stated)

1 Cristian Ronaldo / Manchester United to Real Madrid 2009 / 130 / 80

2 Zlatan Ibrahimovic / Internazionale to Barcelona 2009 / 92 / 56.5

3 Kaka / Milan to Real Madrid 2009 / 90 / 55

4 Fernando Torres / Liverpool to Chelsea 2011 / 81.5 / 50

5 Zinedine Zidane / Juventus to Real Madrid 2001 / 77.5 / 45.7

6 Luis Figo / Barcelona to Real Madrid 2000 / 60 / 37

7 Herman Crespo / Parma to Lazio 2000 / 58 / 35.5

8 Andy Carroll / Newcastle United to Liverpool 2011 / 57 / 35

9 David Villa / Valencia to Barcelona 2010 / 56 / 34.2

10 Gianluigi Buffon / Parma to Juventus 2001 / 53 / 32.6

11 Robinho / Real Madrid to Manchester City 2008 / 53 / 32.6

12 Christian Vieri / Lazio to Internazionale 1999 / 52 / 32

13 Andriy Shevchenko / Milan to Chelsea 2006 / 50.2 / 30.8

14 Dimitar Berbatov / Tottenham Hotspur to Manchester United 2008 / 50.1 / 30.75

15 Pavel Nedved / Lazio to Juventus 2001 / 49.6 / 30.7

16 Karim Benzema / Lyon to Real Madrid 2009 / 48.6 / 29.76

17 Rio Ferdinand / Leeds United to Manchester United 2002 / 47.4 / 29.1

18 Gaizko Mendieta / Valencia to Lazio 2001 / 47.3 / 29

19 Ronaldo / Internazionale to Real Madrid 2002 / 46.4 / 28.49

20 Juan Veron / Lazio to Manchester United 2001 / 45.9 / 28.1

* In Association Football

WORLD CUP GOALSCORERS (Finals only)

Name / Team (number of goals scored)

1 Ronaldo / Brazil (15)

2 Miroslav Klose / Germany (14)

3 Gerd Muller / West Germany (14)

4 Just Fontaine / France (13)

5 Pele / Brazil (12)

6 Jurgen Klinsmann / Germany (11)

7 Sandor Kocsis / Hungary (11)

8 Gabriel Batistuta / Argentina (10)

9 Gary Lineker / England (10)

10 Helmut Rahn / West Germany (10)

11 Teofilo Cubillas / Peru (10)

12 Grzegorz Lato / Poland (10)

13 Ademir / Brazil (9)

14 Jairzinho / Brazil (9)

15 Vava / Brazil (9)

16 Karl-Heinz Rummenigge / West Germany (9)

17 Uwe Seeler / West Germany (9)

18 Roberto Baggio / Italy (9)

19 Paolo Rossi / Italy / 9

20 Christian Vieri / Italy (9)

Did you know? Just Fontaine's tally of 13 goals was scored in a single World Cup tournament the 1958 finals held in Sweden, where France finished in third place.

Did you know?

In the span of a year, Zlatan Ibrahimovic was loaned out to Milan, Emmanuel Adebayor to Real Madrid, Thierry Henry to the New York Red Bulls, Michael Ballack returned to Germany, Raul, too, headed for Germany, while Wayne Rooney re-negotiated his contract for a reported £12.5 million. In 1961, Johnny Haynes became the first British-based player to earn £100 a week.

HIGHEST-PAID FOOTBALLERS PER SEASON

Name / Team / Fee (millions)

1
Wayne Rooney
Manchester United
$20.4 / £12.5

2
Cristiano Ronaldo
Real Madrid
$18.4 / £11.3

3
Zlatan Ibrahimovic
Barcelona
$17 / £10.4

4
Lionel Messi
Barcelona
$14.9 / £9.1

5
Samuel Eto'o
Internazionale
$14.9 / £9.1

6
Kaka
Real Madrid
$14.2 / £8.7

7
Emmanuel Adebayor
Manchester City
$12 / £7.4

8
Karim Benzema
Real Madrid
$12 / £7.4

9
Carlos Tevez
Manchester City
$11.4 / £7

10
John Terry
Chelsea
$10.6 / £6.5

11
Frank Lampard
Chelsea
$10.6 / £6.5

12
Thierry Henry
Barcelona
$10.6 / £6.5

13
Xavi
Barcelona
$10.6 / £6.5

14
Ronaldinho
Milan
$10.6 / £6.5

15
Steven Gerrard
Liverpool
$10.6 / £6.5

16
Daniel Alves
Barcelona
$10 / £6.1

17
Michael Ballack
Chelsea
$9 / £5.6

18
Raul
Real Madrid
$9 / £5.6

19
Rio Ferdinand
Manchester United
$9 / £5.6

20
Kolo Toure
Manchester City
$9 / £5.6

as of 2011

LONGEST REIGNING EUROPEAN MONARCHS

	Monarch	Country	Reign	Years
1	King Louis XIV	France	1643–1715	72
2	Emperor Franz Joseph I	Austria–Hungary	1848–1916	68
3	Queen Victoria	UK	1837–1901	63
4	King Jaime I	Aragón	1213–1276	63
5	King Christian IV	Denmark	1588–1648	60
6	King George III	Great Britain–Hanover	1760–1820	60
7	Queen Elizabeth II	United Kingdom	1952– *	59
8	King Louis XV	France	1715–1774	59
9	King Harald I	Norway	872–930	58
10	King Alfonso VIII	Castile	1158–1214	58
11	King James VI	Scotland (and later England)	1567–1625	58
12	Queen Wilhelmina	Netherlands	1890–1948	58
13	King Henry III	England	1216–1272	56
14	King Eric III	Norway	1389–1442	53
15	Emperor Friedrich III	Holy Roman Emperor	1440–1493	53
16	King Haakon VII	Norway	1905–1957	52
17	King Gorm the Old	Denmark	900–950	50
18	Emperor Heinrich IV	Holy Roman Emperor	1056–1106	50
19	King Edward III	England	1327–1377	50
20	King Alfonso I	Portugal	1139–1185	46

Queen Victoria died in 1901 at the age of 81

EARLIEST PRESIDENTS OF THE USA

Name (lifespan) / Period in office

1 George Washington (1732–1799)* — 1789–1797
2 John Adams (1735–1826) — 1797–1801
3 Thomas Jefferson (1743–1826) — 1801–1809
4 James Madison (1751–1836) — 1809–1817
5 James Monroe (1758–1831) — 1817–1825
6 John Quincy Adams (1767–1848) — 1825–1829
7 Andrew Jackson (1767–1845) — 1829–1837
8 Martin Van Buren (1782–1862) — 1837–1841
9 William Henry Harrison (1773–1841) — 1841–1841
10 John Tyler (1790–1862) — 1841–1845

11 James K. Polk (1795–1841) — 1845–1849
12 Zachary Taylor (1784–1850) — 1849–1850
13 Millard Fillmore (1800–1874) — 1850–1853
14 Franklin Pierce (1804–1869) — 1853–1857
15 James Buchanan (1791–1868) — 1857–1861
16 Abraham Lincoln (1809–1865) — 1861–1865
17 Andrew Johnson (1808–1875) — 1865–1869
18 Ulysses S. Grant (1822–1885) — 1869–1877
19 Rutherford B. Hayes (1822–1893) — 1877–1881
20 James A. Garfield (1831–1881) — 1881-1881

* George Washington was the first President of the United States following ratification of the Constitution.

Source: The Whitehouse.gov

GREATEST US PRESIDENTS*

1 Ronald Reagan (19%)
2 Abraham Lincoln (14%)
3 Bill Clinton (13%)
4 John F. Kennedy (11%)
5 George Washington (10%)
6 Franklin Roosevelt (8%)
7 Barack Obama (5%)
8 No opinion (5%)
9 Theodore Roosevelt (3%)
10 Harry Truman (3%)
11 George W. Bush (2%)
12 Thomas Jefferson (2%)
13 Jimmy Carter (1%)
14 Dwight Eisenhower (1%)
15 George H. W. Bush (1%)
16 Other (1%)
17 None (1%)
18 Andrew Jackson (less than 0.5%)
19 Lyndon Johnson (less than 0.5%)
20 Richard Nixon (less than 0.5%)

* Figures taken from a poll of 1015 adults asked, "Who do you regard as the greatest United States president?"

Source: Gallup 2011

The International Amateur Athletics Federation (now known as the International Association of Athletics Federations) first ratified a world record for the mile in 1913, with John Paul Jones running the mile in 4:14.4. Roger Bannister recorded the first sub-four minute mile on May 6, 1954, and held the record for 46 days. Since then the record has been held by the following athletes:.

FASTEST MILE RUNNERS

Name / Country of origin / Time / Year

1 Roger Bannister / UK / 3:59.4 (1954)

2 John Landy / Australia / 3:57.9 (1954) **3** Derek Ibbotson / UK / 3:57.2 (1957)

4 Herb Elliott / Australia / 3:54.5 (1958) **5** Peter Snell / New Zealand / 3:54.4 (1962)

6 Peter Snell / New Zealand / 3:54.04 (1964) **7** Michel Jazy / France / 3:53.6 (1965) **8** Jim Ryun / USA / 3:51.3 (1966)

9 Jim Ryun / USA / 3:51.1 (1967) **10** Filbert Bayi / Tanzania / 3:51.0 (1975) **11** John Walker / New Zealand / 3:49.4 (1975)

12 Sebastian Coe / UK / 3:48.95 (1979) **13** Steve Ovett / UK / 3:48.8 (1980) **14** Sebastian Coe / UK / 3:48.53 (1981)

15 Steve Ovett / UK / 3:48.40 (1981) **16** Sebastian Coe / UK / 3:47.33 (1981) **17** Steve Cram / UK / 3:46.32 (1985)

18 Noureddine Morceli / Algeria / 3:44.39 (1993) **19** Hicham El Guerrouj / Morocco / 3:43.13 (1999)

20 The record has not been bettered since 1999.

FASTEST MEN OVER 100 METERS

Name (country of origin) / Time / Year

1 Usain Bolt (Jamaica) / 9.76 / 2008

2 Asafa Powell (Jamaica) / 9.77 / 2005

3 Maurice Green (USA) / 9.79 / 1999

4 Donovan Baily (Canada) / 9.84 / 1999

5 Benny Surin (Canada) / 9.84 / 1999

6 Leroy Burrel (USA) / 9.85 / 1994

7 Justin Gatlin (USA) / 9.85 / 2004

8 Carl Lewis (USA) / 9.86 / 1991

9 Frankie Fredericks (Namibia) / 9.86 / 1996

10 Ato Boldon (Trinidad & Tobago) / 9.86 / 1998

11 Francis Obikwelu (Portugal) / 9.86 / 2004

12 Obadale Thompson (Barbados) / 9.87 / 1998

13 Darvis Patton (USA) / 9.89 / 2008

14 Tim Harden (USA) / 9.92 / 1999

15 Michael Marsh (USA) / 9.93 / 1992

16 Patrick Johnson (Australia) / 9.93 / 2003

17 Olusoji Fasuba (Nigeria) / 9.93 / 2006

18 Walter Dix (USA) / 9.93 / 2007

19 Richard Thompson (Trinidad & Tobago) / 9.93 / 2008

20 Calvin Smith (USA) / 9.93 / 1983

Did you know?
A total of 74 men have beaten the ten-second barrier for the 100 meters, with Linford Christie the first European to achieve the feat in 1988 (9.97 seconds). Three men also had their records expunged for drug and doping offences—Justin Gatlin, Tim Montgomery and Ben Johnson.

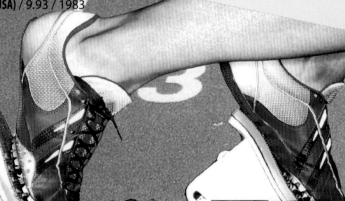

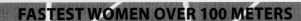

FASTEST WOMEN OVER 100 METERS

Name (country of origin) / Time / Year

1 Florence Griffith-Joyner / USA / 10.49 / 1988

2 Carmelita Jeter / USA / 10.64 / 2009

3 Marion Jones / USA / 10.65 / 1998

4 Christine Arron / France / 10.73 / 1998

5 Shelly-Ann Fraser / Jamaica / 10.73 / 2009

6 Merlene Ottey / Jamaica / 10.74 / 1996

7 Kerron Stewart / Jamaica / 10.75 / 2009

8 Evelyn Ashford / USA / 10.76 / 1984

9 Irina Privalova / Russia / 10.77 / 1994

10 Ivet Lalova / Bulgaria / 10.77 / 2004

11 Dawn Sowell / USA / 10.78 / 1989

12 Torri Edwards / USA / 10.78 / 2008

13 Veronica Campbell-Brown / Jamaica / 10.78 / 2010

14 Li Xuemi / China / 10.79 / 1997

15 Inger Miller / USA / 10.79 / 1999

16 Marlie Gohr / East Germany / 10.81 / 1983

17 Gail Devers / USA / 10.82 / 1992

18 Gwen Torrence / USA / 10.82 / 1994

19 Zhanna Block / Ukraine / 10.82 / 2001

20 Sherone Simpson / Jamaica / 10.82 / 2006

Source: IAAF

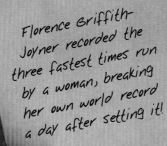

Florence Griffith-Joyner recorded the three fastest times run by a woman, breaking her own world record a day after setting it!

LANGUAGE AND LITERATURE

BESTSELLING BOOKS NOT IN ENGLISH*

Title (date and language of first publication) / Author / Sales (millions)

1. *Dream of the Red Chamber* (1759–91, Chinese)
   Cao Xueqin / 100+
2. *The Alchemist* (1988, Portugese)
   Paulo Coelho / 65
3. *The Name of the Rose* (1980, Italian)
   Umberto Eco / 50
4. *How the Steel Was Tempered* (1932, Russian)
   Nikoalai Ostrovsky / 36.4
5. *War and Peace* (1932, Russian)
   Leo Tolstoy / 36
6. *100 Years of Solitude* (1967, Spanish)
   Gabriel Garcia Marquez / 30
7. *The Girl with the Dragon Tattoo* (2005, Swedish)
   Stieg Larsson / 30
8. *Wolf Totem* (2004, Chinese)
   Jiang Rong / 20
9. *Perfume* (1985, German)
   Patrick Süskind / 15
10. *The Shadow of the Wind* (2001, Spanish)
    Carlos Ruiz Zafó / 15

11. *Follow Your Heart* (1994, Italian) Susanna Tamaro / 14
12. *The Girl Who Kicked the Hornet's Nest* (2007, Swedish)
    Stieg Larsson / 12
13. *Norwegian Wood* (1987, Chinese) Haruki Murakami / 12
14. *The Plague* (1947, French) Albert Camus / 12
15. *No Longer Human* (1948, Japanese) Osamu Dazai / 12
16. *Santa Evita* (1995, Spanish) Tomás Eloy Martínez / 10
17. *Night* (1958, Yiddish) Elie Wiesel / 10
18. *Dan's Gain from the Analects* (2006, Chinese) Yu Dan / 10
19. *Knowledge-value Revolution* (1985, Japanese)
    Taichi Sakaiya / 10
20. *Problems in China's Socialist Economy* (1979, Chinese)
    Xue Muqiao / 10

* When first published.

BESTSELLING CHILDREN'S BOOKS IN ENGLISH

Title (year first published) / Author / Estimated sales (millions)

1. *Harry Potter series* (1997) J.K. Rowling / 400
2. *Goosebumps series* (1992) R.L. Stine / 350
3. *The Baby-sitters Club* (1986) Ann Martin / 335
4. *Berenstein Bears* (1962) Stan and Jan Berenstein / 260
5. *Noddy* (1949) Enid Blyton / 200
6. *Thomas the Tank Engine series* (1945) Rev. W. Audrey / 200
7. *Peter Rabbit* (1902) Beatrix Potter / 150
8. *The Lord of the Rings* (1954–55) J.R.R. Tolkien / 150
9. *Chronicles of Narnia* (1949) C.S. Lewis / 120
10. *Clifford the Big Red Dog* (1963) Norman Bridwell / 110
11. *The Mr. Men series* (1971) Roger Hargreaves / 100
12. *The Hobbit* (1937) J.R.R. Tolkien / 100
13. *The Little Prince* (1943) Antoine de Sainte-Exupéry / 80
14. *Winnie the Pooh* (1926) A.A. Milne / 70
15. *A Series of Unfortunate Events* (1999) Daniel Handler* / 60
16. *Heidi's Years of Wandering and Learning* (1880) Johanna Spyri / 50
17. *Anne of Green Gables* (1908) Lucy Maud Montgomery / 50
18. *Black Beauty* (1877) Anna Sewell / 50
19. *Charlotte's Web* (1952) E.B. White / 45
20. *The Adventures of Pinocchio* (1881) Carlo Collodi / 35

* Writing as Lemony Snicket

LONGEST NOVELS EVER WRITTEN

Title (year of first publication) / Author / Number of words

1. *The Blah Story* (2008) / Nigel Tomm / 11,300,000
2. *Demi-God* (1977) / Mohiuddin Nawab / 11,206,310
3. *The Story of the Vivian Girls* (1912) /
   Henry Darger / 9,000,000
4. *Gordana* (1966) / Marija Juric Zagorka / 3,120,000
5. *Cyrus the Great* (1849) /
   Madeleine & George de Scudéry / 2,100,000
6. *The Men of Good Will* (1932) / Jules Romains / 2,070,000
7. *In Search of Lost Time* (1913) / Marcel Proust / 1,500,000
8. *Sironia, Texas* (1952) / Madison Cooper / 1,100,000
9. *The Man Without Qualities* (1930) /
   Robert Musil / 1,020,000 (est.)
10. *Bottom's Dream* (1970) / Arno Schmidt / 1,000,000
11. *Clarissa* (1748) / Samuel Richardson / 969,000
12. *Poor Fellow My Country* (1975) / Herbert / 850,000
13. *Miss MacIntosh, My Darling* (1965) / Marguerite Young /
    700,000
14. *Varney the Vampire* (1847) / James Malcolm Rymer / 667,000
15. *Atlas Shrugged* (1957) / Ayn Rand / 645,000
16. *The Vicomte of Bragelonne: Ten Years Later* (1847)
    Alexander Dumas, père / 626,000
17. *A Suitable Boy* (1993) / Vikram Seth / 591,552
18. *War and Peace* (1869) / Leo Tolstoy / 560,000
19. *Remembrance Rock* (1948) / Carl Sandberg / 532,030
20. *The Wretched* (1862) / Victor Hugo / 513,000

If E-books were included the longest work would be Marienbad My Love (2008) by Mark Leach, which is 17,000,000 words long!

BIGGEST EARTHQUAKES

Location / Year / Magnitude / Deaths

1
Valdivia, Chile
May 22, 1960
9.5 / 6,000+

2
Prince William Sound, Alaska
March 27, 1964
9.2 / 143

3
Sumatra, Indonesia
December 26, 2004
9.1 / 230,000+

4
Kamchatka, Russia
November 4, 1952
9.0 / unknown

5
Arica, Peru (now Chile)
August 13, 1868
9.0 / 25,000+

6
NE Pacific Coast, USA
(Canada)
January 26, 1700
9.0 / unknown

7
Japan
March 11, 2011
8.9 / 15,000+

8
Maule, Chile
February 27, 2010
8.8 / 570

9
Ecuador, Colombia
January 31, 1906
8.8 / 1,000+

10
Sumatra, Indonesia
November 25, 1833
8.8 / unknown

11
Rat Islands, Alaska
February 4, 1965
8.7 / 0

12
Lisbon, Portugal
November 1, 1755
8.7 / 60,000+

13
Valparaiso, Chile
July 8, 1730
8.7 / 3,000+

14
Sumatra, Indonesia
March 28, 2005
8.6 / 1,350

15
Andreanof Islands, Alaska
March 9, 1957
8.6 / 0

16
Assam, India
(Tibet)
August 15, 1950
8.6 / 1,526

17
Sumatra, Indonesia
September 12, 2007
8.5 / 23

18
Sanriku, Japan
June 15, 1896
8.5 / 22,000+

19
Lima, Peru
October 20, 1687
8.5 / 5,000+

20
Aleppo, Syria
October 11, 1138
8.5 / 230,000+

The earthquake in Haiti in 2010 measured 7 on the magnitude scale and damaged 250,000 homes, forcing many to live in temporary accommodation.

BIGGEST FLOODS

Event (location) / Year / Deaths

1 China Floods (China) 1931 / 2,500,000–3,700,000

2 Yellow River flood (China) 1887 / 900,000–2,000,000

3 Yellow River flood(China) 1938 / 500,000–700,000

4 Yangtze River flood (China) 1935 / 145,000

5 St. Felix's flood (Netherlands) 1530 / 100,000+

6 Hanoi/Red River Delta flood (North Vietnam) 1971 / 100,000

7 Yangtze River flood (China) 1911 / 100,000

8 Banqiao Dam failure (China) 1975 / 86,000

9 St. Lucia's flood (Netherlands) 1287 / 50,000–80,000

10 North Sea flood (Netherlands) 1212 / 60,000

11 Eastern Guatemala flood (Guatemala) 1949 / 40,000

12 St. Marcellus flood (Netherlands) 1219 / 36,000

13 Yangtze River flood (China) 1954 / 30,000

14 Bangladesh monsoon (Bangladesh) 1974 / 28,700

15 Grote Mandrenke storm tide (Netherlands/Germany/ Denmark) 1362 / 25,000–40,000

16 Vargas mudslide (Venezuela) 1999 / 20,006

17 All Saint's flood (Netherlands) 1570 / 20,000

18 Tianjin flood (China) 1939 / 20,000

19 Christmas flood (Netherlands/Germany/Denmark) 1717 / 14,000

20 St. Elizabeth flood (Netherlands/ Belgium) 1421 / 10,000+

MOST PLATINUM AWARDS IN THE UK (GROUPS)

#	Artist	Awards
1	U2	16
2	Queen	14
3	Oasis	11
4	ABBA	10
5	The Beatles	10
6	Led Zeppelin	10
7	Westlife	9
8	Dire Straits	8
9	Eurythmics	8
10	Paul McCartney/Wings	8
11	R.E.M.	8
12	Take That	8
13	UB40	8
14	Wet Wet Wet	8
15	Beautiful South	7
16	Bon Jovi	7
17	Fleetwood Mac	7
18	Genesis	7
19	Green Day	7
20	Pet Shop Boys	7

Source: BPI

Did you know?

Madonna is listed by the Guinness Book of Records as the most successful female recording artist of all time. Since the beginning of her career, she has sold over 200 million records worldwide.

MOST PLATINUM AWARDS IN THE UK (FEMALE)
ARTIST / NUMBER OF AWARDS   Source: BPI

1 Madonna 18
2 Tina Turner 8
3 Kate Bush 7
4 Mariah Carey 7
5 Kylie Minogue 7
6 Celine Dion 6
7 Enya 6
8 Whitney Houston 6
9 Diana Ross 6
10 Barbra Streisand 6
11 Cher 5
12 Gloria Estefan 5
13 Janet Jackson 5
14 Pink 5
15 Britney Spears 5
16 Anastacia 4
17 Sheryl Crow 4
18 Rihanna 4
19 Shania Twain 4
20 Elaine Paige 4

ARTISTS WITH THE MOST PLATINUM AWARDS (UK)

1 Oasis *(What's The Story) Morning Glory*	(14x)	**12** Shania Twain *Come On Over* (10x)
2 ABBA *Gold Greatest Hits*	(13x)	**13** Robbie Williams *I've Been Expecting You* (10x)
3 Dire Straits *Brothers In Arms*	(13x)	**14** James Blunt *Back To Bedlam* (10x)
4 Michael Jackson *Bad*	(13x)	**15** Pink Floyd *Dark Side Of The Moon* (10x)
5 Madonna *The Immaculate Collection*	(12x)	**16** Elton John *The Very Best Of Elton John* (9x)
6 Simply Red *Stars*	(12x)	**17** The Corrs *Talk On Corners* (9x)
7 Queen *Queen's Greatest Hits*	(11x)	**18** Travis *The Man Who* (9x)
8 Michael Jackson *Thriller*	(11x)	**19** David Gray *White Ladders* (9x)
9 Fleetwood Mac *Rumours*	(10x)	**20** Dido *No Angel* (9x)
10 Alanis Morisette *Jagged Little Pill*	(10x)	*Source: BPI*
11 Spice Girls *Spice*	(10x)	

BESTSELLING ALBUMS IN THE USA

RIAA introduced a Diamond Award in 1999 to any album that sold more than ten million copies domestically. These are the current bestsellers.

1 The Eagles *Their Greatest Hits 1971–1975*	(29 million)	**12** Garth Brooks *No Fences* (17 million)
2 Michael Jackson *Thriller*	(29 million)	**13** Boston *Boston* (17 million)
3 Pink Floyd *The Wall*	(23 million)	**14** Whitney Houston *The Bodyguard* Soundtrack (17 million)
4 Led Zeppelin *Led Zeppelin IV*	(23 million)	**15** The Beatles *The Beatles 1967–1970* (17 million)
5 AC/DC *Back In Black*	(22 million)	**16** Hootie & The Blowfish *Cracked Rear View Mirror* (16 million)
6 Garth Brooks *Double Live*	(21 million)	**17** Elton John *Greatest Hits* (16 million)
7 Billy Joel *Greatest Hits Volumes I & II*	(21 million)	**18** The Eagles *Hotel California* (16 million)
8 Shania Twain *Come On Over*	(20 million)	**19** Alanis Morisette *Jagged Little Pill* (16 million)
9 The Beatles *The Beatles (White Album)*	(19 million)	**20** Led Zeppelin *Physical Graffiti* (16 million)
10 Fleetwood Mac *Rumours*	(19 million)	*Source: RIAA*
11 Guns N Roses *Appetite For Destruction*	(18 million)	

MOST COMPETITORS AT THE OLYMPIC GAMES

Country (Olympic year) / Number of games

1 Beijing, China (2008) 10,942
2 Sydney, Australia (2000) 10,651
3 Athens, Greece (2004) 10,625
4 Atlanta, USA (1996) 10,318
5 Barcelona, Spain (1992) 9,356
6 Seoul, South Korea (1988) 8,391
7 Munich, West Germany (1972) 7,134
8 Los Angles, USA (1984) 6,829
9 Montreal, Canada (1976) 6,084
10 Mexico City, Mexico (1968) 5,516

11 Rome, Italy (1960) 5,338
12 Moscow, Soviet Union (1980) 5,179
13 Tokyo, Japan (1964) 5,151
14 Helsinki, Finland (1952) 4,955
15 London, UK (1948) 4,104
16 Berlin, Germany (1936) 3,963
17 Melbourne, Australia (1956) 3,314
18 Paris, France (1924) 3,089
19 Amsterdam, Netherlands (1928) 2,883
20 Antwerp, Belgium (1920) 2,626

MOST PARALYMPIC GOLD MEDALS IN ONE SPORT

1 Trischa Zorn (USA) Swimming / 32
2 Reinhold Moller (Germany) Alpine Skiing / 16
3 Jonas Jacobsson (Sweden) Shooting /16
4 Ragnhild Myklebust (Norway) Cross Country Skiing / 16
5 Mike Kenny (Great Britain) Swimming / 16
6 Beatrice Hess (France) Swimming / 15
7 Mayumi Narita (Japan) Swimming / 15
8 Franz Nietlispach (Switzerland) Athletics / 14
9 Chantal Petitclerc (Canada) Athletics / 14
10 Erin Popovich (USA) Swimming / 14
11 Michael Edgson (Canada) Swimming / 14
12 Erling Trondsen (Norway) Swimming / 13
13 Claudia Hengst (Germany) Swimming / 13
14 Bart Dodson (USA) Athletics / 13
15 John Morhan (USA) Swimming / 13
16 Gerd Schoenfelder (Germany) Alpine Skiing / 12
17 Rolf Heinzmann (Switzerland) Alpine skiing / 12
18 Sarah Will (USA) Alpine Swimming / 12
19 Heinz Frei (Switzerland) Athletics / 11
20 David Roberts (Great Britain) Swimming / 11

Source: IOC

OLYMPIANS WITH
MOST GOLD MEDALS

Name (country) / Sport / Medals won

1   Michael Phelps (USA) / Swimming / 14
2   Larissa Latynina (Soviet Union) / Gymnastics / 9
3   Paavo Nurmi (Finland) / Athletics / 9
4   Mark Spitz (USA) / Swimming / 9
5   Carl Lewis (USA) / Athletics / 9
6   Bjorn Daehlie (Norway) / Cross Country Skiing / 8
7   Birgit Fischer (Germany) / Canoeing / 8
8   Sawao Kato (Japan) / Gymnastics / 8
9   Jenny Thompson (USA) / Swimming / 8
10   Matt Biondi (USA) / Swimming / 8
11   Ray Ewry (USA) / Athletics / 8
12   Nikolai Andrianov (Soviet Union) / Gymnastics / 7
13   Boris Shakhlin (Soviet Union) / Gymnastics / 7
14   Vera Asavska (Czechoslovakia) / Gymnastics / 7
15   Viktor Chukarin (Soviet Union) / Gymnastics / 7
16   Aladar Gerevich (Hungary) / Fencing / 7
17   Hubert Van Innis (Belgium) / Archery / 6
18   Nedo Nadi (Italy) / Fencing / 6
19   Edoardo Mangiarotti (Italy) / Fencing / 6
20   Pal Kovacs (Hungary) / Fencing / 6

Did you know?
Michael Phelps has won an amazing overall 16 Olympic medals!

Fabio Scozzoli (Italy) in 50m breaststroke at European Swimming Championships, August 15, 2010.

MOST PROFITABLE FILMS WITH A BUDGET UNDER $1 MILLION

Title	Cost	Gross box office	Year
1. The Blair Witch Project	$35,000	$248,300,000	1999
2. Rocky	$1,000,000	$225,000,000	1976
3. Paranormal Activity	$15,000	$196,681,656	2009
4. Mad Max	$200,000	$99,750,000	1980
5. Deep Throat	$22,500	$45,000,000	1972
6. Super Size Me	$65,000	$29,529,368	2004
7. Night of the Living Dead	$114,000	$30,000,000	1968
8. Texas Chainsaw Massacre	$140,000	$26,572,439	1974
9. The Brothers MacMullen	$25,000	$10,426,506	1985
10. Facing the Giants	$100,000	$10,178,331	2006
11. Birth of a Nation	$110,000	$9,300,000	1915
12. Cat People	$134,000	$8,000,000	1942
13. Eraserhead	$100,000	$7,000,000	1977
14. Roger & Me	$140,000	$6,706,368	1989
15. Pi	$68,000	$4,678,513	1998
16. Clerks	$27,000	$3,894,240	1994
17. The Road to Ruin	$2,500	$2,500,000	1928
18. In the Company of Men	$25,000	$2,883,261	1997
19. El Mariachi	$7,000	$2,040,920	1992
20. Tarnation	$218.32	$1,162,014	2004

Source: Box Office Mojo

MOST EXPENSIVE FILMS EVER MADE

Title / Year / Cost

#	Title	Year	Cost
1	Pirates of the Caribbean: At World's End	2007	$300m
2	The Hobbit Part 2	2013	$270m
3	The Hobbit Part 1	2012	$270m
4	Tangled	2010	$260m
5	Spiderman 3	2013	$258m
6	Harry Potter and the Half-Blood Prince	2009	$250m
7	Avatar	2009	$237m
8	Superman Returns	2006	$232m
9	Quantum of Solace	2008	$230m
10	Pirates of the Caribbean: Dead Man's Chest	2006	$225m
11	Chronicles of Narnia: Prince Caspian	2008	$225m
12	Robin Hood	2010	$210m
13	Transformers: Revenge of the Fallen	2010	$210m
14	X-Men: The Last Stand	2009	$210m
15	King Kong	2005	$207m
16	His Dark Materials: Golden Compass	2007	$205m
17	Titanic	1997	$200m
18	Spiderman 2	2004	$200m
19	Prince of Persia: Sands of Time	2010	$200m
20	Toy Story 3	2010	$200m

Source: Variety

MOST WORLD SERIES APPEARANCES (PLUS WINS)

1 New York Yankees / 40 (27)   **2** San Francisco Giants / 18 (6)   **3** Los Angeles Dodgers / 18 (6)

4 St. Louis Cardinals / 17 (10)   **5** Oakland Athletics / 14 (9)

6 Boston Red Sox / 11 (7)   **7** Detroit Tigers / 10 (4)   **8** Chicago Cubs / 10 (2)

9 Cinncinnati Reds / 9 (5)   **10** Atlanta Braves / 9 (3)   **11** Pittsburgh Pirates / 7 (5)

12 Baltimore Orioles / 7 (3)   **13** Philadelphia Phillies / 7 (2)

14 Minnesota Twins / 6 (3)   **15** Chicago White Sox / 5 (3)

16 Cleveland Indians / 5 (2)   **17** New York Mets / 5 (2)

18 Florida Marlins / 2 (2)   **19** Toronto Blue Jays / 2 (2)   **20** Kansas City Royals / 2 (1)

Did you know?
The United States has won the most Little League World Series events, with 32 of the 64 competitions won.

PITCHERS WITH THE MOST STRIKEOUTS

1 Nolan Ryan / 5,714
2 Randy Johnson / 4,875
3 Roger Clemens / 4,672
4 Steve Carlton / 4,136
5 Bert Blyleven / 3,701
6 Tom Seaver / 3,640
7 Don Sutton / 3,574
8 Gaylord Perry / 3,534
9 Walter Johnson / 3,509
10 Greg Maddux / 3,371
11 Phil Niekro / 3,342
12 Ferguson Jenkins / 3,192
13 Pedro Martinez / 3,154
14 Bob Gibson / 3,117
15 Curt Schilling / 3,116
16 John Smoltz / 3,084
17 Jim Bunning / 2,855
18 Mickey Lolich / 2,832
19 Mike Mussina / 2,813
20 Cy Young / 2,803

Source: Baseball Almanac

From this list of pitchers, only Pedro Martinez is still playing.

MOST HOME RUNS IN BASEBALL

1 Barry Bonds 762
2 Hank Aaron 755
3 Babe Ruth 714
4 Willie Mays 660
5 Ken Griffey Jr 630
6 Alex Rodriguez 613
7 Sammy Sosa 609
8 Jim Thorne 589
9 Frank Robinson 586
10 Mark McGwire 583
11 Harmon Killebrew 573
12 Rafael Palmeiro 569
13 Reggie Jackson 563
14 Manny Ramirez 555
15 Mike Schmidt 548
16 Mickey Mantle 536
17 Jimmy Foxx 534
18 Willie McCovey 521
19 Frank Thomas 521
20 Ted Williams 521

Source: Baseball Almanac

Alex Rodriguez, Jim Thorne and Manny Ramirez are still playing and so could add to their tallies.

MOST POPULAR EXHIBITIONS AT THE NATIONAL GALLERY, LONDON

Exhibition (date)	Attendance	Free/Paid
1 Manet to Picasso (2006–07)	1,110,044	Free
2 Van Gogh to Picasso: The Berggruen Collection (1991)	530,000	Free
3 London's Monets (1997)	400,000	Free
4 Seeing Salvation (1999–2000)	355,175	Free
5 Tradition and Revolution in French Art: Paintings and Drawings from Lille (1993)	334,000	Paid
6 Velázquez (2006–07)	302,520	Paid
7 Degas: Beyond Impressionism (1996)	283,000	Paid
8 Vermeer and the Delft School (2001)	276,174	Paid
9 Titian (2003)	267,939	Paid
10 Venice through Canaletto's Eyes (1998)	247,000	Free
11 Caravaggio: The Final Years (2005)	244,955	Paid
12 Raphael: from Urbino to Rome (2004)	230,649	Paid
13 Picasso's Prints: Challenging the Past (2009)	227,831	Free
14 Rembrandt by Himself (1999)	226,000	Paid
15 Cezanne in Britain (2006–07)	225,957	Free
16 Kienholz: The Hoerengracht (2010)	223,183	Free
17 Making and Meaning: The Young Michelangelo (1994–95)	223,000	Free
18 El Greco (2004)	221,542	Paid
19 Picasso: Challenging the Past (2009)	204,862	Paid
20 Masterpieces from the Doria Pamphilj Gallery (1996)	204,000	Free

Source: National Gallery, London

MOST VISITED ART MUSEUMS

Art Museum / Number of visitors per year (2009)

1 Musée du Louvre, Paris, France / **8,500,000** **2** British Museum, London, UK / **5,842,138**
3 Metropolitan Museum of Art, New York City, USA / **5,216,988** **4** Tate Modern, London, UK / **5,061,172**

5 National Gallery, London, UK / **4,954,914** **6** National Gallery of Art, Washington, DC, USA / **4,775,114**
7 Museum of Modern Art, New York City, USA / **3,131,238** **8** Centre Georges Pompidou, Paris, France / **3,130,000**

9 National Museum of Korea, Seoul, South Korea / **3,067,909** **10** Musee d'Orsay, Paris, France / **2,985,510**
11 Museo del Prado, Madrid, Spain / **2,732,000** **12** Victoria and Albert Museum, London, UK / **2,629,065**

13 Hermitage Museum, St. Petersburg, Russia / **2,426,203** **14** Centro Cultural Banco do Brasil, Rio de Janeiro, Brazil / **2,317,772**
15 Museo Reina Sofía, Madrid, Spain / **2,313,532** **16** M.H. de Young Memorial Museum, San Francisco, USA / **2,043,854**

17 The National Art Center, Tokyo, Japan / **2,027,980**
18 The National Portrait Gallery, London, UK / **1,819,442**
19 Galleria degli Uffizi, Florence, Italy / **1,651,210**
20 Art Institute of Chicago, Chicago, USA / **1,846,889**

The average amount of time visitors spend looking a each painting when visiting an art gallery is 3 seconds.

MOST POINTS IN AN NBA CAREER

1 Kareem Abdul-Jabbar / 38,387
2 Karl Malone / 36,928
3 Michael Jordan / 32,292
4 Wilt Chamberlain / 31,419
5 Shaquille O'Neal / 28,590
6 Moses Malone / 27,409
7 Elvin Hayes / 27,313
8 Kobe Bryant / 27,279
9 Hakeem Olajuwon / 26,946
10 Oscar Robertson / 26,710
11 Dominique Wilkins / 26,668
12 John Havlicek / 26,395
13 Alex English / 25,613
14 Reggie Miller / 25,279
15 Jerry West / 25,192
16 Patrick Ewing / 24,815
17 Allen Iverson / 24,368
18 Charles Barkley / 23,737
19 Robert Parish / 23,334
20 Adrian Dantley / 23,177

Source: Basketball-reference.com

Shaquille O'Neal and Kobe Bryant are still playing today in the NBA.

MOST GAMES PLAYED IN AN NBA CAREER

1 Robert Parish 1,611
2 Kareem Abdul-Jabbar 1,560
3 John Stockton 1,504
4 Karl Malone 1,476
5 Kevin Willis 1,424
6 Reggie Miller 1,389
7 Clifford R. Robinson 1,380
8 Gary Payton 1,335
9 Moses Malone 1,329
10 Buck Williams 1,307
11 Elvin Hayes 1,303
12 Mark Jackson 1,296
13 Sam Perkins 1,286
14 Charles Oakley 1,282
15 A.C. Green 1,278
16 Terry Porter 1,274
17 John Havlicek 1,270
18 Otis Thorpe 1,257
19 Paul Silas 1,254
20 Hakeem Olajuwon 1,238

Kevin Garnett shooting during an NBA Lakers-Celtics Finals

HIGHEST ANNUAL NBA SALARIES

1 Kobe Bryant (LA Lakers) $24,806,250 **2** Rashard Lewis (Washington) $20,514,000 **3** Kevin Garnett (Boston) $18,800,00

4 Tim Duncan (San Antonio) $18,700,00 **5** Michael Redd (Milwaukee) $18,300,000 **6** Pau Gasol (LA Lakers) $17,822,187

7 Andrei Kirilenko (Utah) $17,822,187 **8** Gilbert Arenas (Orlando) $17,730,694 **9** Yao Ming (Houston) $17,686,100

10 Zach Randolph (Memphis) $17,333,333 **11** Dirk Nowitzki (Dallas) $17,300,000

12 Vince Carter (Phoenix) $17,300,000 **13** Carmelo Anthony (New York) $17,149,243

14 Dwight Howard (Orlando) $16,509,600 **15** Amare Stoudemire (New York) $16,486,611

16 Joe Johnson (Atlanta) $16,324,500 **17** Kenyon Martin (Denver) $15,959,099

18 Elton Brand (Philadelphia) $15,959,099

19 Pedraq Stojakovic (Dallas) $15,602,138

20 Chris Paul (New Orleans) $14,940,152

Did you know?

Basketball was first played in 1891, having been invented by a Canadian called Dr. James Naismith. The Basketball Association of America was set up in 1946 and became the National Basketball Association (NBA) later that same year. The first title was won by the Philadelphia Warriors in 1947. Rashard Lewis (shown right) was born in 1979 and ranks second in the highest paid players in the NBA.

WORST AVALANCHES

Location / Country / Date / Deaths

1
Yungay (Peru)
May 31, 1970
20,000

2
Tyrolian Alps
(Italy–Austria)
1916
10,000

3
Huascaran (Peru)
1962
4,000

4
Plurs (Switzerland)
September 4, 1618
2,500

5
Swiss–Austrian Alps
(Switzerland–Austria)
Winter 1950–51
265+

6
Blons (Austria)
Jan 12, 1954
200+

7
Lahaul Valley
(India)
March 1979
200+

8
Salang
(Afghanistan)
February 8–9,
2010
172

9
North Ossetia
(Russia)
September 21, 2002
150

10
Washington (USA)
March 1, 1910
118

11
Kohistan
(Pakistan)
February 17, 2010
102

12
Obergesteln
(Switzerland)
Winter 1720
88

13
Saas (Switzerland)
Winter 1689
73

14
Rogers Pass
(Canada)
March 4, 1910
62

15
Bayburt Üzengili
(Turkey)
January 18, 1993
59

16
Møre og Romsdal
(Norway)
1679
55

17
Siglunes (Iceland)
1613
50

18
Val d'Isère (France)
February 10, 1970
39

19
Galtür (Austria)
February 23, 1999
31

20
Seyoisfjorour
(Iceland)
February 18, 1884
24

WORST VOLCANIC ERUPTIONS

Volcano / Country / Date / Deaths

#	Volcano (Country)	Date / Deaths
1	Tambora (Indonesia)	1815 / 92,000
2	Krakatau (Indonesia)	1883 / 36,417
3	Mount Pelée (Martinique)	1902 / 29,025
4	Ruiz (Colombia)	1985 / 25,000
5	Unzen (Japan)	1792 / 14,300
6	Laki (Iceland)	1783 / 9,350
7	Kelut (Indonesia)	1919 / 5,110
8	Galunggung (Indonesia)	1882 / 4,011
9	Vesuvius (Italy)	1631 / 3,500
10	Vesuvius (Italy)	79 AD / 3,360
11	Papandayan (Indonesia)	1772 / 2,957
12	Lamington (Papua New Guinea)	1951 / 2,942
13	El Chichon (Mexico)	1982 / 2,000
14	Soufriere (St. Vincent)	1902 / 1,680
15	Oshima (Japan)	1741 / 1,475
16	Asama (Japan)	1783 / 1,377
17	Taal (Philippines)	1911 / 1,335
18	Mayon (Philippines)	1814 / 1,200
19	Agung (Indonesia)	1963 / 1,184
20	Cotopaxi (Ecuador)	1877 / 1,000

HIGHEST ACTIVE VOLCANOES

Name / Location / Height in feet/meters / Last erupted

1 Nevados Ojos del Salado / Chile / 22,595 / 6,887 / 1993

2 Volcan Llullaillaco / Chile, Argentina / 22,057 / 6,723 / 1877

3 Tipas / Argentina / 21,850 / 6,660 / unknown

4 Cerro El Condor / Argentina / 21,430 / 6,532 / unknown

5 Nevado Coropuna / Peru / 21,079 / 6,425 / unknown

6 Volcan Parinacota / Chile, Bolivia / 20,827 / 6,348 / c.290AD

7 Chimborazo / Ecuador / 20,702 / 6,310 / unknown

8 Pular / Chile / 20,449 / 6,233 / 1990 unconfirmed

9 Cerro Aucanquilcha / Chile / 20,262 / 6,176 / unknown

10 San Pedro / Chile / 20,160 / 6,145 / 1960

11 Aracar / Argentina / 19,954 / 6,082 / 1993

12 Guallatiri / Chile / 19,918 / 6,071 / 1985

13 Tupungatito / Chile / 19,685 / 6,000 / 1986

14 Damavand / Iran / 18,603 / 5,670 / unknown

15 Elbrus / Russia / 18,510 / 5,642 / 50AD

16 Pico de Orizaba / Mexico / 18,410 / 5,611 / 1687

17 Popocatepetl / Mexico / 17,930 / 5,465 / 1994–present

18 Ararat (Agri Dagi) / Turkey / 16,945 / 5,165 / 1840

19 Klyuchevskoy / Russia / 15,584 / 4,750 / continuous

20 Mt. Meru / Tanzania / 14,978 / 4,565 / 1910

WORLD'S DEEPEST CAVES

Name / Country / Depth in feet / meters

1 Krubera (Voronja) Cave / Georgia 7,188 / 2,191

2 Illyuzia-Mezhonnogo–Snezhnaya / Georgia 5,751 / 1,753

3 Lamprechtsofen Vogelschacht Weg Schacht / Austria 5,354 / 1,632

4 Gouffre Mirolda / France 5,335 / 1,626   **5** Reseau Jean Bernard / France 5,256 / 1,602

6 Torca del Cerro del Cuevon (T.33)–Torca de las Saxifragas / Spain 5,213 / 1,589   **7** Sarma / Georgia 5,062 / 1,543

8 Shakta Vjacheslav Pantjukhina / Georgia 4,948 / 1,508   **9** Sima de la Cornisa–Torca Magali / Spain 4,944 / 1,507

10 Cehi 2 / Slovenia 4,928 / 1,502   **11** Sistema Cheve (Cuicateco) / Mexico 4,869 / 1,484

12 Sistema Huautla / Mexico 4,839 / 1,475   **13** Sistema del Trave / Spain 4,728 / 1,441

14 Evren Gunay Dudeni (Mehmet Ali Ozel Sinkhole) / Turkey 4,688 / 1,429

15 Sustav Lukina jama–Trojama (Manual II) / Croatia 4,662 / 1,421   **16** Boj–Bulok / Uzbekistan 4,642 / 1,415

17 Gouffre de la Pierre–Saint–Martin / France, Spain 4,619 / 1,408

18 Sima de las Puertas de Illaminako Ateeneko Leizea (BU.56) / Spain 4,619 / 1,408

19 Kuzgun Cave / Turkey 4,593 / 1,400   **20** Abisso Paolo Roversi / Italy 4,429 / 1,350

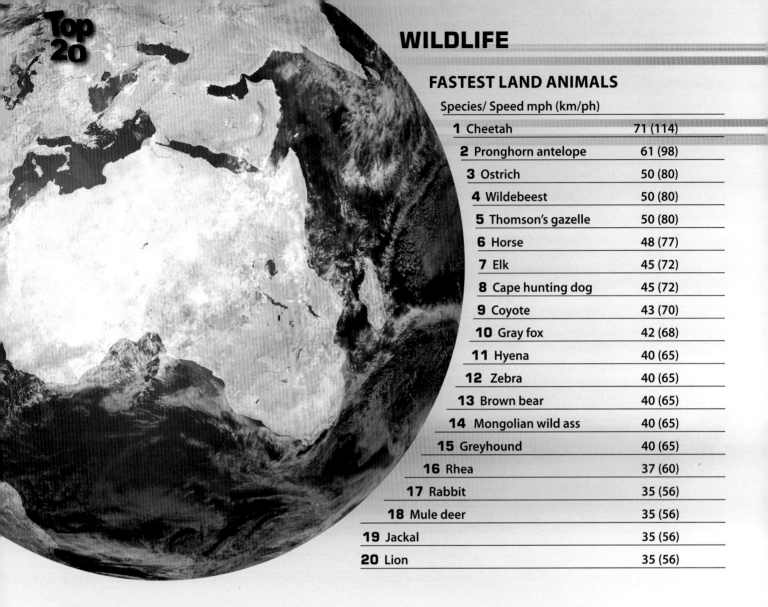

Top 20

WILDLIFE

FASTEST LAND ANIMALS

Species / Speed mph (km/ph)	
1 Cheetah	71 (114)
2 Pronghorn antelope	61 (98)
3 Ostrich	50 (80)
4 Wildebeest	50 (80)
5 Thomson's gazelle	50 (80)
6 Horse	48 (77)
7 Elk	45 (72)
8 Cape hunting dog	45 (72)
9 Coyote	43 (70)
10 Gray fox	42 (68)
11 Hyena	40 (65)
12 Zebra	40 (65)
13 Brown bear	40 (65)
14 Mongolian wild ass	40 (65)
15 Greyhound	40 (65)
16 Rhea	37 (60)
17 Rabbit	35 (56)
18 Mule deer	35 (56)
19 Jackal	35 (56)
20 Lion	35 (56)

BIGGEST LAND MAMMALS

Species / Maximum weight (lb/kg)

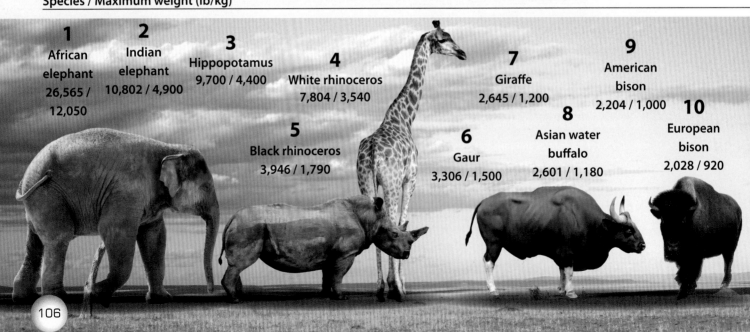

1 African elephant 26,565 / 12,050

2 Indian elephant 10,802 / 4,900

3 Hippopotamus 9,700 / 4,400

4 White rhinoceros 7,804 / 3,540

5 Black rhinoceros 3,946 / 1,790

6 Gaur 3,306 / 1,500

7 Giraffe 2,645 / 1,200

8 Asian water buffalo 2,601 / 1,180

9 American bison 2,204 / 1,000

10 European bison 2,028 / 920

FASTEST BIRDS IN FLIGHT

Species / Speed mph (km/ph)

1 Peregrine falcon (*Falco peregrinus*) ....200 (322)*
2 Spine tailed swift (*Hirundapus caudacutus*) 106 (171)
3 Golden eagle (*Aquila chrysaetos*) ....98 (158)*
4 White-rumped swift (*Apus caffer*).....................97 (124)
5 SGreat frigatebird (*Fregata minor*) 95 (153)
6 Spur-winged goose (*Plectropterus gambensis*) . 88 (142
7 Red-breasted merganser (*Mergus serrator*) 88 (129)
8 Trumpeter swan (*Cygnus buccinator*) 80 (130)
9 Canvasback duck (*Aythya valisineria*) 72 (116)
10 Eider duck (*Somateria mollissimal*) 70 (113)

11 Common teal (*Anas crecca*) 68 (109)
12 Mallard (*Anas platyrhynchos*).............................65 (105)
13 Northern pintail (*Anas acuta*) 65 (105)
14 Long-tailed skewer (*Stercorarius longicaudus*) ...60 (97)
15 Rock dove (*Columba livia*) 60 (97)
16 Anna's hummingbird (*Calypte anna*) 58 (93)
17 Common pochard (*Aythya farina*) 52 (84)
18 Long-tailed duck (*Clangula hyemalis*) 52 (84)
19 European turtle dove (*Streptopelia turtur*) 50 (80)
20 Common scooter (*Melanitta nigra*) 49 (79)

* Diving flight

11 African water buffalo 1,984 / 900

12 Moose 1,587 / 720

13 Polar bear 1,499 / 680

14 Brown bear 1,433 / 650

15 Elk (Wapiti) 1,332 / 600

16 Arabian camel 1,332 / 600

17 Sambar deer 1,203 / 546

18 Black bear 992 / 450

19 Siberian tiger 661 / 300

20 Lion 551 / 250

HIGHEST BRIDGES

Name / Location / Height feet (meters) / Maximum vertical drop / Year completed

1. **Siduhe River Bridge** Yesanguanzhen, China 1,550 (472) 2009
2. **Hegigo Gorge Bridge** Otoma, Papua 1,289 (393) 2005
3. **Balinghe River Bridge** Guanling, China 1,280 (70) 2009
4. **Beipanjiang River 2003 Bridge** Xingbeizhen, China 1,200 (366) 2003
5. **Beipanjiang River 2009 Bridge** Qinglong, China 1,083 (330) 2009
6. **Liuguanghe Bridge** Liu Guangzhen, China 975 (297) 2001
7. **Zhijinghe River Bridge** Dazhipingzhen, China 965 (294) 2009
8. **Royal Gorge Bridge** Cañon City, Colorado, USA 955 (291) 1929
9. **Millau Viaduct** Millau, France 909 (277) 2004
10. **Beipanjiang River Railway Bridge** Liupanshui, China 902 (275) 2001
11. **Mike O'Callaghan–Pat Tilman Memorial Bridge** Boulder City, Nevada, USA 890 (271) 2010
12. **New River Gorge Bridge** Fayetteville, W. Virginia, USA 876 (267) 1977
13. **Wulingshan Bridge** Pengshui, China 863 (263) 2009
14. **Italia Viaduct** Laino Borgo, Italy 850 (259) 1974
15. **Jiangiehe Bridge** Weng'an, China 840 (256) 1995
16. **Sfalassa Bridge** Bagnara Calabra, Italy 820 (250) 1974
17. **Azhihe River Bridge** Changliuxiang, China 810 (247) 2003
18. **Vajont Dam Footbridge** Longarone, Italy 750 (229) 1963
19. **Zhuchanghe River Bridge** Sanbanqiaozhen, China 735 (224) 2008
20. **Auburn-Foresthill Bridge** Auburn, California, USA 730 (223) 1973

Source: highestbridges.com

LONGEST BRIDGES

Name / Location	Type	Length feet / meters	Year
1. Danyang-Kunshan Grand Bridge / China	Rail	540,700 / 164,800	2011
2. Tianjin Bridge / China	Rail	373,000 / 113,700	2011
3. Weinan Weihe Grand Bridge / China	Rail	261,588 / 79,732	2010
4. Bang Na Expressway / Thailand	Road	177,000 / 54,000	2000
5. Beijing Grand Bridge / China	Rail	157,982 / 48,153	2011
6. Qingdao Haiwan Bridge / China	Road	139,400 / 42,500	2011
7. Lake Pontchartrain Causeway / USA	Road	126,122 / 38,442	1969
8. Manchac Swamp Bridge / USA	Road	120,440 / 36,710	1970
9. Yangcun Bridge / China	Rail	117,490 / 35,812	2007
10. Hangzhou Bay Bridge / China	Road	117,037 / 35,673	2007

LONGEST TUNNELS

Name / Location / Length feet / meters / Year

Name	Location	Length feet	meters	Year
1. Delaware Aqueduct	New York State, USA	85.1	137.0	1945
2. Päijänne Water Tunnel	South Finland, Finland	74.6	120.0	1982
3. Dhuofang Water Tunnel	Liaoning, China	53.0	85.32	2009
4. Orange/Fish River Tunnel	South Africa	51.4	82.8	1972
5. Bolmen Water Tunne	Kronoberg/Scania Sweden	51.0	82.0	1987
6. Seiken Tunnel	Tsugaru Strait, Japan	33.5	53.85	1988
7. Zelivka Water Tunnel	Bohemia, Czech Republic	31.7	51.07	1972
8. Channel Tunnel	English Channel, UK/France	31.3	50.45	1994
9. Subway Line 5	Seoul, South Korea	29.6	47.6	1995
10. Metro Line 9	Moscow, Russia	25.8	41.5	2002
11. Metro Sur (L–12)	Madrid, Spain	25.4	40.9	2003
12. Metro Toei Oedo Line	Tokyo, Japan	25.3	40.7	2000
13. Kárahnjúkar Powerplant	Austerland, Iceland	24.7	39.7	2007
14. Quabbin Aqueduct	Massachusetts, USA	24.6	39.6	1905
15. Metro Line 6	Moscow, Russia	23.4	37.6	1990
16. Lötschberg Base Tunnel	Bernese Alps, Switzerland	21.5	34.57	2007
17. Metro L–7	Madrid, Spain	20.5	32.91	2007
18. New Guanjiao Tunnel	Qinhai, China	20.3	32.6	2012
19. U–Bahn U7	Berlin, Germany	19.8	31.8	1984
20. Metro Line 2 Orange	Montreal, Canada	19.1	30.79	2007

Name / Location	Type	Length feet / meters	Year
11. Runyang Bridge / China	Road	116,990 / 35,660	2005
12. Donghai Bridge / China	Road	106,600 / 32,500	2005
13. Shanghai Maglev Bridge / China	Rail	98,123 / 29,908	2003
14. Atchafalaya Basin Bridge / USA	Road	96,100 / 29,290	1973
15. Yanshi Bridge / China	Rail	93,645 / 28,543	2009
16. Jintang Bridge / China	Road	87,070 / 26,540	2009
17. Jinbin Light Rail No 1 Bridge / China	Metro	84,600 / 25,800	2003
18. King Fahd Causeway / Saudi Arabia / Bahrain	Road	82,000 / 25,000	1986
19. Suvarnabhumi Airport Link / Bangkok	Rail	80,400 / 24,500	2010
20. Chesapeake Bay Bridge–Tunnel / USA	Road	79,200 / 24,140	1999

BIGGEST EMPIRES IN HISTORY*

Empire / Principal regions / Total land area (million square miles/km)

1 British Colonial / Worldwide / 12.8 (33.1)

2 Mongol / Asia / 12.7 (33.0)

3 Russian / Europe–Asia / 9.1 (23.7)

4 Spanish / Americas–Far East / 7.7 (20.0)

5 Quing / China / 5.7 (14.7)

6 Yuan / China / 5.4 (14.0)

7 French Colonial / Worldwide / 5.0 (13.0)

8 Umayaad Caliphate / Middle East–N. Africa / 4.3 (11.1)

9 Abbasid Caliphate / Middle East–N. Africa / 4.3 (11.1)

10 Portuguese / Africa–America / 4.1 (10.4)

11 Rashidun Caliphate–Middle East–N. Africa / 3.4 (9.0)

12 Brazilian / South America / 3.2 (8.5)

13 Persian (Achaemenid) / Middle East N. Africa / 3.0 (8.0)

14 Japanese / Pacific / 2.8 (7.4)

15 Han / China / 2.6 (6.5)

16 Ming / China / 2.6 (6.5)

17 Roman / Europe–Asia–North Africa 2.6 (6.5)

18 Gok Turk / Central Asia / 2.3 (6.0)

19 Golden Horde / Eastern Europe / 2.3 (6.0)

20 Ottoman Empire / Middle East–N. Africa / 2.0 (5.2)

* Total land area at its largest.

* Based on archeological evidence of settled communities living in permanent structures and practicing farming, and or irrigation, and religious (spiritual) beliefs.

EARLIEST CIVILIZATIONS*

Name / Location / Established (approximate date BC)

1 Çatal Hüyük Community / Turkey / 7500

2 Jarmo Community / Iraq / 7000

3 Halaf Culture / Syria / 6100

4 Samarran Culture / Iraq / 5500

5 Ubaid Period (Early Sumer) Iraq / 5300

6 Amratian Culture / Egypt / 4000

7 Uruk Period (Mid Sumer) / Iraq / 4100

8 Valdivia Culture / Ecuador / 3500

9 Gerzean Culture / Egypt / 3500

10 Protodynastic Period / Egypt / 3200

11 Early Sumerian Dynasty / Iraq / 3000

12 Canaris Culture / Ecuador / 3000

13 Chibchas Culture / Panama (Columbia) / 3000

14 Second Egyptian Dynasty / Egypt / 2890

15 Caral Civilization / Peru / 2600

16 Indus Valley Civilization / India (Pakistan) / 2600

17 Longshan Culture / China / 2500

18 Akkadian Empire / Iraq / 2330

19 Xia Dynasty / China / 2100

20 Assyrian Empire / Iraq / 2000

FIRST COUNTRIES TO GIVE THE VOTE TO WOMEN

Country / Year

1 Pitcairn Islands 1838

2 Isle of Man 1881

3 Cook Islands 1893

4 New Zealand 1893

5 Australia 1902

6 Finland 1906

7 Norway 1913

8 Denmark 1915

9 Canada 1917*

10 Russia 1917*

11 Azerbaijan 1918

12 Estonia 1918

13 Georgia 1918

14 Germany 1918

15 Hungary 1918

16 Kyrgyz Republic 1918

17 Latvia 1918

18 Lithuania 1918

19 Moldova 1918

20 Poland 1918

* Initially for women aged over 21. In all other countries listed, for women aged 18 or over.

50c U.S. POSTAGE
LUCY STONE

Did you know?
Lucy Stone was at the forefront of the women's rights movement in the US. She championed the wearing of bloomers, designed by Amelia Bloomer, as they gave greater [...] for women.

RICHEST PEOPLE IN THE WORLD

Name (country of birth) / Wealth ($/£ billion)

1 Carlos Slim Helu (Mexico) 74/45

2 Bill Gates (USA) 56/34

3 Warren Buffett (USA) 50/31

4 Bernard Arnault (France) 41/25

5 Larry Ellison (USA) 39.5/24

6 Lakshmi Mittal (India) 31.1/19

7 Amancio Ortega (Spain) 31/19

8 Eike Batista (Brazil) 30/18

9 Mukesh Ambani (India) 27/16.5

10 Christy Walton (USA) 26.5/16

11 Li Ka-shing (Hong Kong) 26/15.94

12 Karl Albrecht (Germany) 25.5/15.6

13 Stefan Persson (Sweden) 22.4/13.7

14 Vladimir Lisin (Russia) 24/14.7

15 Liliane Bettencourt (France) 23.5/14.4

16 Sheldon Adelson (USA) 23.3/14.2

17 David Thomson (Canada) 23/14.1

18 Charles Koch (USA) 22/13.4

19 David Koch (USA) 22/13.4

20 Jim Walton (USA) 21.3/13.06

RICHEST ROYALS

Name / Country / Wealth ($/£ billion)

1 King Bhumibol Adulyadej (Thailand) 30/18.39
2 Prince Azim (Brunei) 22/13.49
3 Sultan Haji Hassanal Bolkiah (Brunei) 20/12.26
4 Prince Alwaleed bin Talal Alsaud (Saudi Arabia) 19.6/12.01
5 King Abdullah bin Abdul Aziz Saud (Saudi Arabia) 18/11.03
6 Crown Prince Sheik Hamdan bin Mohammed (Dubai) 18/11.03
7 Sheikh Khalifa bin Zayed al-Nahyan (United Arab Emirates) 15/9.2
8 Sheikh Mohammed bin Rashid al-Maktoum (Dubai) 4.5/2.76
9 Prince Hans-Adam II (Liechtenstein) 3.5/2.15
10 King Mohammed VI (Morocco) 2.5/1.53
11 Sheikh Hamad bin Khalifa al- Thani (Qatar) 2.4/1.47
12 Prince Albert von Thurn und Taxis (Germany) 2.2/1.35
13 Prince Albert II (Monaco) 1.0/0.61
14 Prince Charles (UK) 0.9/0.55
15 The Aga Khan (Iran) 0.8/0.49
16 Sultan Qaboos bin Said (Oman) 0.7/0.43
17 Queen Elizabeth II (UK) 0.45/0.28
18 Sheikh Nasser Al-Mohammad Al-Ahmad Al-Jaber Al-Sabah (Kuwait) 0.35/0.21
19 Queen Beatrix Wilhelmina Armgard (Netherlands) 0.2/0.12
20 King Mswati III (Swaziland) 0.1/0.06

The King of Thailand, Bhumibol Adulyadej, is known as Rama IX.

RICHEST CELEBRITIES

Name / Profession / Pay ($/£ million)

3 U2 (Musicians) 130/80
4 Tyler Perry (Director/Producer) 125/77

5 Michael Bay (Director/Producer) 120/74
6 AC/DC (Musicians) 114/70

1 Oprah Winfrey (TV Personality) 315/193
2 James Cameron (Director/Producer) 210/129

9 Jerry Bruckheimer (Director/Producer) 100/61
10 George Lucas (Director/Producer) 95/58

11 Beyoncé Knowles (Singer/Songwriter) 87/53
12 Simon Cowell (TV Personality) 80/49

7 Tiger Woods (Sports Star) 105/64
8 Steven Spielberg (Director/Producer) 100/61

15 Jerry Seinfeld (Comedian) 75/46.4
16 Bruce Springsteen (Singer/Songwriter) 70/43.3

13 Dr. Phil McGraw (TV Personality) 80/49
14 Johnny Depp (Actor) 75/45.9

17 Howard Stern (Personality) 70/42.9
18 James Patterson (Author) 70/42.9

19 Floyd Mayweather (Sports Star) 65/39.8
20 Britney Spears (Singer/Songwriter) 64/39.23

Source: Forbes

113

HIGHEST INNINGS IN TWENTY20

Score / Teams / Year

1 260/6 Sri Lanka v Kenya (2007)	**4** 218/4 India v England (2007)
2 241/6 South Africa v England (2009)	**5** 215/5 Sri Lanka v India (2009)
3 221/5 Australia v England (2007)	**6** 214/5 Australia v New Zealand (2005)
7 214/6 New Zealand – Australia (2010)	**10** 211/5 South Africa v Scotland (2009)
8 214/4 Australia v New Zealand (2010)	**11** 209/3 Australia v South Africa (2006)
9 211/4 India v Sri Lanka (2009)	**12** 208/2 South Africa v West Indies (2007)
13 208/8 West Indies v England (2007)	**15** 205/6 West Indies v South Africa (2009)
14 206/7 Sri Lanka v India (2009)	**16** 203/5 Pakistan v Bangladesh (2008)
17 202/6 England v South Africa (2009)	**19** 200/6 England v India (2007)
18 201/4 South Africa v Australia (2006)	**20** 198/5 New Zealand v Ireland (2009)

Source: cricinfo.com

In 2004, Andrew Symonds of Australia made the fastest century in Twenty20 cricket, making 100 runs off 34 balls.

Did you know?

Sachin Tendulkar has broken records throughout his career. He is worshipped in his home country, India, and is known throughout the world as one of the greatest batsmen ever to play cricket. He bats, bowls, and throws with his right hand, but writes with his left hand.

Ricky Ponting is the most successful captain in Test match history. He has led his team to victory in 44 Tests.

MOST RUNS IN A TEST CAREER

Name (team) / Number of runs

1 Sachin Tendulkar (India) 14,692		**11** Graham Gooch (England) 8,900
2 Ricky Ponting (Australia) 12,363		**12** Javed Miandad (Pakistan) 8,832
3 Rahul Dravid (India) 12,063		**13** Inzamam-ul-Haq (Pakistan) 8,830
4 Brian Lara (West Indies) 11,953		**14** Matthew Hayden (Australia) 8,625
5 Jacques Kallis (South Africa) 11,947		**15** Viv Richards (West Indies) 8,540
6 Allan Border (Australia) 11,174		**16** Alec Stewart (England) 8,463
7 Steve Waugh (Australia) 10,927		**17** Kumar Sangakkara (Sri Lanka) 8,244
8 Sunny Gavaskar (India) 10,122		**18** David Gower (England) 8,231
9 Mahela Jayawardene (Sri Lanka) 9,527		**19** Geoff Boycott (England) 8,114
10 Shivnarine Chanderpaul (West Indies) 9,063		**20** Garfield Sobers (West Indies) 8,032

Source: cricinfo.com

(1 light year = 6 trillion [6,000,000,000,000] miles, nearly 10 trillion kilometers)

STARS CLOSEST TO EARTH

Common name / Scientific name / Distance in light years (unless otherwise stated)

#	Common name	Scientific name	Distance
1	The Sun	–	93 million miles
2	Proxima Centauri	V645 Cen	4.2
3	Rigil Kentaurus	Alpha Cen A	4.3
4	Alpha Cen B	–	4.3
5	Barnard's Star	–	6.0
6	Wolf 359	CN Leo	7.7
7	–	BD +36 2147	8.2
8	Luyten 726-8A	UV Cet A	8.4
9	Luyten 726-8B	UV Cet B	8.4
10	Sirius A	Alpha CMa A	8.6
11	Sirius B	Alpha CMa B	8.6
12	Ross 154	–	9.4
13	Ross 248	–	10.4
14	–	Epsilon Eri	10.8
15	Ross 128	–	10.9
16	–	61 Cyg A	11.1
17	–	61 Cyg B	11.1
18	–	Epsilon Ind	11.2
19	–	BD +43 44 A	11.2
20	–	BD +44 B	11.2

LARGEST STARS OBSERVED IN THE UNIVERSE

Name / Size by Solar radii

1 VY Canis Major 1,800–2,100

2 VV Cephei A 1,600–1,900

3 RW Cephei 1,650

4 V838 Monocerotis 1,570

5 WOH G64 1,540

6 V354 Cephei 1,520

7 KW Sagittarii 1,460

8 KY Cygni 1,420–2,850

9 Mu Cephei 1,420

10 Betelgeuse 950–1,000

11 Antares 800

12 V382 Carinae 747

13 S Pegasi 580

14 T Cephei 540

15 S Orionis 530

16 W Hydrae 520

17 R Cassiopeiae 500

18 Chi Cygni 470

19 Alpha Herculis 460

20 Rho Cassiopeiae 450

1= radius of the sun, 432,450 miles (695,500 kilometers)

FIRST HUMANS IN SPACE

Name / Craft (country) / Date

(number of orbits)

Yuri Gagarin / Vostok 1 (USSR)
4/12/61 (1)

Alan Shepard / Mercury 3 (USA)
5/5/61 (sub-orbital)

Virgil Grissom / Mercury 4 (USA)
7/21/61 (sub-orbital)

Herman Titov / Vostok 2 (USSR)
8/6/61 (17)

John Glenn / Mercury 6 (USA)
2/20/62 (3)

Scott Carpenter / Mercury 7 (USA)
5/24/62 (3)

Andrian Nikolayev / Vostok 3 (USSR)
8/11/62 (64)

Pavel Popovich / Vostok 4 (USSR)
8/12/62 (48)

Walter Schirra / Mercury 8 (USA)
10/3/62 (6)

Gordon Cooper / Mercury 9 (USA)
5/15/63 (22)

Valeri Bykovsky / Vostok 5 (USSR)
6/14/63 (81)

Valentina Tereshkova / Vostok 6 (USSR)
6/16/63 (48)

Vladimir Komarov / Voskhod 1 (USSR)
10/12/64 (16)

Boris Yegorov / Voskhod 1 (USSR)
10/12/64 (16)

Konstantin Feoktistov / Voskhod 1 (USSR)
10/12/64 (16)

Pavel Belyayev / Voskhod 2 (USSR)
3/18/65 (17)

Alexei Leonov / Voskhod 2 (USSR)
3/18/65 (17)

Virgil Grissom / Gemini 3 (USA)
3/23/65 (3)

John Young / Gemini 3 (USA)
3/23/65 (3)

James McDivitt / Gemini 4 (USA)
6/3/65 (62)

1 AU is the approximate distance of Earth from the Sun. That is 92,955,810 miles or 149,597,870 km.

A monkey called Albert II was sent into space in June 1949 and Laika the dog orbited the earth in Sputnik satellite in November 1957.

COMETS' CLOSEST APPROACH TO EARTH

Name / Date / Distance in AU

#	Name	Date	Distance in AU
1	Lexell	July 1770	0.0151
2	Tempel-Tuttle	October 1366	0.0229
3	IRAS Araki-Alcock	May 1983	0.0312
4	Halley	April 837AD	0.0334
5	Biela	December 1805	0.0366
6	C/1743 C1	February 1743	0.0390
7	Pons–Winnecke	June 1927	0.0394
8	C/1702 H1	April 1702	0.0437
9	Schwassmann–Wachmann	May 1930	0.0617
10	Sugano–Saigusa–Fujikawa	June 1983	0.0628
11	Great Comet	January 1760	0.0682
12	Schwassmann–Wachmann	May 2006	0.0787
13	C/1853 G1	April 1853	0.0839
14	Bouvard–Herschel	August 1797	0.0879
15	Halley	April 1374	0.0884
16	Halley	April 1607	0.0898
17	Messier	September 1763	0.0934
18	Tempel	August 1864	0.0964
19	Schmidt	July 1862	0.0982
20	Hyakutake	March 1996	0.1018

Source: IAU Minor Planet Center, Harvard

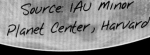

Countries with the lowest life expectancy

	Country / Life expectancy at birth	
1	Angola	38.8
2	Afghanistan	45.0
3	Nigeria	47.6
4	Chad	48.3
5	Swaziland	48.6
6	Guinea-Bissau	48.7
7	South Africa	49.3
8	Zimbabwe	49.6
9	Central African Republic	50.1
10	Somalia	50.4
11	Lesotho	51.6
12	Malawi	51.7
13	Mozambique	51.8
14	Namibia	52.2
15	Zambia	52.4
16	Mali	52.6
17	Tanzania	52.9
18	Uganda	53.2
19	Niger	53.4
20	Burkina Faso	53.7

COUNTRIES WITH THE HIGHEST LIFE EXPECTANCY

	Country / Life expectancy at birth				
1	Monaco	89.7	11	Jersey	81.4
2	Macau	84.4	12	Canada	81.3
3	San Marino	83.0	13	France	81.2
4	Andorra	82.4	14	Spain	81.2
5	Japan	82.3	15	Switzerland	81.1
6	Guernsey	82.2	16	Sweden	81.1
7	Singapore	82.1	17	Israel	80.9
8	Hong Kong	82.0	18	Iceland	80.9
9	Australia	81.8	19	Anguilla	80.8
10	Italy	81.7	20	Bermuda	80.7

World Average 66.7
Source: CIA World Factbook

Jeanne Calment, the oldest woman in the world

OLDEST PEOPLE

1
Jeanne Calment
Born: France, Feb 21 1875
Died: Aug 4 1997
Age: 122 years,
164 days

7
Elizabeth Bolden
Born: USA, Aug 15 1890
Died: Dec 11 2006
Age: 116 years,
118 days

13
Edna Parker
Born: USA, Apr 20 1893
Died: Nov 26 2008
Age: 115 years,
220 days

17
Emiliano Mercado del Toro
Born: Puerto Rico, Aug 21 1891
Died: Jan 24 2007
Age: 115 years, 156 days

2
Sarah Knauss
Born: USA, Sept 24 1880
Died: Dec 30 1999
Age: 119 years,
97 days

8
Carrie C. White
Born: USA, Nov 18 1874
Died: Feb 14 1991
Age: 116 years,
88 days

14
Margaret Skeete
Born: Canada, Oct 28 1878
Died: May 7 1994
Age: 115 years,
192 days

18
Bettie Wilson
Born: USA, Sep 13 1890
Died: Feb 13 2006
Age: 115 years, 153 days

3
Lucy Hannah
Born: USA, Jul 16 1875
Died: Mar 21 1993
Age: 117 years,
248 days

9
Kamato Hongo
Born: Japan, Sept 16 1887
Died: Oct 31 2003
Age: 116 years,
45 days

15
Gertrude Baines
Born: USA, Apr 6 1894
Died: Sep 11 2009
Age: 115 years,
158 days

19
Julie Winnefred Bertrand
Born: Canada, Sept 16 1891
Died: Jan 18 2007
Age: 115 years,
124 days

4
Marie-Louise Meilleur
Born: Canada, Aug 29 1880
Died: Apr 16 1998
Age: 117 years,
230 days

10
Maggie Barnes
Born: USA, Mar 6 1882
Died: Jan 19 1998
Age: 115 years,
319 days

16
Anitica Butariu
Born: Romania, Jun 17 1882
Died: Nov 21 1997
Age: 115 years,
157 days

20
Maria de Jesus
Born: Portugal,
Sept 10 1893
Died: Jan 2 2009
Age: 115 years, 114 days

5
Maria Capovilla
Born: Ecuador, Sept 14 1889
Died: Aug 27 2006
Age: 116 years,
347 days

11
Christian Mortensen
Born: USA, Aug 16 1882
Died: April 25 1998
Age: 115 years
252 days

6
Tane Ikai
Born: Japan, Jan 18 1879
Died: Jul 12 1995
Age: 116 years, 175 days

12
Charlotte Hughes
Born: USA, Aug 1 1877
Died: Mar 17 1993
Age: 115 years,
228 days

MOST NUMBER ONE SINGLES IN THE UK

1.	Elvis Presley	21
2.	The Beatles	17
3.	Cliff Richard	14
4.	Westlife	14
5.	Madonna	13
6.	The Shadows	12
7.	Take That	11
8.	ABBA	9
9.	Spice Girls	9
10.	The Rolling Stones	8
11.	Oasis	8
12.	George Michael	7
13.	Michael Jackson	7
14.	Kylie Minogue	7
15.	U2	7
16.	McFly	7
17.	Eminem	7
18.	Slade	6
19.	Rod Stewart	6
20.	Blondie	6

Source: OCC

MOST NUMBER ONE SINGLES IN THE US

1.	The Beatles	20	8.	Janet Jackson	10	15.	George Michael	8
2.	Mariah Carey	18	9.	Stevie Wonder	10	16.	The Rolling Stones	8
3.	Elvis Presley	17	10.	Rihanna	10	17.	Phil Collins	7
4.	Michael Jackson	13	11.	Elton John	9	18.	Pat Boone	6
5.	Madonna	12	12.	Bee Gees	9	19.	Daryl Hall	
6.	The Supremes	12	13.	Usher	9		& John Oates	6
7.	Whitney Houston	11	14.	Paul McCartney/Wings	9	20.	Diana Ross	6

Source: Billboard

LONGEST AT THE TOP OF THE UK CHART (ALBUMS)

Artist / Album / Number of weeks at number one

#	Artist	Album	Weeks
1.	Film Soundtrack	*South Pacific*	115
2.	Film Soundtrack	*The Sound Of Music*	70
3.	Film Soundtrack	*The King And I*	48
4.	Simon & Garfunkel	*Bridge Over Troubled Water*	33
5.	The Beatles	*Please Please Me*	30
6.	The Beatles	*Sgt Pepper's Lonely Hearts Club Band*	27
7.	Elvis Presley	*G.I. Blues Soundtrack*	22
8.	The Beatles	*With The Beatles*	21
9.	The Beatles	*A Hard Day's Night*	21
10.	Broadway Stage Soundtrack	*My Fair Lady*	19
11.	Elvis Presley	*Blue Hawaii Soundtrack*	18
12.	Film Soundtrack	*Saturday Night Fever*	18
13.	The Beatles	*Abbey Road*	17
14.	The Carpenters	*The Singles 1969–1973*	17
15.	Phil Collins	*But Seriously*	15
16.	Spice Girls	*Spice*	15
17.	Dire Straits	*Brothers In Arms*	14
18.	Cliff Richard & The Shadows	*Summer Holiday Soundtrack*	14
19.	Bob Dylan	*John Wesley Harding*	13
20.	Film Soundtrack	*West Side Story*	13

Source: OCC

LONGEST AT THE TOP OF THE US CHART (ALBUMS)

Artist / Album / Number of weeks at number one

#	Artist	Album	Weeks
1.	Film Soundtrack	*West Side Story*	54
2.	Michael Jackson	*Thriller*	37
3.	Harry Belafonte	*Calypso*	31
4.	Film Soundtrack	*South Pacific*	31
5.	Fleetwood Mac	*Rumours*	31
6.	Film Soundtrack	*Saturday Night Fever*	24
7.	Prince	*Purple Rain*	24
8.	MC Hammer	*Please Hammer Don't Hurt 'Em*	21
9.	Film Soundtrack	*The Bodyguard*	20
10.	Elvis Presley	*Blue Hawaii Soundtrack*	20
11.	Doris Day	*Love Me Or Leave Me Soundtrack*	19
12.	The Monkees	*More Of The Monkees*	18
13.	Film Soundtrack	*Dirty Dancing*	18
14.	Garth Brooks	*Ropin' The Wind*	18
15.	The Police	*Synchronicity*	17
16.	Billy Ray Cyrus	*Some Gave All*	17
17.	Film Soundtrack	*The Sound Of Music*	16
18.	Andy Williams	*Days Of Wine And Roses*	16
19.	Vanilla Ice	*To The Extreme*	16
20.	Film Soundtrack	*Titanic*	16

HIGHEST-EARNING MUSICALS

	Title	US Box office gross	Year		Title	US Box office gross	Year
1.	Grease	$188,389,888	1978	12.	Sweeney Todd:		
2.	Chicago	$170,697,519	2002		The Demon Barber		
3.	Mamma Mia!	$144,130,063	2008		of Fleet Street	$52,898,073	2007
4.	Hairspray	$118,871,849	2007	13.	The Phantom of		
5.	Rocky Horror				the Opera	$51,268,815	2004
	Picture Show	$112,892,319	1975	14.	Evita	$50,047,179	1996
6.	Dreamgirls	$103,365,956	2006	15.	Popeye	$49,823,037	1980
7.	High School Musical 3	$90,559,416	2008	16.	Yentl	$40,218,899	1983
8.	Best Little			17.	Burlesque	$39,440,655	2010
	Whorehouse in Texas	$69,701,637	1982	18.	Funny Lady	$39,000,000	1975
9.	Moulin Rouge!	$57,386,607	2001	19.	Little Shop of Horrors	$38,748,395	1986
10.	The Blues Brothers	$57,229,890	1980	20.	All That Jazz	$37,823,676	1979
11.	Annie	$57,059,003	1982				

Source: Box Office Mojo

HIGHEST-EARNING ANIMATED FILMS

	Title	US Box office gross	Year		Title	US Box office gross	Year
1.	Shrek 2	$441,226,247	2004	12.	Cars	$244,082,982	2006
2.	Toy Story 3	$415,004,880	2010	13.	Shrek		
3.	Finding Nemo	$339,714,978	2003		Forever After	$238,736,787	2010
4.	The Lion King	$328,541,776	1994	14.	WALL-E	$233,808,164	2008
5.	Shrek the Third	$322,719,944	2007	15.	How to Train		
6.	Up	$293,004,164	2009		Your Dragon	$217,581,231	2010
7.	Shrek	$267,665,011	2001	16.	Aladdin	$217,581,231	1992
8.	The Incredibles	$261,441,092	2004	17.	Kung Fu Panda	$215,434,591	2008
9.	Monsters, Inc	$255,873,250	2001	18.	Ratatouille	$206,445,654	2007
10.	Despicable Me	$251,513,985	2010	19.	Monsters Vs Aliens	$198,351,526	2009
11.	Toy Story 2	$245,852,179	1999	20.	Happy Feet	$198,000,317	2006

Source: Box Office Mojo

HIGHEST-EARNING COMIC BOOK FILM ADAPTATIONS

	Title	US Box Office Gross	Year
1.	*The Dark Knight*	$533,345,358	2008
2.	*Spider-Man*	$403,706,375	2002
3.	*Spider-Man 2*	$373,585,825	2004
4.	*Spider-Man 3*	$336,530,303	2007
5.	*Iron Man*	$318,412,101	2008
6.	*Iron Man 2*	$312,433,331	2010
7.	*Batman*	$251,188,924	1989
8.	*Men in Black*	$250,690,539	1997
9.	*X-Men: The Last Stand*	$234,362,462	2006
10.	*X2: X-Men United*	$214,949,694	2003
11.	*300*	$210,614,939	2007
12.	*Batman Begins*	$205,343,774	2005
13.	*Superman Returns*	$200,081,192	2006
14.	*Men in Black II*	$190,418,803	2002
15.	*Batman Forever*	$184,031,112	1995
16.	*X-Men Origins: Wolverine*	$179,299,717	2009
17.	*Batman Returns*	$162,831,698	1992
18.	*X-Men*	$157,299,717	2000
19.	*Fantastic Four*	$154,696,080	2005
20.	*Teenage Mutant Ninja Turtles*	$135,265,915	1990

Source: Box Office Mojo

Source: National Climatic Data Center

COLDEST PLACES ON EARTH

Location / Country / Temperature °F (°C) / Date recorded

1
Vostok Station
Antarctica
−128.6°F (−89.2°C)
7/21/1983

2
Amunsden-Scott South
Pole Station
South Pole
−117°F (−82.8°C)
8/20/2010

3
Dome A
East Antarctica
−116.5°F (−82.5°C)
July 2005

4
Verkhoyansk
Sakha, Russia
−90.0°F (−68.0°C)
2/7/1892

5
Oymyakon
Sakha, Russia
−90.0°F (−68.0°C)
2/6/1933

6
North Ice
Greenland
−87.0°F (−66.1°C)
1/9/1954

7
Snag, Yukon
Canada
−81.0°F (−63.0°C)
2/3/1947

8
Prospect Creek,
Alaska, USA
−80.0°F (−62.0°C)
1/23/1971

9
Ust' Shchugor
Russia
−72.6°F (−58.1°C)
12/31/1978

10
Malgovik
Sweden
−63.4°F (−53.0°C)
12/19/2009

11
Mohe County
China
−62.14°F
(−52.3°C)
2/13/1969

12
Kittilä, Lapland
Finland
−60.7°F (−51.5°C)
1/28/1999

13
Van
Turkey
−51.5°F (−46.4°C)
1/9/1990

14
Lake Futensee
Germany
−50.6°F (−45.9°C)
12/24/2001

15
Mount Everest
Nepal
−49.0°F (−45.0°C)
15/5/1999

16
Chunggangjin
North Korea
−46.48°F (−43.6°C)
1/12/1933

17
Jõgeva
Estonia
−46.0°F (−43.5°C)
1/17/1940

18
Daugavpils
Latvia
−45.8°F (−43.2°C)
2/8/1956

19
Utena
Lithuania
−45.2°F (−42.9°C)
2/1/1956

20
Slavnom
Belarus
−44.0°F (−42.2°C)
1/17/1940

HOTTEST COUNTRIES ON EARTH

Location / Country / Temperature °F (°C) / Date recorded

1 Al 'Azizyah
Libya
136.0°F (57.8°C)
9/13/1922

2 Death Valley,
California, USA
134.0°F (56.7°C)
7/10/1913

3 Mitraba
Kuwait
129.0°F (54.0°C)
6/15/2010

4 Mohenjo-daro, Sindh
Pakistan
128.3°F (53.5°C)
5/26/2010

5 Basra
Iraq
125.7°F (52.0°C)
6/14/2010

6 Jeddah
Saudi Arabia
125.6°F (52.0°C)
6/22/2010

7 Purulia, West Bengal
India 118.0°F (51.1°C)
6/18/2005

8 Oodnadatta,
South Australia
Australia
123.0°F (50.7°C)
1/2/1960

9 Doha
Qatar
122.7°F (50.4°C)
7/14/2010

10 Dunbrody, Eastern Cape
South Africa
122.0°F (50.0°C)
11/3/1918

11 Dongola
Sudan
121.3°F (49.6°C)
6/25/2010

12 Villa de Maria
Argentina
120.4°F (49.1°C)
1/2/1920

13 Mardin
Turkey
119.8°F (48.8°C)
8/4/1993

14 Blima
Niger
118.8°F (48.2°C)
6/23/2010

15 Athens
Greece
118.4°F (48.0°C)
7/10/1977

16 Turpan, Xinjang
China
118.0°F (47.7°C)
7/13/1975

17 Faya
Chad
117.7°F (47.6°C)
6/22/2010

18 Amareleja, Beja
Portugal
117.3°F (47.4°C)
8/1/2003

19 Murcia
Spain
116.9°F (47.2 °C)
4/7/1994

20 Amendola
Italy
116.6°F (47.0°C)
7/25/2007

MOST FORMULA 1 GRAND PRIX WINS	**1** Michael Schumacher (Germany) 91	**2** Alain Prost (France) 51	**3** Ayrton Senna (Brazil) 41	**4** Nigel Mansell (UK) 31	**5** Jackie Stewart (UK) 27
6 Fernando Alonso (Spain) 26	**7** Jim Clark (UK) 25	**8** Niki Lauda (Austria) 25	**9** Juan Manuel Fangio (Argentina) 24	**10** Nelson Piquet (Brazil) 23	**11** Damon Hill (UK) 22
12 Mika Hakkinen (Finland) 20	**13** Kimi Raikkonen (Finland) 18	**14** Stirling Moss (UK) 16	**15** Jack Brabham (Australia) 14	**16** Emerson Fittipaldi (Brazil) 14	**17** Lewis Hamilton (UK) 14
18 Graham Hill (UK) 14	**19** Alberto Ascari (Italy) 13	**20** David Coulthard (UK) 13		Source: Formula1.com	

HORSES BY EARNINGS (US)

	1	2	3	4	5	6	7	8	9	10
Name	Blame	Lookin At Lucky	Zenyatta	Super Saver	Blind Luck	Dangerous Midge	Unrivalled Belle	Paddy O'Prado	Awesome Feather	Big Drama
Earnings	$43,751,467	$2,064,278	$1,830,000	$1,718,534	$1,679,662	$1,620,000	$1,614,659	$1,579,950	$1,495,746	$1,420,810

	11	12	13	14	15	16	17	18	19	20
Name	Gio Ponti	Uncle Mo	Shared Account	Quality Road	Joshua Tree	Fly Down	Goldikova	Dubai Majesty	Court Vision	Life At Ten
Earnings	$1,384,000	$1,296,000	$1,289,800	$1,260,000	$1,185,840	$1,134,700	$1,080,000	$1,009,724	$1,009,091	$999,000

Source: Equibase.com

The best-ranking rider still currently competing is Alberto Contador.

ALL TIME BEST RANKINGS IN THE TOUR DE FRANCE

Name / Country of origin / Points

1 Lance Armstrong / USA / 13050	11 Philippe Thys / Belgium / 5400
2 Eddy Merckx / Belgium / 11850	12 Alberto Contador / Spain / 5400
3 Bernard Hinault / France / 11100	13 Jan Ullrich / Germany / 5250
4 Jacques Anquetil / France / 9450	14 Gino Bartali / Italy / 5100
5 Miguel Indurain / Spain / 9000	15 Nicolas Frantz / Luxemburg / 4800
6 Greg Lemond / USA / 6450	16 Antonin Magne / France / 4650
7 Lucien Van Impe / Belgium / 6450	17 Gustave Garrigou / France / 4500
8 Louison Bobet / France / 6300	18 Fausto Coppi / Italy / 4500
9 Federico Bahamontes / Spain / 5550	19 Laurent Fignon / France / 4200
10 Joop Zoetemelk / Netherlands / 5400	20 Richard Virengue / France / 4200

Source: cyclinghalloffame.com

Did You Know?

The world's most famous cycle race, the Tour de France, is an annual three-week event that takes place in France and, occasionally, neighboring countries. It was founded in 1903 by Henri Desgrange. American cyclist Lance Armstrong (right) has won the event a record seven times in succession.

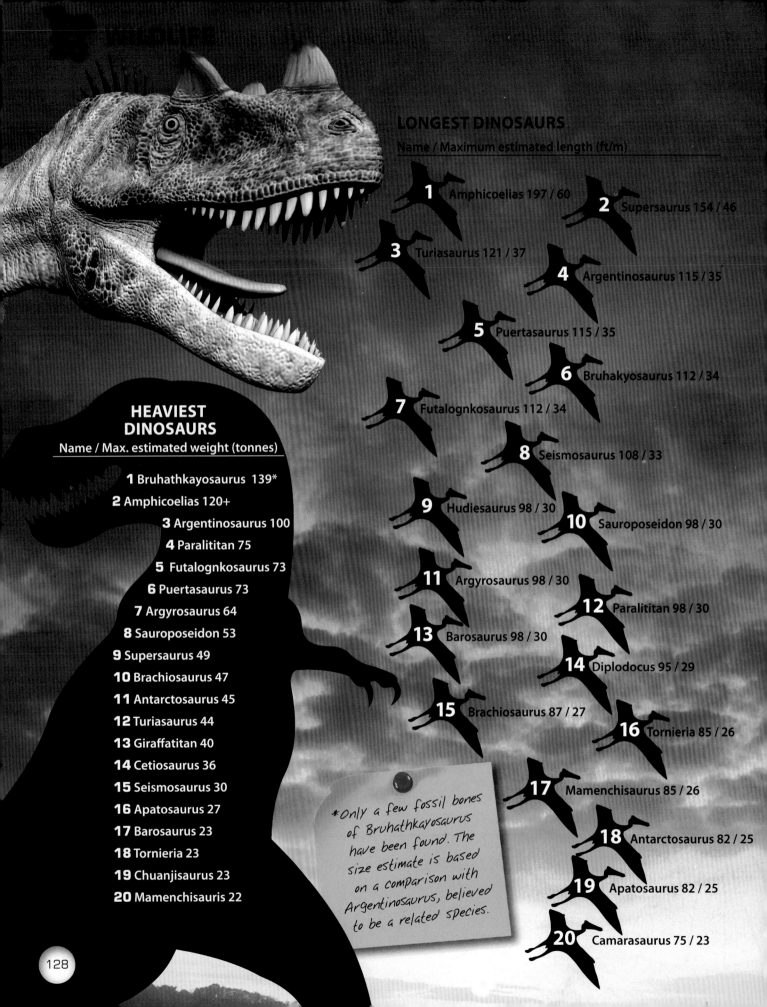

LONGEST DINOSAURS
Name / Maximum estimated length (ft/m)

1 Amphicoelias 197 / 60
2 Supersaurus 154 / 46
3 Turiasaurus 121 / 37
4 Argentinosaurus 115 / 35
5 Puertasaurus 115 / 35
6 Bruhakyosaurus 112 / 34
7 Futalognkosaurus 112 / 34
8 Seismosaurus 108 / 33
9 Hudiesaurus 98 / 30
10 Sauroposeidon 98 / 30
11 Argyrosaurus 98 / 30
12 Paralititan 98 / 30
13 Barosaurus 98 / 30
14 Diplodocus 95 / 29
15 Brachiosaurus 87 / 27
16 Tornieria 85 / 26
17 Mamenchisaurus 85 / 26
18 Antarctosaurus 82 / 25
19 Apatosaurus 82 / 25
20 Camarasaurus 75 / 23

HEAVIEST DINOSAURS
Name / Max. estimated weight (tonnes)

1 Bruhathkayosaurus 139*
2 Amphicoelias 120+
3 Argentinosaurus 100
4 Paralititan 75
5 Futalognkosaurus 73
6 Puertasaurus 73
7 Argyrosaurus 64
8 Sauroposeidon 53
9 Supersaurus 49
10 Brachiosaurus 47
11 Antarctosaurus 45
12 Turiasaurus 44
13 Giraffatitan 40
14 Cetiosaurus 36
15 Seismosaurus 30
16 Apatosaurus 27
17 Barosaurus 23
18 Tornieria 23
19 Chuanjisaurus 23
20 Mamenchisauris 22

*Only a few fossil bones of Bruhathkayosaurus have been found. The size estimate is based on a comparison with Argentinosaurus, believed to be a related species.

SMALLEST DINOSAURS

Name / Minimum estimated length (in/cm)

1 Epidextipteryx
10 / 25

2 Ornithomimus minutus
11 / 30

3 Palaeopteryx
11 / 30

4 Rahonavis
11 / 30

5 Achiornis
13 / 34

6 Protarchaeopteryx
16 / 40

7 Juravenator
16 / 40

8 Parvicursur
18 / 45

9 Xixianykus
20 / 50

10 Alwalkeria
20 / 50

11 Echinodon
20 / 50

12 Chaoyangsaurus
20 / 50

13 Microceratops
20 / 50

14 Jinfengopteryx
22 / 55

15 Shuvuuia
24 / 60

16 Wannanosaurus
24 / 60

17 Fruitadens
26 / 65

18 Mahakala
27 / 68

19 Pneumatoraptor
29 / 73

20 Graciliceratops
31 / 80

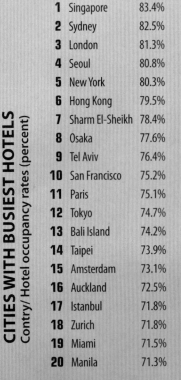

CITIES WITH BUSIEST HOTELS
Contry / Hotel occupancy rates (percent)

1	Singapore	83.4%
2	Sydney	82.5%
3	London	81.3%
4	Seoul	80.8%
5	New York	80.3%
6	Hong Kong	79.5%
7	Sharm El-Sheikh	78.4%
8	Osaka	77.6%
9	Tel Aviv	76.4%
10	San Francisco	75.2%
11	Paris	75.1%
12	Tokyo	74.7%
13	Bali Island	74.2%
14	Taipei	73.9%
15	Amsterdam	73.1%
16	Auckland	72.5%
17	Istanbul	71.8%
18	Zurich	71.8%
19	Miami	71.5%
20	Manila	71.3%

Marina Bay Sands Hotel in Singapore is the largest light and water spectacle in Southeast Asia

MOST POPULOUS CITIES (urban centers, not including suburbs)

City / Country / Population

	City, Country	Population		City, Country	Population		City, Country	Population
1	Shanghai, China	13,830,000	8	Seóul, South Korea	10,460,000	15	Lagos, Nigeria	7,930,000
2	Mumbai (Bombay), India	13,830,000	9	Beijing, China	10,120,000	16	London, UK	7,750,000
3	Karachi, Pakistan	13,050,000	10	Jakarta, Indonesia	9,580,000	17	Lima, Peru	7.600,000
4	Delhi, India	12,560,000	11	Tokyo, Japan	8,880,000	18	Bogotá, Colombia	7,250,000
5	Istanbul, Turkey	12,510,000	12	Mexico City, Mexico	8,870,000	19	Tehran, Iran	7,240,000
6	Sao Paulo, Brazil	11,240,000	13	Kinshasa, Congo	8,750,000	20	Ho Ch Minh City, Vietnam	7,160,000

LONGEST PLACE NAMES IN THE WORLD

Name (country)

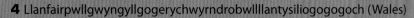

1 Krung Thep Mahanakhon Amon Rattanakosin Mahinthara Ayuthaya Mahadilok Phop Noppharat Ratchathani Burirom Udomratchaniwet Mahasathan Amon Piman Awatan Sathit Sakkathattiya Witsanukam Prasit (Thailand)

2 Taumata-whaka-tangi-hanga-koauau-o-tamatea-turi-pukakapi-ki-maunga-horo-nuku-poka-i-whenua-kitana-tahu (New Zealand)

3 United-Townships-of-Dysart-Bruton-Clyde-Dudley-Eyre-Guilford-Harburn-Harcourt-and-Havelock (Canada)

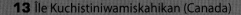

4 Llanfairpwllgwyngyllgogerychwyrndrobwllllantysiliogogogoch (Wales)

5 Lake Chargoggagoggmanchauggagoggchaubunagungamaugg (USA)

6 Tweebuffelsmeteenskootmorsdoodgeskietfontein (South Africa)

7 Äteritsiputeritsipuolilautatsijänkä (Finland)

8 Pekwachnamaykoskwaskwaypinwanik lake (Canada)

9 Sri Venkatanarasimharajuvariipeta (India)

10 Mamungkukumpurangkuntjunya hill (Australia)

11 Tiruchchirapalli Palakarai (India)

12 Gasselterboerveenschemond (Holland)

13 Île Kuchistiniwamiskahikan (Canada)

14 Bullaunancheathrairaluinn (Ireland)

15 Muckanaghederdauhaulia (Ireland)

16 Parangaricutirimicuaro (Mexico)

17 Drehideenglashanatooha (Ireland)

18 Siemieniakowszczyzna (Poland)

19 Siemieniakowszczyzna (Poland)

20 Newtownmountkennedy (Ireland)

MOST POPULAR UK BOYS' NAMES 100 YEARS AGO

1 John
2 William
3 George
4 Thomas
5 James

6 Arthur
7 Frederick
8 Albert
9 Charles
10 Robert

11 Edward
12 Joseph
13 Ernest
14 Alfred
15 Frank

16 Henry
17 Leslie
18 Harold
19 Harry
20 Leonard

Source: Office for National Statistics

MOST POPULAR US GIRLS' NAMES 100 YEARS AGO

1 Mary
2 Helen
3 Margaret
4 Ruth
5 Dorothy
6 Anna
7 Elizabeth
8 Mildred
9 Marie
10 Alice

11 Florence
12 Frances
13 Ethel
14 Lillian
15 Gladys
16 Edna
17 Rose
18 Evelyn
19 Louise
20 Irene

MOST POPULAR US BOYS' NAMES 100 YEARS AGO

1 John
2 William
3 James
4 George
5 Robert
6 Joseph
7 Charles
8 Frank
9 Edward
10 Thomas

11 Henry
12 Walter
13 Willie
14 Harry
15 Albert
16 Harold
17 Paul
18 Arthur
19 Clarence
20 Raymond

Source: Social Security Administration USA

MOST POPULAR UK GIRLS' NAMES 100 YEARS AGO

1 Mary		11	Gladys
2 Margaret		12	Annie
3 Doris		13	Alice
4 Dorothy		14	Phyllis
5 Kathleen		15	Hilda
6 Florence		16	Lilian
7 Elsie		17	Ivy
8 Edith		18	Marjorie
9 Elizabeth		19	Ethel
10 Winifred		20	Violet

Source: Office for National Statistics

LONGEST WARS

War (dates) / Duration (years)

1 Byzantine–Seljuk Turks War (1048–1308) / 260

2 Mongol Conquests (1206–1324) / 118

3 Hundred Years War (1337–1453) / 116

4 Beaver Wars (1640–1701) / 61

5 Dutch–Portuguese War (1602–1661) / 59

7 Greco–Persian War (499–448 BC) / 51

7 Apache Wars (1851-1900) / 49

8 Caucasian War (1817–1864) / 44

9 First War of Scottish Independence (1296–1328) / 32

10 Achinese War (1873–1904) / 30

11 Texas–Indian War (1845–1875) / 30

12 Eritrean War of Independence (1961–1991) / 30

13 Peloponnesian War (431–404 BC) / 27

14 War of 27 Years (1681–1707) / 26

15 Thirty Years War (1618–1643) / 25

16 Franco–Spanish War (1635–1659) / 24

17 South African Border War (1966–1989) / 23

18 First Punic War (264–241 BC) / 23

19 The Great Northern War (1700–1721) / 21

20 Vietnam War (1955–1975) / 20

This list does not include civil wars – wars fought by citizens of the same country.

BLOODIEST BATTLES

Battle (year) / Total deaths

1 Stalingrad (1942–43) / 1,900,000* **2** Leningrad (1941–44) / 1,600,000*

3 Verdun (1916) / 976,000 **4** Moscow (1941–42) / 900,000

5 Passchendaele (1917) / 848,614 **6** Serbian Campaign (1914–15) / 633,500

7 Marne (First) (1914) / 483,000 **8** Gallipoli (1915–16) / 473,000

9 Belorussia (First) 1943 / 375,000 **10** Voronezh–Voroshilovgrad (1942) / 371,000

11 Belorussia (Second) 1944 / 350,000 **12** Kursk (1943) / 325,000

13 Somme (1916) / 306,000 **14** Arras (1917) / 278,000

15 Rzhev–Vyazma (1942) / 272,000 **16** West Ukraine (Second) (1944) / 270,000

17 North Caucasus (1942) / 262,000 **18** Berlin (1945) / 250,000

19 West Ukraine (First) (1941) / 189,000 **20** North France (1940) / 185,000

* Including civilians

SHORTEST WARS*

War / Duration

1 Anglo–Zanzibar War (1896) / 45 mins
2 South Ossetia War (2008) / 4 days
3 Six–Day War (1967) / 6 days
4 Indo–Pakistan War (1971) / 13 days
5 Serbo–Bulgarian War (1885) / 14 days
6 Agacher Christmas War (1985) / 16 days
7 Georgian–Armenian War (1918) / 24 days
8 Sino–Vietnamese War (1979) / 27 days
9 Greco–Turkish War (1897) / 30 days
10 Iraq War (2006) / 31 days

11 Second Balkan War (1913) / 32 days
12 Sino–Indian War (1962) / 32 days
13 Lebanon War (2006) / 33 days
14 Polish–Lithuanian War (1920) / 37 days
15 Falklands War (1982) / 42 days
16 Neapolitan War (1815) / 66 days
17 Austro–Prussian War (1866) / 68 days
18 Second Italian War of Independence (1859) / 74 days
19 Spanish–American War (1898) / 109 days
20 100 Days War (1815) / 111 days

* This list does not include civil wars

135

MOST ENDANGERED MAMMALS*

1 Long-beaked echidna (*Zaglossus attenboroughi*)

2 Mountain pygmy possum (*Burramys parvus*)

3 Riverine rabbit (*Bunolagus monticularis*)

4 Sumatran rhinoceros (*Dicerorhinus sumatrensis*)

5 Northern hairy-nosed wombat
   (*Lasiorhinus krefftii*)

6 Pygmy three-toed sloth (*Bradypus pygmaeus*)

7 Greater funnel-eared bat
   (*Natalus jamaicensis*)

8 Bolivian chinchilla rat
   (*Abrocoma boliviensis*)

9 Talaud bear cuscus
   (*Ailurops melanotis*)

10 Monk seal
   (*Monachus monachus*)

11 Rondo dwarf galago
   (*Galagoides rondoensis*)

12 Greater bamboo lemur
   (*Prolemur simus*)

13 Gilbert's potoroo
   (*Potorous gilbertii*)

14 Hirola (*Beatragus hunteri*)

15 Saola (*Pseudoryx nghetinhensis*)

16 Sumatran orangutan (*Pongo abelii*)

17 Perrier's sifaka (*Propithecus perrier*)

18 Vaquita (*Phocoena sinus*)

19 African wild ass (*Equus asinus*)

20 Western gorilla (*Gorilla gorilla*)

Source: Zoological Society of London's list of Top 100 Evolutionarily Distinct and Globally Endangered Mammals. All are on the critically endangered list.

LONGEST-LIVING LAND ANIMALS

Animal / Oldest recorded age (years)

1 Giant tortoise 255

2 Radiated tortoise 188

3 Greek tortoise 160

4 Crocodile 130

5 Human 122

6 Turkey buzzard 118

7 Macaw 111

8 Tuatara 110

9 Andean condor 100

10 Elephant 86

11 Alligator 80

12 Cockatoo 77

13 Great horned owl 68

14 Northern royal
   albatross 61

15 Crow 59

16 Bald eagle 50

17 Horse 50

18 Komodo dragon 50

19 White rhino 50

20 Hippopotamus 49

CLOSEST ANIMAL RELATIVES TO HUMANS*

Species / Diverged from man (million years ago)

1
Common chimpanzee
(*Pan troglodytes*) 6

2
Bonobo
(*Pan paniscus*) 6

3
Western gorilla
(*Gorilla gorilla*) 7

4
Eastern gorilla
(*Gorilla berengei*) 7

5
Bornean Orang-utan
(*Pongo pygmaeus*)
13–16

6
Sumatran Orang-utan
(*Pongo abeli*)
13–16

7
Lar gibbon
(*Hylobates lar*)
20–25

8
Agile gibbon
(*Hylobates agilis*)
20–25

9
Muller's Bornean gibbon
(*Hylobates mullerei*)
20–25

10
Silvery gibbon (*Hylobates moloch*) 20–25

11
Pileated gibbon (*Hylobates pileatus*) 20–25

12
Kloss's gibbon (*Hylobates klossi*) 20–25

13
Western and Eastern hoolock gibbon
(*Hoolock sp.*) 20–25

14
Sianmang gibbon
(*Symphalangus syndactylus*) 20–25

15
Northern buffed-cheeked gibbon (*Nomascus annamensis*) 20–25

16
Black crested gibbon
(*N. concolor*) 20–25

17
Eastern black-crested gibbon
(*N. nasutus*) 20–25

18
Northern white-cheeked gibbon (*N. nasutus*) 20–25

19
Southern white-cheeked gibbon (*N. siki*) 1–20

20
Yellow-cheeked gibbon
(*N. gabriella*) 25–30

*Old world monkeys including macaque and colobus monkeys are the next closest relatives to humans.

137

MOST DOGS PER COUNTRY

Country / Number of dogs

1 USA 61,080,000

2 Brazil 30,051.000

3 China 22,908,000

4 Japan 9,600,000

5 Russia 9,600,000

6 South Africa 9,100,000

7 France 8,150,000

8 India 8,000,000

9 Italy 7,600,000

10 Poland 7,520,000

11 Thailand 6,900,000

12 UK 6,100,000

13 Italy 5,800,000

14 Canada 5,700,000

15 Germany 5,000,000

16 Australia 3,972,000

17 Netherlands 3,000,000

18 Spain 1,500,000

19 Argentina 1,000,000

20 South Korea 1,000,000

MOST CATS PER COUNTRY

Country / Number of cats

1. USA 76,430,000
2. China 53,100,000
3. Mexico 14,000,000
4. Russia 12,700,000
5. Brazil 12,466,000
6. France 9,600,000
7. Italy 9,400,000
8. UK 7,700,000
9. Ukraine 7,350,000
10. Japan 7,300,000
11. Germany 7,100,000
12. Canada 4,500,000
13. Australia 3,000,000
14. Spain 3,000,000
15. Netherlands 2,300,000
16. Hungary 1,900,000
17. New Zealand 1,500,000
18. Austria 1,400,000
19. Sweden 1,300,000
20. Switzerland 1,200,000

MOST AGGRESSIVE DOGS

Breed of dog / Origin

1
Daschund
Germany

2
Chihuahua
Mexico

3
Beagle
Greece

4
Jack Russell
UK

5
Australian Cattle Dog
Australia

6
Cocker Spaniel
UK

7
Border Collie
UK

8
Pit Bull
USA

9
Great Dane
Germany/Denmark

10
Sprinter Spaniel
UK

11
Shetland Sheepdog
UK

12
Airedale terrier
UK

13
Bichon Frise
France

14
Doberman Pinscher
Germany

15
Rottweiler
Germany

16
Boxer
Germany

17
German Shepherd
Germany

18
Wheaten Terrier
Ireland

19
Akita
Japan

20
Collie
UK

The European Cup includes both variations of the competition (European Champion Clubs' Cup and UEFA Champions League), the Cup Winners Cup was discontinued in 1999 and the Europa League listing includes the Inter-Cities Fairs Cup and UEFA Cup statistics. Where teams are level on the number of competitions won, they have been separated according to their performance in the premier competition, then the Cup Winners Cup and finally, the Europa League.

Kristine Lilly of the USA is the most capped female player, having represented her country 352 times between 1987 and 2001 and scored 130 goals. She also picked up two gold medals at the Olympic Games, helping the USA win in 1996 and 2004.

MOST SUCCESSFUL CLUB SIDES IN EUROPEAN COMPETITION (FOOTBALL)

Team	European Cup Winners	Cup	Europa League	Total
1 Real Madrid	9	–	2	11
2 Barcelona	3	4	3	10
3 AC Milan	7	2	–	9
4 Liverpool	5	–	3	8
5 Ajax	4	1	1	6
6 Bayern Munich	4	1	1	6
7 Internazionale	3	3	–	6
8 Juventus	2	1	3	6
9 Manchester United	3	1	–	4
10 Valencia	–	1	3	4
11 Porto	2	–	1	3
12 Feyenoord	1	–	2	3
13 Anderlecht	–	2	1	3
14 Tottenham Hotspur	–	1	2	3
15 Benefica	2	–	–	2
16 Nottingham Forest	2	–	–	2
17 Hamburg	1	1	–	2
18 Borussia Dortmund	1	1	–	2
19 PSV Eindhoven	1	–	1	2
20 Chelsea	–	2	–	2

MOST INTERNATIONAL CAPS (MEN'S FOOTBALL)

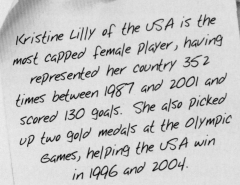

1 Mohamed Al-Deayea, Saudi Arabia, 178

2 Claudio Suarez, Mexico, 178

3 Ahmed Hassan, Egypt, 175

4 Hossam Hassan, Egypt, 169

5 Ivan Hurtado, Ecuador, 167

6 Vitalijs Astafjevs, Latvia, 167

7 Cobi Jones, USA, 164

8 Adnan Al-Talyani, United Arab Emirates, 164

9 Sami Al-Jaber, Saudi Arabia, 158

10 Martin Reim, Estonia, 157

11 Lothar Matthaus, West Germany/Germany, 150

12 Ali Daei, Iran, 149

13 Pavel Pardo, Mexico, 146

14 Mohammed Al-Khilaiwi, Saudi Arabia, 143

15 Marko Kristal, Estonia, 143

16 Thomas Ravelli, Sweden, 143

17 Cafu, Brazil, 142

18 Lilian Thuram, France, 142

19 Majed Abdullah, Saudi Arabia, 139

20 Javier Zanetti, Argentina, 138

Source: rsssf.com

MOST INTERNATIONAL GOALS

1 Ali Daei (Iran) 109
2 Ferenc Puskas (Hungary) 84
3 Pele (Brazil) 77
4 Sandor Kocsis (Hungary) 75
5 Bashar Abdullah (Kuwait) 75
6 Stern John (Trinidad & Tobago) 69
7 Hossam Hassan (Egypt) 69
8 Gerd Muller (West Germany) 68
9 Majed Abdullah (Saudi Arabia) 67
10 Diego Forlan (Uruguay) 65

11 Kiatisuk Senamuang (Thailand) 65
12 Ronaldo (Brazil) 62
13 Hussain Saeed Mohammed (Iraq) 61
14 Imre Schlosser (Hungary) 59
15 Mirolsav Klose (Germany) 59
16 Gabriel Batistuta (Argentina) 56
17 Carlos Pavon (Honduras) 56
18 Kazuyoshi Miura (Japan) 55
19 Kunishige Kamamoto (Japan) 55
20 Romario (Brazil) 55

Source: rsssf.com

FIFA WORLD CUP-WINNING COUNTRIES AND PLACINGS

Country	Winners	Runners-up	3rd place	4th place
1 Brazil	5	2	2	1
2 Italy	4	2	1	1
3 Germany	3	4	4	1
4 Argentina	2	2	-	-
5 Uruguay	2	-	-	-
6 France	1	1	2	1
7 England	1	-	-	1
8 Spain	1	-	-	1
9 Holland	-	3	1	1
10 Czech Republic	-	2	-	-
11 Hungary	-	2	-	-
12 Sweden	-	1	2	1
13 Austria	-	-	1	1
14 Portugal	-	-	1	1
15 USA	-	-	1	-
16 Chile	-	-	1	-
17 Croatia	-	-	1	-
18 Turkey	-	-	1	-
19 Yugoslavia	-	-	-	2
20 Soviet Union	-	-	-	1

PETS AND ANIMALS

COUNTRIES FARMING CHICKENS

Country / Annual production

Source: FAO

2 USA 1.97 billion

4 Brazil 1.1 billion

6 Nigeria 740 million

8 India 425 million

10 Japan 286 million

1 China 3.86 billion

3 Indonesia 1.2 billion

5 UK 850 million

7 Mexico 540 million

9 Russia 340 million

COUNTRIES FARMING CATTLE

Country / Total herd numbers (millions)

Source: The Beef market

1 India 281

2 Brazil 187

3 China 139

4 USA 100.8

5 Argentina 55

6 Australia 29.6

7 Russian Federation 25.8

8 France 23.2

9 Mexico 22.44

10 Denmark 18.6

11 UK 14.3

12 South Africa 14.2

13 Spain 14.1

14 Canada 12.6

15 Poland 10.7

16 Italy 9.9

17 Ireland 6.3

18 Netherlands 6.1

19 Romania 4.9

20 Austria 2.16

12 Turkey 250 million

14 Malaysia 160 million

16 Bangladesh 140 million

18 Thailand 121 million

20 Australia 93 million

11 Iran 280 million

13 Vietnam 163 million

15 Pakistan 153 million

17 Philippines 125 million

19 South Korea 107 million

COUNTRIES FARMING PIGS

	Country	Total numbers (millions)
1.	China	425.6
2.	USA	61.7
3.	Russia	60.0
4.	Brazil	35.9
5.	Germany	27.1
6.	Japan	27.0
7.	Vietnam	26.6
8.	Spain	26.1
9.	South Korea	23.0
10.	Denmark	22.0
11.	Poland	18.1
12.	Ukraine	17.0
13.	Mexico	15.5
14.	Canada	14.9
15.	France	12.7
16.	Netherlands	11.7
17.	Italy	6.3
18.	Belgium	4.8
19.	UK	4.5
20.	Portugal	2.5

Source: Live Swine Selected Countries USDA

Did you know?

A male pig is called a boar and a female is known as a gilt until she has piglets, when she is known as a sow.

BESTSELLING SINGLES IN THE UK

1. **Elton John** *Candle In The Wind 1997/Something About The Way You Look Tonight* (4.9 million)

2. **Band Aid** *Do They Know It's Christmas?* (3.6 million)

3. **Queen** *Bohemian Rhapsody* (2.2 million)

4. **Wings** *Mull Of Kintyre* (2.1 million)

5. **Boney M** *Rivers Of Babylon/Brown Girl In The Ring* (2 million)

6. **John Travolta & Olivia Newton-John** *You're The One That I Want* (2 million)

7. **Frankie Goes To Hollywood** *Relax* (1.91 million)

8. **The Beatles** *She Loves You* (1.89 million)

9. **Robson Green & Jerome Flynn** *Unchained Melody/White Cliffs Of Dover* (1.8 million)

10. **Boney M** *Mary's Boy Child–Oh My Lord* (1.8 million)

11. **Will Young** *Evergreen/Anything Is Possible* (1.8 million)

12. **Wet Wet Wet** *Love Is All Around* (1.8 million)

13. **Stevie Wonder** *I Just Called To Say I Love You* (1.8 million)

14. **The Beatles** *I Want To Hold Your Hand* (1.8 million)

15. **Aqua** *Barbie Girl* (1.7 million)

16. **Cher** *Believe* (1.7 million)

17. **Various Artists** *Perfect Day* (1.5 million)

18. **Bryan Adams** *(Everything I Do) I Do It For You* (1.5 million)

19. **Ken Dodd** *Tears* (1.5 million)

20. **The Beatles** *Can't Buy Me Love* (1.5 million)

Source: OCC

BESTSELLING ALBUMS IN THE UK

1. Queen *Greatest Hits* (5.4 million)
2. The Beatles *Sgt Pepper's Lonely Hearts Club Band* (4.8 million)
3. Oasis *(What's The Story) Morning Glory* (4.3 million)
4. Dire Straits *Brothers In Arms* (4 million)
5. ABBA *Gold Greatest Hits* (3.9 million)
6. Pink Floyd *Dark Side Of The Moon* (3.8 million)
7. Queen *Greatest Hits II* (3.6 million)
8. Michael Jackson *Thriller* (3.6 million)
9. Michael Jackson *Bad* (3.6 million)
10. Madonna *The Immaculate Collection* (3.4 million)
11. Simply Red *Star* (3.4 million)
12. Shania Twain *Come On Over* (3.3 million)
13. Fleetwood Mac *Rumours* (3.1 million)
14. The Verve *Urban Hymns* (3.1 million)
15. Dido *No Angel* (3 million)
16. Simon & Garfunkel *Bridge Over Troubled Water* (3 million)
17. The Corrs *Talk On Corners* (2.9 million)
18. The Spice Girls *Spice* (2.9 million)
19. James Blunt *Back To Bedlam* (2.9 million)
20. David Gray *White Ladder* (2.9 million)

Source: OCC

TOP UK SINGLE DOWNLOADS

1. Black Eyed Peas *I Gotta Feeling*
2. Lady Gaga *Poker Face*
3. Black Eyed Peas *Boom Boom Pow*
4. Jason Mraz *I'm Yours*
5. Coldplay *Viva la Vida*
6. Lady Gaga *Just Dance*
7. Flo Rida *Low (feat. T-Pain)*
8. Taylor Swift *Love Story*
9. Leona Lewis *Bleeding Love*
10. Ke$ha *Tik Tok*
11. Rihanna *Disturbia*
12. P!nk *So What*
13. Katy Perry *I Kissed a Girl*
14. Beyoncé *Bad Single Ladies (Put a Ring On It)*
15. Katy Perry *Hot N Cold*
16. Kanye West *Stronger*
17. T.I. *Live Your Life (feat. Rihanna)*
18. Plain White T's *Hey There Delilah*
19. Flo Rida Featuring *Right Round*
20. Miley Cyrus *Party In the U.S.A.*

Source: OCC

Did you know?
The official download chart in the UK was first launched in September 2004 and the first number one single was Westlife's *Flying Without Wings*.

PETS AND ANIMALS

COUNTRIES FARMING DUCKS

Country / Production ($1000)

Source: United Nations Food Organization

1 France 270,506

2 Malaysia 151,471

3 Vietnam 114,815

4 Thailand 108,416

5 India 87,320

6 Taiwan 76,779

7 USA 67,041

8 Hungary 62,484

9 Republic of Korea 62,380

10 Germany 58,611

11 Egypt 50,978

12 UK 49,589

13 Myanmar 38,998

14 Indonesia 30,461

15 Philippines 28,639

16 Mexico 26,361

17 Poland 26,035

18 Netherlands 18,094

19 Bangladesh 16,345

20 Madagascar 13,851

COUNTRIES FARMING SHEEP

Country / Production ($1000)

Source: United Nations Food Organization

1
Australia
1,319,506

2
New Zealand
1,007,057

3
Iran
771,536

4
UK
621,177

5
Turkey
538,333

6
Syria
483,030

7
India
472,509

8
Spain
462,915

9
Sudan
360,045

10
Pakistan
328,393

11
Algeria
328,136

12
France
248,471

13
Russia
246,580

14
South Africa
222,079

15
Kazakhstan
209,974

16
Morocco
203,841

17
Nigeria
194,761

18.
USA
179,033

19
Turkmenistan
178,044

20
Romania
175,782

TOP 20 PEOPLE

GIRLS' NAMES IN THE UK TODAY

	Name	Usage
1	Olivia	5,201
2	Ruby	4,555
3	Chloe	4,479
4	Emily	4,462
5	Sophie	4,452
6	Jessica	4,291
7	Grace	4,291
8	Lilly	3,967
9	Amelia	3,625
10	Evie	3,389
11	Mia	2,836
12	Ava	2,827
13	Ella	2,818
14	Charlotte	2,778
15	Isabella	2,607
16	Lucy	2,597
17	Isabelle	2,546
18	Daisy	2,449
19	Holly	2,263
20	Megan	2,250

BOYS' NAMES IN THE UK TODAY

	Name	Usage
1	Oliver	7,364
2	Jack	7,090
3	Harry	6,143
4	Alfie	5,536
5	Joshua	5,526
6	Thomas	5,520
7	Charlie	5,409
8	William	5,247
9	James	4,544
10	Daniel	4,444
11	George	4,347
12	Samuel	4,314
13	Ethan	3,729
14	Joseph	3,613
15	Benjamin	3,319
16	Mohammed	3,300
17	Lucas	3,276
18	Jacob	3,214
19	Dylan	3,201
20	Archie	3,069

Source: Office for National Statistics

The fastest growing surnames in the UK are Zhang, Wang, Yang, Huang and Lin.

148

Did you know?
Facebook Jamal Ibrahim was born in Egypt in 2011.

MOST COMMON SURNAMES IN SCOTLAND

Name / Percentage of population

	Name	Percentage of population
1	Smith	1.28
2	Brown	0.94
3	Wilson	0.89
4	Robertson	0.78
5	Thomson	0.78
6	Campbell	0.77
7	Stewart	0.73
8	Anderson	0.70
9	Scott	0.55
10	Murray	0.53
11	MacDonald	0.52
12	Reid	0.52
13	Taylor	0.49
14	Clark	0.47
15	Ross	0.43
16	Young	0.42
17	Mitchell	0.41
18	Watson	0.41
19	Paterson	0.40
20	Morrison	

MOST COMMON SURNAMES IN ENGLAND

Surname / Percentage of population

	Surname	Percentage of population
1	Smith	1.26
2	Jones	0.77
3	Taylor	0.59
4	Brown	0.56
5	Williams	0.39
6	Wilson	0.39
7	Johnson	0.37
8	Davis	0.34
9	Robinson	0.32
10	Wright	0.32
11	Thompson	0.31
12	Evans	0.30
13	Walker	0.30
14	White	0.30
15	Roberts	0.28
16	Green	0.28
17	Hall	0.28
18	Wood	0.27
19	Jackson	0.27
20	Clarke	0.26

HISTORY AND WARFARE

Sources:
US Naval History
and Heritage.

BIGGEST BATTLESHIPS OF WORLD WAR II

	Name	Country	Weight (tonnes)	Length ft (m)
1	Yamato	Japan	71,659	928 (283)
2	Musashi	Japan	71,659	928 (283)
3	Iowa	US	52,834	889 (271)
4	New Jersey	US	52,834	889 (271)
5	Missouri	US	52,834	889 (271)
6	Wisconsin	US	52,834	889 (271)
7	Bismarck	Germany	50,900	823 (251)
8	Tirpitz	Germany	50,900	823 (251)
9	Richelieu	France	48,950	813 (248)
10	Jean Bart	France	48,950	813 (248)
11	Hood	UK	47,430	859 (262)
12	North Carolina	US	45,089	725 (221)
13	Washington	US	45,089	725 (221)
14	King George V	UK	43,300	744 (227)
15	Prince of Wales	UK	43,300	744 (227)
16	Duke of York	UK	43,300	744 (227)
17	Anson	UK	43,300	744 (227)
18	Howe	UK	43,300	744 (227)
19	Nagato	Japan	42,850	725 (221)
20	Mutsu	Japan	42,850	725 (221)

Did you know?

Neither of the two largest battleships, Yamato and Musashi, survived World War II. Yamamoto was sunk on April 7, 1945, by US bombers off the coast of Japan and Musashi was destroyed in October 1944.

The US ships, Iowa, New Jersey, Missouri and Wisconsin were also commissioned for use in World War II. Wisconsin was still in use in 1991 and was used in Operation Desert Storm in Iraq. She is now berthed in a museum in Virginia, USA.

MILITARY AIR FLEETS WORLDWIDE
Country / Number of combat aircraft*

Did you know?
The idea of the jet engine was first developed by British engineer Frank Whittle in 1928. The idea was used by the Germans and the Heinkel He 178, the first jet aircraft, took off in 1939.

1 USA 2,600
2 Russia 2,300
3 China 2,200
4 India 740
5 North Korea 620
6 Pakistan 500
7 South Korea 460
8 Egypt 440
9 UK 420
10 Israel 410
11 Turkey 410
12 Taiwan 400
13 Saudi Arabia 390
14 France 380
15 Iran 310
16 Greece 290
17 Sweden 250
18 Italy 230
19 Ukraine 200
20 Spain 160

* Fixed wing aircraft rather then rotary winged, such as helicopters.

An airforce pilot inside the cockpit of a fighter plane

INTERNET RETAIL SITES (UK)

Website / Percentage of total visits at any one time

1	eBay UK 22.49%	**11**	John Lewis 0.70%
2	Amazon UK 6.53%	**12**	SupaPrice 0.69%
3	Argos 1.69%	**13**	Groupon UK 0.63%
4	Gumtree 1.50%	**14**	Boots 0.62%
5	Tesco 1.19%	**15**	HotUKDeals 0.62%
6	eBay 1.10%	**16**	New Look 0.61%
7	Your M&S 1.08%	**17**	Debenhams 0.61%
8	Next 0.91%	**18**	Tesco Direct 0.57%
9	Play.com 0.88%	**19**	ASOS 0.57%
10	Amazon.com 0.86%	**20**	MoneySavingExpert.com 0.51%

Source: Hitwise

MOST POPULAR ONLINE PURCHASES

Category / Percentage of total spend (%)

	Category	Percentage
1	Books	13.8
2	Clothing and shoes	12.0
3	Airline travel	8.0
4	Electronic/digital goods	7.7
5	Music CDs/downloads	6.0
6	Cosmetics/health supplements	6.0
7	Computer equipment	5.0
8	Hotels/cruises/tours	5.0
9	Entertainment events	5.0
10	Groceries	4.6
11	Computer software	4.5
12	DVDs	4.3
13	Games	4.0
14	Sports goods/memorabilia	3.7
15	Toys	3.0
16	Pet supplies	2.0
17	Home furnishings	1.6
18	Motorcars/autoparts	1.4
19	Pharmaceuticals	1.3
20	Other	1.1

Sources: National Retail Federation, Forrester Research, Nielsen Co.

5 282610899287 7

NEWS WEBSITES

Website / Address (http://...) / Individual visitors (million/month)

1 Yahoo! News (news.yahoo.com) 70.0

2 CNN (www.cnn.com) 48.0

3 MSNBC (www.msnbc.msn.com) 45.0

4 Google News (news.google.com) 46.0

5 *Daily Mail* Online (www.dailymail.co.uk) 43.0

6 *New York Times* (news.google.com) 38.0

7 *Guardian* Online (www.guardian.co.uk) 35.3

8 *Telegraph* (www.telegraph.co.uk) 33.6

9 Huffington Post (news.google.com) 28.0

10 digg (digg.com/news) 27.5

11 Fox News (www.foxnews.com) 24.0

12 *Washington Post* (www.washingtonpost.com) 22.0

13 *LA Times* (www.washingtonpost.com) 21.9

14 Reuters (uk.reuters.com) 21.0

15 ABC News (abcnews.go.com) 20.0

16 USA Today (www.usatoday.com) 19.0

17 BBC News (www.bbc.co.uk/news) 18.5

18 Drudge Report (www.drudgereport.com) 14.0

19 *Daily Mirror* (www.mirror.co.uk) 11.0

20 *The Independent* (www.independent.co.uk) 10.6

Top Viral Advert

The world's most successful viral advert is Nike's three-minute "Write the Future" ad, attracting 7.8 million viewers in its first week. Shown in May 2010 to promote FIFA's football World Cup it features a host of international soccer stars. The previous record, set by "Earl and Tiger," with golfer Tiger Woods, had 6.3 million hits in its first week.

Source: various including Alexa and Audit Bureau of Circulation Electronic.

The Vatican

SMALLEST COUNTRIES IN THE WORLD

Country / Area (miles / km squared)

	Country	Area
1	The Vatican	0.2 / 0.44
2	Monaco	0.8 / 1.95
3	Pitcairn Islands	1.9 / 5
4	Gibraltar	2.3 / 6
5	Tokelau	4.6 / 12
6	Nauru	8.1 / 21
7	Tuvalu	10 / 26
8	Norfolk Island	14 / 36
9	Bermuda	21 / 54
10	San Marino	24 / 61
11	Guernsey	30 / 78
12	Ascension Island	34 / 88
13	Anguilla	35 / 91
14	Tristan da Cunha	38 / 98
15	Montserrat	39 / 102
16	Jersey	45 / 116
17	Saint Helena	47 / 122
18	Wallis & Futuna	55 / 142
19	British Virgin Islands	58 / 151
20	Liechtenstein	62 / 160

LARGEST COUNTRIES IN THE WORLD

Country / Area (miles / km squared)

	Country	Area		Country	Area
1	Russia	6,600 / 17,098,242	11	Algeria	920 / 2,381,741
2	Canada	3,850 / 9,984,670	12	Congo	905 / 2,344,858
3	USA	3,700 / 9,629,091	13	Greenland	836 / 2,166,086
4	China	3,700 / 9,598,094	14	Saudi Arabia	772 / 2,000,000
5	Brazil	3,288 / 8,514,877	15	Mexico	758 / 1,964,375
6	Australia	2,970 / 7,692,024	16	Indonesia	735 / 1,904,569
7	India	1,270 / 3,287,263	17	Libya	679 / 1,759,540
8	Argentina	1,070 / 2,780,400	18	Iran	636 / 1,648,195
9	Kazakhstan	1,050 / 2,724,900	19	Mongolia	604 / 1,564,100
10	Sudan	967 / 2,505,813	20	Peru	496 / 1,285,216

view of an iceberg off the coast of Greenland.

Mongolia, the western coast.

1 Greenland 0.067 / 0.026 **2** Falkland Islands 0.67 / 0.26 **3** Mongolia 4.4 / 1.7
4 Western Sahara 4.9 / 1.9 **5** French Guiana 5.4 / 2.1
6 Namibia 6.7 / 2.6 **7** Australia 7.5 / 2.9

LEAST DENSELY POPULATED COUNTRIES
Country / Population per square mile/km

8 Iceland 8 / 23.1 **9** Suriname 8.3 / 3.2
10 Mauritania 8.3 / 3.2 **11** Botswana 8.8 / 3.4
12 Canada 8.8 / 3.4 **13** Guyana 9.1 / 3.5 **14** Libya 9.3 / 3.6 **17** Central African Republic 19 / 7.1 **20** Chad 23 / 8.8
15 Gabon 14 / 5.5 **16** Kazakhstan 15 / 5.8 **19** Russia 21 / 8.3
18 Niue (NZ) 20 / 7.7

RICHEST
CHILD STARS

Actor(s)	Nett worth (US$)	Actor(s)	Nett worth (US$)
1. Miley Cyrus	$1 billion	11. Angus T. Jones	$7.8 million
2. Daniel Radcliffe	$50 million	12. Dakota Fanning	$4 million
3. Olsen Sisters	$38 million	13. Miranda Cosgrove	$2 million
4. Emma Watson	$30 million	14. Selena Gomez	$1 million
5. Jonas Brothers	$20 million	15. Dylan and Cole Sprouse	$1 million
6. Zac Efron	$10 million	16. Keke Palmer	$500,000
7. Macauley Culkin	$17 million	17. Rico Rodriguez	$300,000
8. Drew Barrymore	$15 million	18. Demi Lovato	$200,000
9. River Phoenix	$9.5 million	19. Victoria Justice	$200,000
10. Jaden Smith	$8 million	20. Shirley Temple	$100,000

Source: Forbes.com

COUNTRIES WITH THE MOST CINEMAS

1.	USA	31,640
2.	India	21,801
3.	Germany	4,712
4.	Italy	4,603
5.	Spain	3,354
6.	Mexico	2,320
7.	Japan	2,221
8.	France	2,150
9.	UK	2,019
10.	Australia	1,748
11.	Russia	1,416
12.	Brazil	1,400
13.	Sweden	1,167
14.	Kazakhstan	1,129
15.	Indonesia	1,009
16.	Czech Republic	823
17.	Cuba	728
18.	Argentina	780
19.	Poland	695
20.	Canada	692

Source: BFI

CINEMA-GOERS BY COUNTRY

Country/Admissions (millions annually) Source: Nation Master

1.	India	2,860	11.	Canada	112.8
2.	USA	1,421	12.	Italy	104.9
3.	Indonesia	190.0	13.	Australia	80.0
4.	France	155.4	14.	Brazil	80.0
5.	Germany	149.0	15.	South Korea	54.7
6.	Japan	145.0	16.	Argentina	32.5
7.	China	140.0	17.	Turkey	31.5
8.	UK	139.5	18.	Poland	27.5
9.	Spain	131.4	19.	Iran	26.0
10.	Mexico	120.0	20.	Belgium	21.9

MOST INFLUENTIAL BLOGS

Blog / Web address

1 The Huffington Post http://www.huffingtonpost.com
2 Techcrunch http://techcrunch.com
3 Mashable http://mashable.com
4 Gawker http://uk.gawker.com
5 TMZ http://www.tmz.com
6 Boing Boing http://www.boingboing.net
7 The Daily Beast http://www.thedailybeast.com
8 Bad Science http://www.badscience.net
9 The Official Google Blog http://googleblog.blogspot.com
10 Marbury http://www.marbury.typepad.com
11 CNN Political Ticker http://politicalticker.blogs.cnn.com
12 Students for a Free Tibet http://www.studentsforafreetibet.org
13 Jezebel http://uk.jezebel.com
14 Craig Murray http://craigmurray.org.uk
15 Environmental Graffiti http://www.environmentalgraffiti.com
16 Engadget http://www.engadget.com
17 Gizmodo http://uk.gizmodo.com
18 The Sartorialist http://www.thesartorialist.blogspot.com
19 BBC Internet Blog http://www.bbc.co.uk/blogs/bbcinternet
20 ReadWriteWeb http://www.readwriteweb.com

Search — MOST POPULAR WEBSITES

Website / Individual users

#	Website	Individual users	#	Website	Individual users
1	Google	349,758,716	11	Amazon	111,945,278
2	MSN/WindowsLive/Bing	271,929,865	12	Blogger	110,738,193
3	Yahoo!	233,479,611	13	Ask	100,846,108
4	Microsoft	220,410,208	14	Fox Interactive Media	92,899,123
5	Facebook	218,860,914	15	Mozilla	67,949,332
6	YouTube	203,258,182	16	Real Network	61,513,698
7	Wikipedia	154,174,390	17	Adobe	53,002,496
8	AOL	128,146,575	18	About	52,543,328
9	eBay	121,740,943	19	PayPal	48,552,302
10	Apple	119,232,527	20	Weather Channel	48,048,043

Source: BBC

MOST UNUSUAL DEATHS OF THE LAST TWO DECADES

2010

A Los Angeles woman suffocated while trying to enter her boyfriend's home by climbing down the Chimney and becoming trapped. (Source: *Los Angeles Times*).

2009

A Ukrainian chemistry student blew himself up when he dipped his chewing gum into liquid explosive, thinking it citric acid flavouring. (Source: *Independent*)

2008

A Brazilian priest drowned after flying out to sea suspended from a collection of party balloons he had filled with helium. (Source: Associated Press)

2007

A Californian man was struck and killed by a fire hydrant that had been hit by a car, which then took off with explosive force. (Source: Associated Press).

2006

A girl died of asphyxiation after being sucked into the intake pipe of swimming pool in Saitama, Japan after its covering had slipped off. (Source: *Japan Times*)

2005

A South Korean man died of exhaustion after playing an internet video game for 50 hours non-stop. (Source: *Times* Online)

2004

A man in Washington State, USA, died when his faulty electric lava lamp exploded. He was heating it on the stove to make it work. (Source: *Times* Online)

2003

A Texas surgeon was decapitated when his neck became trapped in lift doors and the safety over-ride failed to stop the lift rising. (Source: *Houston Chronicle*)

2002

An ice hockey fan died when she was struck on the head by the puck during a game at Columbus, Ohio, USA. (Source: ESPN.com)

2001

A boy was struck and killed by a metal oxygen tank that was attracted by the powerful pulling power of the magnetic resonance imaging machine as he lay inside. (Source: *New York Times*)

2000

A man died while trying to take off from Niagara Falls, USA, on board a jet ski to which he had attached a jet pack and parachute, and both failed to operate. (Source: *Los Angeles Times*)

1999

Three men died while playing dare in a Cambodian bar by kicking an unexploded tank mine between them, the mine exploded. (Source: Reuters)

1998

An entire football team were killed by lightning during a match in the Republic of Congo. They were the visitors—the home team were uninjured. (Source: BBC)

1997

A German couple were crushed inside a car they had just sold to a scrap metal yard after getting inside to shelter from the rain. (Source: *Daily Mirror*).

1996

A man was asphyxiated by his python. The man had been cutting up raw chicken and the python could smell it on him. (Source: *New York Times*).

1995

A Michigan man died while hanging under a moving farm truck after his clothes got caught in the drive shaft. He was trying to locate a mystery noise while a friend drove. (Source: *Kalamazoo Gazette*)

1994

An angry golfer died when he threw his golf club against a bench and the shaft split, flying back and stabbing him in the chest. (Source: *New York Times*)

1993

A Toronto lawyer fell to his death after crashing through the window of his 24th-floor office while demonstrating the glass was "unbreakable." (Source: UPI)

1992

A North Carolina man shot himself in the head after he was awoken by his bedside phone and picked up his gun in error. (Source: *Hickory Daily Record*).

1991

A Californian woman was killed by a tall "umbrella" that was part of an art installation that blew over in a gale. (Source: *New York Times*)

most followed people on twitter

Home   Profile   Find   People   Settings   Helps   Sign out

Name (website) / Number of followers*

#	Name (website)	Followers
1	Lady Gaga (www.ladygaga.com)	10,313,490
2	Justin Bieber (www.youtube.com/justinbieber)	9,854,198
3	Barack Obama (www.barackobama.com)	8,149,252
4	Britney Spears (www.britneyspears.com)	7,904,855
5	Kim Kardashian (www.kimkardashian.celebuzz.com)	7,560,772
6	Katy Perry (www.katyperry.com)	7,449,295
7	Ashton kutcher (www.facebook.com/Ashton)	6,795,097
8	Ellen DeGeneres (www.ellentv.com)	6,711,047
9	Taylor Swift (www.twitter.com/taylorswift13)	6,451,877
10	Shakira (www.shakira.com)	6,132,730
11	Oprah Winfrey (www.oprah.com)	5,927,906
12	Selena Gomez (www.selenagomez.com)	5,494,621
13	Rihanna (www.rihannanow.com)	5,172,791
14	Justin Timberlake (www.justintimberlake.com)	4,614,228
15	50cent (http://listn.to/50cent)	4,612,052
16	Ryan Seacrest (www.ryanseacrest.com)	4,485,649
17	Mariah Carey (www.mariahcarey.com)	4,426,321
18	Eminem (www.twitter.com/eminem)	4,346,456
19	Ashley Tisdale (www.ashleytisdale.com)	4,325,124
20	P!nk (www.pinkspage.com)	4,031,266

source: http://twitterholic.com

*At time of printing

SOCIAL NETWORKING SITES

Network / Registered users

#	Network / Registered users	#	Network / Registered users
1	Facebook / 500,000,000	11	Friendster / 90,000,000
2	Qzone / 200,000,000	12	Badoo / 86,000,000
3	Twitter / 175,000,000	13	hi5 / 80,000,000
4	Habbo / 162,000,000	14	LinkedIn / 80,000,000
5	Windows Live Spaces / 120,000,000	15	Netlog / 70,000,000
6	Bebo / 117,000,000	16	Flixter / 63,000,000
7	Vkontakte / 110,578,500	17	MyLife / 51,000,000
8	MySpace / 100,000,000+	18	Classmates.com / 50,000,000
9	Tagged / 100,000,000	19	douban / 46,850,000
10	Orkut / 100,000,000	20	Odnoklassniki / 45,000,000

Source: Internet World Stats

COUNTRIES USING THE INTERNET

Country / Number of internet users / Percentage of the population

1	China	420,000,000	31.6	**11** Argentina	41,343,201	64.4
2	USA	266,224,500	77.4	**12** South Korea	39,440,000	81.1
3	Japan	99,143,700	78.2	**13** Turkey	35,000,000	45.0
4	India	81,000,000	6.9	**14** Iran	33,200,000	43.2
5	Brazil	75,943,600	37.8	**15** Mexico	30,600,000	27.2
6	Germany	65,123,800	79.1	**16** Italy	30,026,400	51.7
7	Russia	59,700,000	42.8	**17** Indonesia	30,000,000	12.3
8	UK	51,442,100	82.5	**18** Philippines	29,700,000	29.7
9	France	44,625,300	68.9	**19** Spain	29,093,984	62.6
10	Nigeria	43,982,200	28.9	**20** Poland	22,450,600	58.4

HIGHEST POPULATIONS AGED UNDER 15

Country / Percentage of population aged under 15

1. Niger 50.0
2. Mali 49.2
3. Burkina Faso 48.9
4. Angola 47.5
5. Guinea-Bissau 47.1
6. Burundi 46.9
7. Congo 46.8
8. Chad 46.7
9. Zambia 46.5
10. Malawi 46.2
11. Palestine 46.1
12. Ethiopia 45.7
13. Benin 45.6
14. Eritrea 45.5
15. Tanzania 45.3
16. Rwanda 45.2
17. Sierra Leone 44.2
18. Guinea 44.0
19. Mozambique 44.0
20. Swaziland 43.7

Source: United Nations Development Program (Human Development Report)

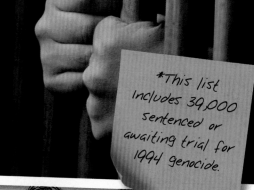

*This list includes 39,000 sentenced or awaiting trial for 1994 genocide.

WORLD'S HIGHEST PRISON POPULATIONS

Country / Prisoners (per 100,000 of the population)

1
USA
756

2
Russian Federation
629

3
Rwanda
604*

4
St. Kitts and Nevis
588

5
Cuba
531

6
Virgin Islands (USA)
512

7
Virgin Islands (UK)
488

8
Palau
478

9
Belarus
468

10
Belize
455

11
Bahamas
422

12
Georgia
415

13
American Samoa
410

14
Grenada
408

15
Anguilla
401

16
Bermuda
394

17
Cayman Islands
380

18
Barbados
379

19
Kazakhstan
378

20
French Guiana
365

Source: King's College London—World Prison Population List

Imperial Palace in Tokyo, Japan

LARGEST MONARCHIES
Monarchy / Number of subjects (millions)

1 UK/Commonwealth..........134
2 Japan.................128.1
3 Thailand..............64.2
4 Spain.................43.1
5 Morocco...............31.5
6 Malaysia..............25.4
7 Saudi Arabia..........24.6
8 Netherlands...........16.3
9 Cambodia..............14.1
10 Belgium...............10.4
11 Sweden.................9.0
12 Papua New Guinea.......5.9
13 Jordan.................5.7
14 Denmark................5.4
15 Norway.................4.6
16 United Arab Emirates...4.5
17 Kuwait.................2.7
18 Oman...................3.0
19 Lesotho................1.9
20 Swaziland..............1.4

BIGGEST BIRDS BY WINGSPAN

Species / Maximum recorded length (in / cm)

1 Wandering albatross (*Diomedea exulans*) 146 / 370

2 Andean condor (*Vultur gryphus*) 126 /220

3 Cinereous vulture (*Aegypius monachus*) 122 / 310

4 Lammergeier (*Gypaetus barbatus*) 121 / 308

5 Lappet-faced vulture (*Torgos tracheliotos*) 118 / 300

6 Trumpeter swan (*Cygnus buccinator*) 118 / 300

7 Southern Royal Albatross (*Diomedea epomophora*) 118 / 300

8 Dalmatian Pelican (*Pelecanus crispus*) 118 / 300

9 Himalayan vulture (*Gyps himalayensis*) 114 / 289

10 Griffon vulture (*Gyps fulvus*) 114 / 289

11 Jabiru (*Jabiru mycteria*) 110 / 280

12 Great White pelican (*Pelecanus onocrotalus*) 110 / 280

13 Whooper swan (*Cygnus cygnus*) 108 / 275

14 Saddle-billed stork (*Ephippiorhynchus senegalensis*) 106 / 270

15 Ruppels Vulture (*Gyps rueppellii*) 102 / 260

16 Wattled Crane Q(*Bugeranus carunculatus*) 102 / 260

17 Sarus crane (*Grus antigone*) 98 / 250

18 Brown pelican (*Pelecanus occidentalis*) 98 / 250

19 Australian Pelican (*Pelecanus conspicillatus*) 98 / 250

20 White-tailed eagle (*Haliaeetus albicilla*) 96 / 244

HEAVIEST BIRDS

Species / Maximum recorded weight lb / kg

1 Ostrich (*Struthio camelus*) 286 / 130

2 Cassowary (*Casuarius casuarius*) 128 / 58

3 Emu (*Dromaius novaehollandiae*) 106 / 48

4 Emperor penguin (*Aptenodytes forsteri*) 99 / 45

5 Greater rhea (*Rhea americana*) 88 / 40

6 Darwin's rhea (*Rhea pennata*) 55 / 25

7 Great bustard (*Otis tarda*) 46 / 21

8 Whooper swan (*Cygnus cygnus*) 44 / 20

9 Trumpeter swan (*Cygnus buccinator*) 37 / 17

10 King penguin (*Aptenodytes patagonicus*) 35 / 16

11 Andean condor (*Vultur gryphus*) 33 / 15

12 Dalmatian pelican (*Pelecanus crispus*) 33 / 15

13 Cinereous vulture (*Aegypius monachus*) 31 / 14

14 Griffon vulture (*Gyps fulvus*) 29 / 13

15 Australian pelican (*Pelecanus conspicillatus*) 29 / 13

16 Mute swan (*Cygnus olor*) 26 / 12

17 Wandering albatross (*Diomedea exulans*) 24 / 11

18 Red-crowned crane (*Grus japonensis*) 22 / 10

19 Maribou stork (*Leptoptilos crumeniferus*) 20 / 9

20 Harpy eagle (*Harpia harpyja*) 20 / 9

FARTHEST MIGRATING BIRDS

Species / Migration distance (miles/km)*

1
Arctic tern
(*Sterna paradisae*)
21,748 / 35,000

2
Sooty Shearwater
(*Pufinus griseus*)
19,883 / 32,000

3
Pied wheatear
(*Oenanthe pleschanke*)
11,184 / 18,000

4
Short-tailed shearwater
(*Puffinis tenuiostris*)
10,563 / 17,000

5
Ruff sandpiper
(*Philomachus pugnax*)
9,320 / 15,000

6
Pectoral sandpiper
(*Calidris melanotos*)
8,699 / 14,000

7
Peregrine falcon
(*Falco peregrinus*)
8,388 / 13,500

8
Red knot
(*Calidris canutus*)
8,264 / 13,300

9
Oriental honey buzzard
(*Pernis ptilorhynchus*)
7,208 / 11,600

10
Bar-tailed godwit
(*Limosa lapponica*)
7,146 / 11,500

11
Common buzzard
(*Buteo buteo*)
6,213 / 10,000

12
Swainson's hawk
(*Buteo swainsoni*)
6,213 / 10,000

13
Lesser yellowleg
(*Tringa flavipes*)
5,778 / 9,300

14
Eleanor's falcon
(*Falco eleonorae*)
5,592 / 9,000

15
Dark-sided flycatcher
(*Muscicapa sibirica*)
5,592 / 9,000

16
New world blackbird
(*Dolichonyx oryzivorus*)
4,225 / 6,800

17
Common nighthawk
(*Chordeiles minor*)
4,225 / 6,800

18
Cliff swallow
(*Petrochelidon pyrrhomata*)
4,225 / 6,800

19
Grey-cheeked thrush
(*Catharus minimus*)
3,852 / 6,200

20
Cuckoo
(*Cuculus canorus*)
3,106 / 5,000

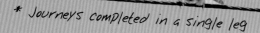

* Journeys completed in a single leg

EARTH AND SPACE

BIGGEST ASTEROIDS

Name / Diameter (miles / km) / Date discovered

1	**2**	**3**	**4**	**5**	**6**	**7**	**8**	**9**	**10**
Ceres	2 Pallas	4 Vesta	10 Hygiea	704 Interamnia	52 Europa	511 Davida	87 Sylvia	65 Cybele	15 Eunomia
391 miles	338 miles	328 miles	267 miles	202 miles	187 miles	179 miles	175 miles	169 miles	166 miles
952km	544km	529km	431km	326km	301km	289km	286km	273km	268km
1801	1802	1807	1849	1910	1858	1903	1866	1861	1851

11	**12**	**13**	**14**	**15**	**16**	**17**	**18**	**19**	**20**
3 Juno	10199	31 Euphrosyne	624 Hektor	2060 Chiron	88 Thisbe	324	19 Fortuna	451 Patientia	532
160 miles	Chariklo	159 miles	149 miles	145 miles	144 miles	Bamberga	139 miles	139 miles	Herculina
258km	160 miles	256km	241km	233km	232km	142 miles	225km	225km	137 miles
1804	258km	1854	1854	1977	1866	229km	1852	1899	222km
	1997					1892			1904

BIGGEST METEOR CRATERS

Name (location) / Diameter (miles / km) / Age (million years)

Name (location)	Diameter (miles/km)	Age	Name (location)	Diameter (miles/km)	Age
1 Vredefort (FreeState, South Africa)	186 / 300	2020	**10** Kara (Nenetsia, Russia)	40 / 65	70
2 Sudbury (Ontario, Canada)	155 /250	1850	**11** Beaverhead (Idaho/Montana, USA)	37 / 60	600
3 Chicxulub (Yucatan, Mexico)	112/180	65	**12** Tookoonooka (Queensland, Australia)	34 / 55	128
4 Manicouagan (Quebec, Canada)	62 /100	214	**13** Charlevoix (Quebec, Canada)	33 / 54	342
5 Popigai (Siberia, Russia)	62 / 100	35.7	**14** Siljan (Dalarna, Sweden)	32 / 52	377
6 Chesapeake Bay (Virginia, USA)	56 / 90	35.5	**15** Karakul (Pamir Mountains, Tajikistan)	32 / 52	5
7 Acraman (South Australia, Australia)	56 / 90	590	**16** Montagnais (Nova Scotia, Canada)	28 / 45	50
8 Puchezh-Katunki (Nizhny Novgorod Oblast, Russia)	50 / 80	167	**17** Araguainha (Central Brazil)	25 / 40	244
9 Morokweng (Kalahari Desert, South Africa)	43 / 70	145	**18** Saint Martin (Manitoba, Canada)	25 / 40	220
			19 Mjølnir (Barents Sea, Norway)	25 / 40	142
			20 Woodleigh (Western Australia, Australia)	25 / 40	364

EARLIEST SATELLITES AND SPACE PROBES

Name (year of launch) / Country / Mission

1 **Sputnik 1 (1957)**
USSR
World's first orbiter

2 **Sputnik 2 (1957)**
USSR
First to carry animal, a dog, Laika

3 **Explorer 1 (1958)**
USA
First US orbiter

4 **Vanguard 1 (1958)**
USA
First solar powered satellite

5 **Explorer 3 (1958)**
USA
First with tape recorder for
delayed transmission of data

6 **Explorer 4 (1958)**
USA
Elliptical orbit

7 **Project SCORE (1958)**
USA
First communications satellite

8 **Explorer 6 (1959)**
USA
First to send pictures of Earth
from orbit

9 **Explorer 7 (1959)**
USA

10 **Luna 1 (1959)**
USSR
Lunar impactor, partial success

11 **Pioneer 4 (1959)**
USA
Lunar fly-by, partial success

12 **Luna 2 (1959)**
USSR
First to impact on the
moon's surface

13 **Luna 3 (1959)**
USSR
Fly-by, first pictures of the
moon's hidden side

14 **Pioneer 5 (1960)**
USA
First mission to monitor
the sun

15 **TIROS 1 (1960)**
USA
Weather satellite

16 **Courier 1B (1960)**
USA
Communications satellite

17 **OSCAR1 (1961)**
USA
First amateur satellite

18 **Mariner 2 (1962)**
USA
First satellite to return data from Venus

19 **Telstar 1 (1962)**
USA
First satellite relaying TV pictures

20 **Ariel 1 (1962)**
UK
First non-US or USSR satellite

CALORIE-BURNING ACTIVITIES

Activity for 30 minutes / Calories burned by a 155-lb (70-kg) person / Calories burned by a 190-lb (86-kg) person

Activity	155-lb (70-kg)	190-lb (86-kg)
1. Running (fast)	440	540
2. Cycling (fast)	422	520
3. Riding exercise bike (vigorous)	370	450
4. Freestyle swimming (vigorous)	350	430
5. Martial arts (vigorous)	350	430
6. Skipping (moderate)	350	430
7. Ice skating (vigorous)	320	390
8. Cross-country skiing (vigorous)	320	390
9. Riding mountain bike (vigorous)	300	370
10. Rowing (vigorous)	300	370
11. Jogging (moderate)	280	350
12. Freestyle swimming (moderate)	280	350
13. Cycling (moderate)	280	350
14. Playing basketball/tennis	280	350
15. Cross-country skiing (moderate)	280	350
16. Riding exercise bike (moderate)	250	300
17. Rowing (moderate)	250	300
18. Hiking	250	300
19. Playing soccer	250	300
20. Brisk walking (uphill)	210	260

Source: Men's Fitness magazine

FASTEST CROSS-CHANNEL SWIMS

Name (country of birth) / Year / Time

(*) Fastest man, (**) Fastest woman, (***) Fastest crossing France to England.

1 Petar Stoychev * (Bulgaria) 2007 / 6 hrs 57 mins

3 Yuiy Kudinov (Russia) 2007 / 7 hrs 05 mins

2 Yvetta Hlavacova ** (Czech Republic) 2006 / 7 hrs 5 mins

5 Chad Undeby (USA) 1994 / 7 hrs 7 mins

4 Rostidslav Vitek (Czech Republic) 2009 / 7 hrs 6 mins

6 Petar Stoychev (Bulgaria) 2006 / 7 hrs 21 mins

7 Penny Lee Dean (USA) 1978 / 7 hrs 40 mins

8 Christoph Wandratsch (Germany) 2005 / 7 hrs 52 mins

9 Yvetta Hlavacova (Czech Republic) 2007 / 7 hrs 53 mins

10 Tamara Bruce (Australia) 1994 / 7 hrs 53 mins

Source: Channel Swimming and Piloting Association.

12 Richard Davey*** (UK) 1988 / 8 hrs 5 mins

11 Hans Van Goor (Holland) 1995 / 8 hrs 2 mins

13 Irene van der Laan (Holland) 1982 / 8 hrs 6 mins

17 Paul Asmuth (USA)1985 / 8 hrs 12 mins

14 Irene van der Laan (Holland) 1983 / 8 hrs 10 mins

20 Javier Gutierrez (Mexico) 1999 / 8 hrs 16 mins

15 Natalia Pankina (Russia) 2007 / 8 hrs 11 mins

16 Philip Rush (New Zealand) 1988 / 8 hrs 11 mins

18 Gail Rice (USA) 1999 / 8 hrs 12 mins

19 Anita Sood (India) 1987 / 8 hrs 15 mins

FIRST CLIMBERS TO REACH THE SUMMIT OF EVEREST

Climber(s) / Country of birth / Year of ascent

1 Edmund Hillary (New Zealand) 1953
2 Tenzing Norgay Sherpa (Nepal) 1953
3 Ernst Schmied (Switzerland) 1956
4 Jürg Marmet (Switzerland) 1956
5 Dölf Reist (Switzerland) 1956
6 Hansrudolf von Gunten (Switzerland) 1956
7 Wang Fu-Chou (China) 1960
8 Chu Yin-Hua (China) 1960
9 Gonbu (Gingbu) (Tibet) 1960
10 Jim Whittaker (USA) 1963
11 Nawang Gombu Sherpa (Nepal) 1963
12 Lute Jerstad (USA) 1963
13 Barry Bishop (USA) 1963
14 Tom Hornbein (USA) 1963
15 Willi Unsoeld (USA) 1963
16 A.S. Cheema (India) 1965
17 Nawang Gombu Sherpa * (Nepal) 1965
18 Sonam Gyatso (India) 1965
19 Sonam Wangyal (India) 1965
20 C.P. Vohra and Ang Kami** (India) 1965

* The first person to reach the summit twice.
**Vohra and Kami linked arms. Five separate climbing expeditions are represented here.

TENORS OF THE RECORDING ERA*

Name (dates) / Nationality

1 Plácido Domingo (1941-) Spanish
2 Enrico Caruso (1873–1921) Italian
3 Luciano Pavarotti (1935-2007) Italian
4 Fritz Wunderlich (1930-66) German
5 Jussi Bjorling (1911–1960) Swedish
6 Lauritz Melchior (1890–1973) Danish
7 Beniamino Gigli (1890–1957) Italian
8 Jon Vickers (1926–) Canadian
9 Nicolai Gedda (1925–) Swedish
10 Peter Pears (1910–86) English
11 Tito Schipa (1880–1965) Italian
12 Carlo Bergonzi (1924–) Italian
13 Juan Diego Flórez (1973–) Peruvian
14 Peter Schreier (1935–) German
15 Franco Corelli (1921–2003) Italian
16 John McCormack (1884–1945) Irish
17 Anthony Rolfe Johnson (1940–2010) English
18 Alfredo Kraus (1927–1999) Spanish
19 Wolfgang Windgasssen (1914–1974) French
20 Sergey Lemeshev (1902–1977) Russian

SOPRANOS OF THE RECORDING ERA*

Name (dates) / Nationality

1 Maria Callas (1923–77) / Greek
2 Joan Sutherland (1926–2010) / Australian
3 Victoria de los Angeles (1923–2005) / Spanish
4 Leontyne Price (1927–) / American
5 Birgit Nilsson (1918–2005) / Swedish
6 Montserrat Caballé (1933–) / Spanish
7 Lucia Popp (1939–93) / Slovak
8 Margaret Price (1941–2011) / Welsh
9 Kirsten Flagstad (1895–1962) / Norwegian
10 Emma Kirkby (1949–) / English
11 Elizabeth Schwarzkopf (1915–2006) German-born Austrian/British
12 Régine Crespin (1927–2007) / French
13 Galina Vizhnevskaya (1926–) / Russian
14 Gundula Janowitz (1937–) / Austrian
15 Karita Mattila (1960–) / Finnish
16 Elisabeth Schumann (1888–1952) / German
17 Christine Brewer (1955) / American
18 Renata Tebaldi (1922–2004) / Italian
19 Rosa Ponselle (1897–1981) / American
20 Elly Ameling (1933–) / Dutch

* Based on a poll of professional opera critics.

50c Australian Legends AUSTRALIA
Dame Joan Sutherland OM AC

Leontyne Price in 2008.

MOST FREQUENTLY PERFORMED OPERAS*

	Title	Year of premiere	Composer
1	*Madame Butterfly*	(1904)	Giacomo Puccini
2	*La bohème*	(1896)	Giacomo Puccini
3	*La traviata*	(1853)	Giuseppe Verdi
4	*Carmen*	(1875)	Georges Bizet
5	*The Barber of Seville*	(1816)	Gioachino Rossini
6	*The Marriage of Figaro*	(1786)	Wolfgang Amadeus Mozart
7	*Don Giovanni*	(1787)	Wolfgang Amadeus Mozart
8	*Tosca*	(1900)	Giacomo Puccini
9	*Rigoletto*	(1851)	Giuseppe Verdi
10	*The Magic Flute*	(1791)	Wolfgang Amadeus Mozart
11	*La Cenerentola*	(1817)	Gioachino Rossini
12	*Turandot*	(1926)	Giacomo Puccini
13	*Lucia di Lammermoor*	(1835)	Gaetano Donizetti
14	*Pagliacci*	(1892)	Ruggero Leoncavallo
15	*Così fan tutte*	(1790)	Wolfgang Amadeus Mozart
16	*Aida*	(1871)	Giuseppe Verdi
17	*Il Trovatore*	(1853)	Giuseppe Verdi
18	*Faust*	(1859)	Charles Gounod
19	*Die Fledermaus*	(1874)	Johann Strauss II
20	*L'elisir d'amore*	(1832)	Gaetano Donizetti

* In North America in the first decade of the 21st century.

Source: OperaAmerica.com.

MOST RECENT CELEBRITIES
WHO DIED YOUNG

Name (age) / Profession / Year of death

	Name (age)	Profession	Year of death
1	Alexander McQueen (40)	Fashion designer	2010
2	Justin Mentell (27)	Actor	2010
3	Stephen Gately (33)	Singer–songwriter	2009
4	Brittany Murphy (32)	Singer–actress	2009
5	Heath Ledger (28)	Actor	2008
6	Brad Renfro (25)	Actor	2008
7	Anna Nicole Smith (39)	Actress–model	2007
8	Nicole DeHuff (30)	Actress	2005
9	Kellie Waymire (36)	Actress	2003
10	Hanse Cronje (32)	Cricketer	2002
11	Aaliyah Haughton (22)	Singer–actress	2001
12	Charlotte Coleman (33)	Actress	2001
13	Kim Walker (32)	Actress	2001
14	Dana Plato (34)	Actress	1999
15	Jill Dando (37)	TV presenter	1999
16	Florence Griffith-Joyner (38)	Athlete	1998
17	Michael Hutchence (37)	Actor–musician	1997
18	Christopher Wallace (24) *	Rap singer	1997
19	Chris Farley (33)	Actor	1997
20	Jeff Buckley (30)	Musician	1997

We have based this list on celebrities under the age of 40 who have died most recently.

* AKA Biggie Smalls, or The Notorious B.I.G

CAUSES OF DEATH WORLDWIDE

Cause of death / Total deaths per year (millions) / percentage of total deaths

	Cause of death	Total deaths per year (millions)	percentage of total deaths
1	Coronary heart disease	7.2	12.2%
2	Stroke	5.7	9.7%
3	Respiratory infection	4.2	7.1%
4	Chronic obstructive pulmonary disease	3.0	5.1%
5	Diarrhoea	2.2	3.7%
6	HIV/AIDS	2.0	3.5%
7	Tuberculosis	1.5	2.5%
8	Lung cancer	1.3	2.3%
9	Traffic accident	1.3	2.2%
10	Premature birth	1.2	2.0%
11	Malaria	1.2	2.0%
12	Childhood diseases	1.1	1.8%
13	Hypertensive heart disease	0.9	1.6%
14	Suicide	0.9	1.5%
15	Stomach cancer	0.9	1.5%
16	Cirrhosis of the liver	0.8	1.4%
17	Kidney disease	0.7	1.2%
18	Bowel cancer	0.6	1.1%
19	Liver cancer	0.6	1.1%
20	Measles	0.6	1.1%

Source: World Health Organization (The World Health Report)

MOST COMMON PHOBIAS

Phobia / Percentage of respondents with a phobia*

1 Snakes 50%
2 Public speaking 41%
3 Heights 36%
4 Confined spaces 34%
5 Spiders and insects 27%
6 Injections 21%
7 Mice 20%
8 Flying 18%
9 Visiting the doctor 13%
10 Thunder 11%
11 Dogs 11%
12 Crowds 11%
13 The dark 6%
14 Open spaces 5%
15 Social situations 5%
16 Dirt 4%
17 Strangers 4%
18 Being alone 3%
19 Clowns 3%
20 Dead things 2%

* Some respondents may have had more than one phobia.

MOST POPULAR CAT BREEDS (USA)

Breed

1. Persian
2. Maine Coon
3. Exotic Shorthair
4. Siamese
5. Abyssinian
6. Ragdoll
7. Birman
8. American Shorthair
9. Oriental
10. Sphynx
11. Norwegian Forest Cat
12. Burmese
13. Cornish Rex
14. Devon Rex
15. Tonkinese
16. British Shorthair
17. Scottish Fold
18. Ocicat
19. Russian Blue
20. Egyptian Mau

MOST POPULAR DOG BREEDS IN UK

Breed / Number of registrations

	Breed	Registrations		Breed	Registrations		Breed	Registrations
1.	Labrador Retriever	45,700	5.	Staffordshire Bull Terrier	12,729	13.	Miniature Schnauzer	4,396
2.	Cocker Spaniel	20,459	6.	King Charles Spaniel	11,411	14.	Lhasa Apso	4,154
3.	Springer Spaniel	15,133	7.	Golden Retriever	9,373	15.	Yorkshire Terrier	4,042
4.	German Shepherd	12,857	8.	West Highland Terrier	9,300	16.	Bulldog	3,522
			9.	Boxer	9,066	17.	Dobermann	3,388
			10.	Border Terrier	8,916	18.	Bull Terrier	3,361
			11.	Rottweiler	6,575	19.	Weimaraner	2,744
			12.	Shih Tzu	4,436	20.	Pug	2,681

Source: Kennel Club

TYPES OF FISH CAUGHT AND LANDED (IN TONNES)

Fish / Tonnes
Source: United Nations Food Organization

1 Peruvian anchoveta 9,703,000

2 Chilean Jack Mackerel 1,750,000

3 Blue Whiting 1,589,000

4 Largehead Hairtail 1,371,000

5 Atlantic Cod 835,000

6 European Anchovy 483,000

7 Argentine Hake 409,000

8 Pollock 370,000

9 Araucanian Herring 347,000

10 Cape Hakes 306,000

11 Haddock 244,000

12 Atlantic Herring 259,000

13 Sole 176,000

14 Indian Mackerels 173,000

15 South pacific Hake 162,000

16 Ponyfish 141,000

17 Patagonia Grenadier 132,000

18 North Pacific Hake 130,000

19 Nantian 128,000

20 European Plaice 99,000

CHICKEN-EATING NATIONS

Country / Consumption per capita lb (kg)
Source: Food Market Exchange: World Poultry consumption

#	Country	lb (kg)	#	Country	lb (kg)	#	Country	lb (kg)	#	Country	lb (kg)
1.	China	110 (50.0)	6.	Saudi Arabia	71 (32.4)	11.	Spain	58 (26.2)	16.	Greece	50 (22.6)
2.	US	109 (49.6)	7.	Taiwan	71 (32.3)	12.	Portugal	58 (25.3)	17.	Netherlands	49 (22.1)
3.	Israel	99 (45.0)	8.	Australia	61 (27.7)	13.	France	55 (24.9)	18.	Argentina	47 (21.1)
4.	Canada	77 (35.1)	9.	UK	60 (27.2)	14.	Brazil	54 (24.4)	19.	Mexico	44 (20.1)
5.	Singapore	76 (34.4)	10.	Ireland	59 (27.0)	15.	South Africa	52 (23.9)	20.	Italy	43 (19.3)

MOST OBESE NATIONS

Countries / Proportion of population registered as obese* (%)

1 USA 30.6
2 Mexico 24.2
3 UK 23.0
4 Slovakia 22.4
5 Greece 21.9
6 Australia 21.7
7 New Zealand 20.9
8 Hungary 18.8
9 Luxembourg 18.4
10 Czech Republic 14.8
11 Canada 14.3
12 Spain 13.1
13 Ireland 13.0
14 Germany 12.9
15 Portugal 12.8
16 Finland 12.8
17 Iceland 12.4
18 Turkey 12.0
19 Belgium 11.7
20 Netherlands 10.0

* Defined as percentage of the population with Body Mass Index (BMI) over 30. BMI is a number that relates an individual's weight to height (weight/height squared).

TALLEST MEN IN THE WORLD EVER

Name / Height / Country of origin / Year of birth and death

1 Robert Wadlow 8ft 11 in (272cm), USA, 1918–1940
2 John Rogan 8ft 8in (267cm), USA, 1868–1905
3 John F. Carroll 8ft 7in (264cm), USA, 1932–1969
4 Vaino Myllrinne 8ft 3in (261cm), Finland, 1909–1963
5 Don Koehler 8ft 2in (249cm), USA 1925–1981
6 Bernard Coyne 8ft 2in (249cm), USA 1897–1921
7 Vikas Uppal 8ft 2in (249cm), India 1986–2007
8 Sultan Kosen 8ft 2in (249cm), Turkey 1982–
9 Patrick Cotter O'Brien 8ft 1in (246cm), Ireland 1760–1806
10 Gabriel Estevao Monjane 8ft 1in (246cm), Mozambique 1944–1990
11 Julius Koch 8ft 1in (246cm) Germany, 1872–1902
12 Suleiman Ali Nashnush 8ft 0.4in (245cm), Libya 1943–1991
13 Anton de Franchpoinct 8ft 0 in (244cm), Germany unknown
14 Zhang Juncai 7ft 11in (242 cm), China 1983–
15 Suparwono 7ft 11in (242cm), Indonesia 1985–
16 Alexander Sizonenko 7ft 10.9in (241cm), Russia 1959–
17 Grgo Kusic 7ft 10in (238cm), Croatia 1892–1918
18 Bao Xishun 7ft 9in (236cm), China 1951–
19 Angus MacAskill 7ft 9in (236cm), Scotland 1825–1863
20 Sun Ming-Ming 7ft 9in (236cm), China 1983–

Source: Organization for Economic Co-operation and Development (OECD Health Data)

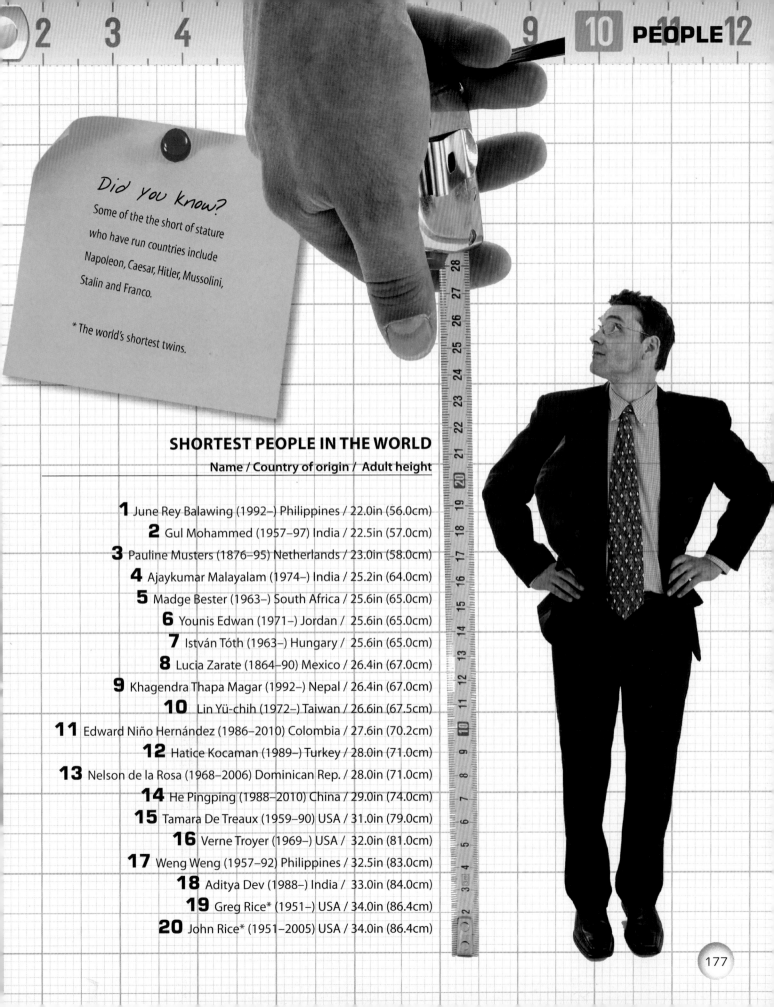

Did you know?
Some of the the short of stature who have run countries include Napoleon, Caesar, Hitler, Mussolini, Stalin and Franco.

* The world's shortest twins.

SHORTEST PEOPLE IN THE WORLD

Name / Country of origin / Adult height

1 June Rey Balawing (1992–) Philippines / 22.0in (56.0cm)

2 Gul Mohammed (1957–97) India / 22.5in (57.0cm)

3 Pauline Musters (1876–95) Netherlands / 23.0in (58.0cm)

4 Ajaykumar Malayalam (1974–) India / 25.2in (64.0cm)

5 Madge Bester (1963–) South Africa / 25.6in (65.0cm)

6 Younis Edwan (1971–) Jordan / 25.6in (65.0cm)

7 István Tóth (1963–) Hungary / 25.6in (65.0cm)

8 Lucia Zarate (1864–90) Mexico / 26.4in (67.0cm)

9 Khagendra Thapa Magar (1992–) Nepal / 26.4in (67.0cm)

10 Lin Yü-chih (1972–) Taiwan / 26.6in (67.5cm)

11 Edward Niño Hernández (1986–2010) Colombia / 27.6in (70.2cm)

12 Hatice Kocaman (1989–) Turkey / 28.0in (71.0cm)

13 Nelson de la Rosa (1968–2006) Dominican Rep. / 28.0in (71.0cm)

14 He Pingping (1988–2010) China / 29.0in (74.0cm)

15 Tamara De Treaux (1959–90) USA / 31.0in (79.0cm)

16 Verne Troyer (1969–) USA / 32.0in (81.0cm)

17 Weng Weng (1957–92) Philippines / 32.5in (83.0cm)

18 Aditya Dev (1988–) India / 33.0in (84.0cm)

19 Greg Rice* (1951–) USA / 34.0in (86.4cm)

20 John Rice* (1951–2005) USA / 34.0in (86.4cm)

OLYMPIC GOLD MEDALS: WINTER GAMES

Country / Number of medals (in Olympic history)

1 Norway 107

2 Germany 89

3 USA 87

4 Soviet Union 78

5 Austria 55

6 Canada 52

7 Sweden 48

8 Switzerland 44

9 Finland 41

10 East Germany 39

11 Italy 37

12 Russia 36

13 Netherlands 29

14 France 27

15 South Korea 23

16 Great Britain 9

17 China 9

18 Japan 9

19 Unified Team 9

20 Australia 5

OLYMPIC GOLD MEDALS: ATHLETICS

1 USA / 311
2 Soviet Union / 64
3 Great Britain / 49
4 Finland / 48
5 East Germany / 38
6 Kenya / 22
7 Poland / 22
8 Australia / 9
9 Sweden / 19
10 Italy / 19

11 Russia / 18
12 Ethiopia / 18
13 Germany / 15
14 Jamaica / 13
15 France / 13
16 Canada / 13
17 West Germany / 12
18 Romania / 11
19 Czech Republic / 11
20 Cuba / 10

Source: IOC

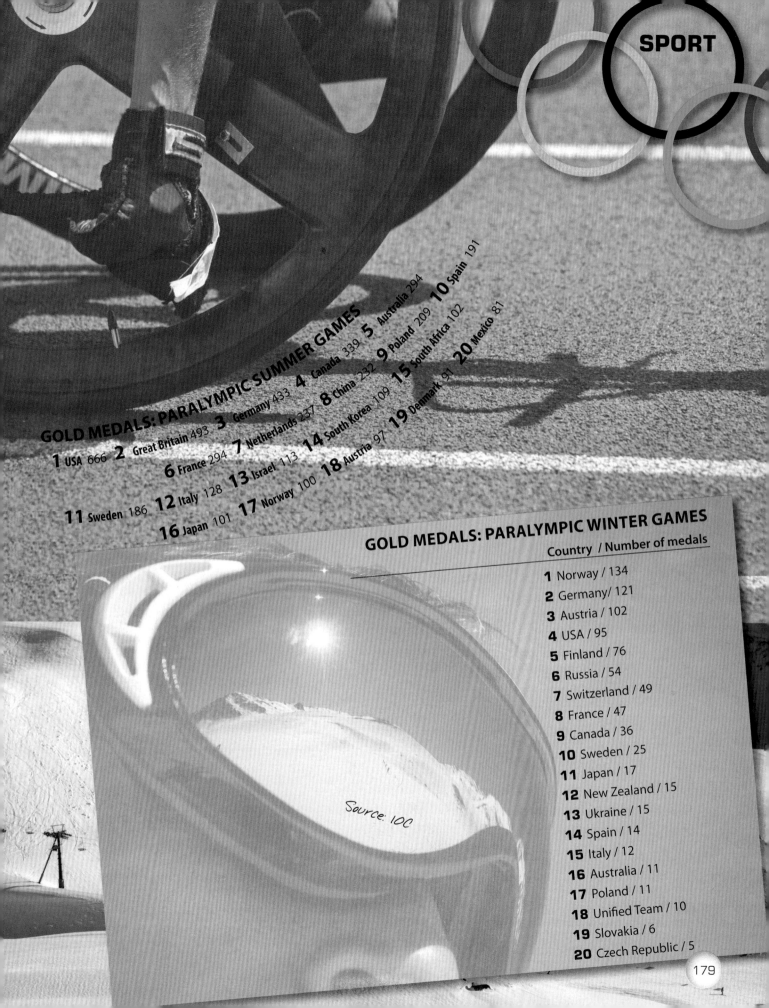

GOLD MEDALS: PARALYMPIC SUMMER GAMES

1 USA 666   **2** Great Britain 493   **3** Germany 433   **4** Canada 339   **5** Australia 294

6 France 294   **7** Netherlands 237   **8** China 232   **9** Poland 209   **10** Spain 191

11 Sweden 186   **12** Italy 128   **13** Israel 113   **14** South Korea 109   **15** Denmark 91

16 Japan 101   **17** Norway 100   **18** Austria 97   **19** South Africa 102   **20** Mexico 81

Source: IOC

GOLD MEDALS: PARALYMPIC WINTER GAMES

Country / Number of medals

1 Norway / 134
2 Germany / 121
3 Austria / 102
4 USA / 95
5 Finland / 76
6 Russia / 54
7 Switzerland / 49
8 France / 47
9 Canada / 36
10 Sweden / 25
11 Japan / 17
12 New Zealand / 15
13 Ukraine / 15
14 Spain / 14
15 Italy / 12
16 Australia / 11
17 Poland / 11
18 Unified Team / 10
19 Slovakia / 6
20 Czech Republic / 5

EARTH AND SPACE

LONGEST RIVERS

Name (location) / Length in miles/km

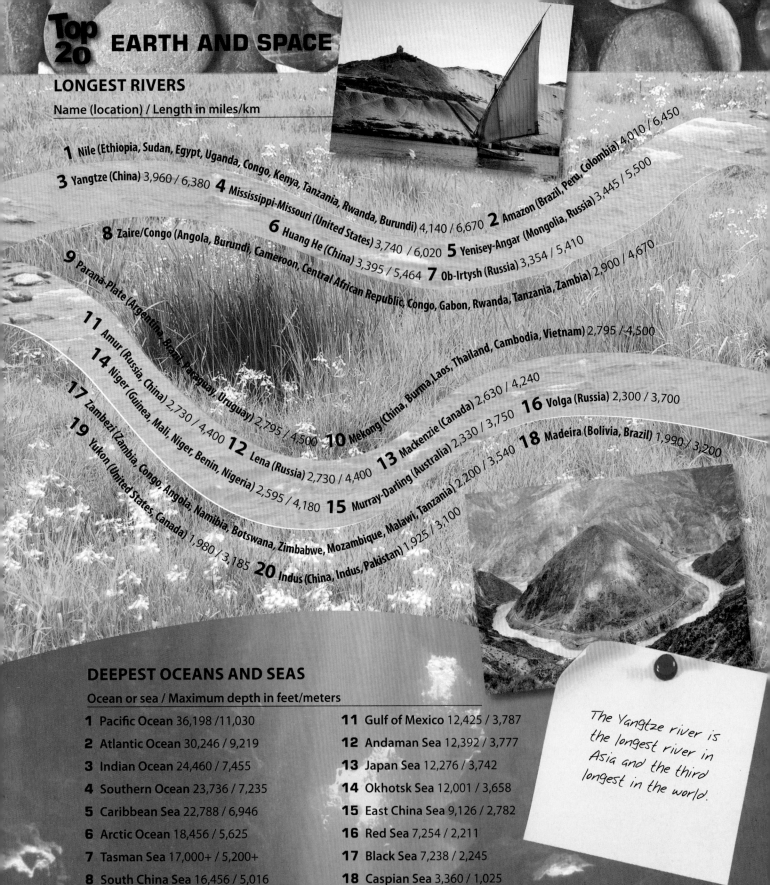

1 Nile (Ethiopia, Sudan, Egypt, Uganda, Congo, Kenya, Tanzania, Rwanda, Burundi) 4,140 / 6,670

2 Amazon (Brazil, Peru, Colombia) 4,010 / 6,450

3 Yangtze (China) 3,960 / 6,380

4 Mississippi-Missouri (United States) 3,740 / 6,020

5 Yenisey-Angar (Mongolia, Russia) 3,445 / 5,500

6 Huang He (China) 3,395 / 5,464

7 Ob-Irtysh (Russia) 3,354 / 5,410

8 Zaire/Congo (Angola, Burundi, Cameroon, Central African Republic, Congo, Gabon, Rwanda, Tanzania, Zambia) 2,900 / 4,670

9 Paraná-Plate (Argentina, Brazil, Paraguay, Uruguay) 2,795 / 4,500

10 Mekong (China, Burma, Laos, Thailand, Cambodia, Vietnam) 2,795 / 4,500

11 Amur (Russia, China) 2,730 / 4,400

12 Lena (Russia) 2,730 / 4,400

13 Mackenzie (Canada) 2,630 / 4,240

14 Niger (Guinea, Mali, Niger, Benin, Nigeria) 2,595 / 4,180

15 Murray-Darling (Australia) 2,330 / 3,750

16 Volga (Russia) 2,300 / 3,700

17 Zambezi (Zambia, Congo, Angola, Namibia, Botswana, Zimbabwe, Mozambique, Malawi, Tanzania) 2,200 / 3,540

18 Madeira (Bolivia, Brazil) 1,990 / 3,200

19 Yukon (United States, Canada) 1,980 / 3,185

20 Indus (China, Indus, Pakistan) 1,925 / 3,100

The Yangtze river is the longest river in Asia and the third longest in the world.

DEEPEST OCEANS AND SEAS

Ocean or sea / Maximum depth in feet/meters

1 Pacific Ocean 36,198 / 11,030

2 Atlantic Ocean 30,246 / 9,219

3 Indian Ocean 24,460 / 7,455

4 Southern Ocean 23,736 / 7,235

5 Caribbean Sea 22,788 / 6,946

6 Arctic Ocean 18,456 / 5,625

7 Tasman Sea 17,000+ / 5,200+

8 South China Sea 16,456 / 5,016

9 Bering Sea 15,659 / 4,773

10 Mediterranean Sea 15,197 / 4,632

11 Gulf of Mexico 12,425 / 3,787

12 Andaman Sea 12,392 / 3,777

13 Japan Sea 12,276 / 3,742

14 Okhotsk Sea 12,001 / 3,658

15 East China Sea 9,126 / 2,782

16 Red Sea 7,254 / 2,211

17 Black Sea 7,238 / 2,245

18 Caspian Sea 3,360 / 1,025

19 North Sea 2,165 / 660

20 Baltic Sea 1,380 / 421

TALLEST WATERFALLS

Name / Location / Height in feet/meters

1
Angel Falls (Venezuela)
3,212 / 979

2
Tugela Falls (South Africa)
3,110 / 948

3
Tres Hermanas (Peru)
3,000 / 914

4
Olo'upena Falls (USA)
2,953 / 900

5
Yumbilla (Peru)
2,938 / 895

6
Vinnufossen (Norway)
2,822 / 860

7
Balaifossens (Norway)
2,788 / 850

8
Pu'uka'oka Falls (USA)
2,756 / 840

9
James Bruce Falls (Canada)
2,755 / 839

10
Browne Falls (New Zealand)
2,744 / 836

11
Strupenfossen (Norway)
2,690 / 820

12
Ramnefjellsfossen (Norway)
2,685 / 818

13
Waihilau Falls (Hawaii)
2,600 / 792

14
Colonial Creek Falls (USA)
2,584 / 788

15
Mongefossen (Norway)
2,535 / 773

16
Gocta Falls (Peru)
2,531 / 771

17
Mutarazi Falls (Zimbabwe)
2,499 / 762

18
Kjelfossen (Norway)
2,477 / 755

19
Yosemite Falls (USA)
2,425 / 739

20
Trou de Fer (Réunion)
2,380 / 725

Did you know?
Angel Falls was named after Jimmie Angel from the US, who was the first person to fly over the falls on November 18,1933, while looking for valuable ore beds. He achieved legendary status in Venezuela for his exploits and his ashes were scattered over the falls in 1960.

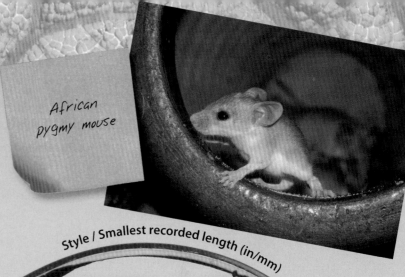

African pygmy mouse

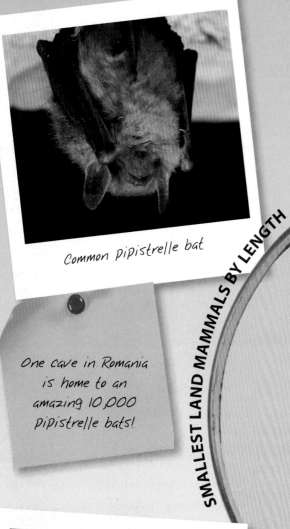

Common pipistrelle bat

One cave in Romania is home to an amazing 10,000 pipistrelle bats!

SMALLEST LAND MAMMALS BY LENGTH

Style / Smallest recorded length (in/mm)

1 **Bumblebee bat** (Craseonycteris thonglongya) 1.14 / 29
2 **Baluchistan pygmy jerboa** (Salpingotulus michaelis) 1.18 / 30
3 **Etruscan shrew** (Suncus etruscus) 1.18 / 30
4 **African pygmy mouse** (Mus minutoides) 1.18 / 30
5 **American pygmy shrew** (Sorex hoyi) 1.18 / 30
6 **Soprano pipistrelle bat** (Pipistrellus pygmaeus) 1.38 / 35
7 **Common pipistrelle bat** (Pipistrellus pipistrellus) 1.38 / 35
8 **Northern pygmy mouse** (Baiomys taylori) 1.42/ 36
9 **Lesser bamboo bat** (Tylonycteris pachypus) 1.57 / 40
10 **Eurasian pygmy shrew** (Sorex minutus) 1.57 / 40
11 **Tasmanian pygmy possum** (Cercartetuds lepidus) 1.97 / 50
12 **European harvest mouse** (Micromys minutus) 2.17 / 55
13 **Henley's gerbil** (Gerbillus henleyi) 2.75 / 70
14 **Meadow jumping mouse** (Zapus hudsonius) 2.83 / 72
15 **Southern pygmy mouse** (Baiomys musculus) 3.07 / 78
16 **Ural (pygmy) field mouse** (Apodemus uralensis) 3.54 / 90
17 **Berthe's mouse lemur** (Microcebus berthae) 3.62 / 92
18 **Mountain tarsier** (Tarsius pumilus) 3.74 / 95
19 **Pygmy marmoset** (Callithrix pygmaea) 4.60 / 117
20 **Pygmy mouse lemur** (Microcebus myoxinus) 4.72 / 120

A pygmy marmoset

The American pygmy shrew is found in Alaska Canada and the USA.

BIGGEST BEARS

Name / Maximum recorded size (lb/kg)

1 Kodiak bear (*Ursus arctos middendorffi*) 1,543 / 700+

2 Polar bear (*Ursus maritimus*) 1,499 / 680

3 Kamchatka brown bear (*Ursus arctos beringianus*) 1,433 / 650

4 Siberian brown bear (*Ursus arctos collaris*) 1,322 / 600

5 Himalayan brown bear (*Ursus arctos isabellinus*) 1,279 / 580

6 Tibetan blue bear (*Ursus arctos pruinosus*) 1,212 / 550

7 Eurasian brown bear (*Ursus arctos arctos*) 1,058 / 480

8 Grizzly bear (*Ursus arctos horribilis*) 992 / 450

9 American black bear (*Ursus americanus*) 992 / 450

10 European brown bear (*Ursus arctos subsp.*) 782 / 355

11 Cinnamon bear (*Ursus arctos cinnamomum*) 595 / 270

12 Kermode bear (*Ursus americanus kermode*) 496 / 225

13 Spectacled bear (*Tremarctos ornatus*) 441 / 200

14 Giant panda (*Ailuropoda melanoleuca*) 331 / 150

15 Sloth bear (*Melursus ursinus*) 309 / 140

16 Marsican brown bear (*Ursus arctos marsicanus*) 287 / 130

17 Asian black bear (*Ursus thibetanus*) 256 / 116

18 Formosan black bear (*Ursus thibetanus formosanus*) 243 / 110

19 Gobi bear (*Ursus arctos gobiensis*) 220 / 100

20 Sun bear (*Ursus malayanus*) 132 / 60

UK HITS OF THE 1970s

1 Wings *Mull Of Kintyre*
2 Boney M *Rivers Of Babylon/ Brown Girl In The Ring*
3 John Travolta & Olivia Newton-John *You're The One That I Want*
4 Boney M *Mary's Boy Child/Oh My Lord*
5 John Travolta & Olivia Newton John *Summer Nights*
6 John Lennon *Imagine*
7 Village People *Y.M.C.A.*
8 Queen *Bohemian Rhapsody*
9 Blondie *Heart Of Glass*
10 David Soul *Don't Give Up On Us*
11 Slade *Merry Xmas Everybody*
12 Art Garfunkel *Bright Eyes*
13 Gary Glitter *I Love You Love Me Love*
14 Ian Dury & The Blockheads *Hit Me With Your Rhythm Stick*
15 ABBA *Dancing Queen*
16 Brotherhood Of Man *Save Your Kisses For Me*
17 Simon Park Orchestra *Eye Level*
18 New Seekers *I'd Like To Teach The World To Sing (In Perfect Harmony)*
19 Julie Covington *Don't Cry For Me Argentina*
20 Little Jimmy Osmond *Long Haired Lover From Liverpool*

Source: OCC

US HITS OF THE 1970s

1 Debbie Boone *You Light Up My Life*
2 Bee Gees *Night Fever*
3 Rod Stweart *Tonight's The Night (Gonna Be Alright)*
4 Andy Gibb *Shadow Dancing*
5 Chic *Le Freak*
6 My Sharona *The Knack*
7 Roberta Flack *The First Time Ever I Saw Your Face*
8 Gilbert O' Sullivan *Alone Again*
9 Three Dog Night *Joy To The World*
10 Simon & Garfunkel *Bridge Over Troubled Water*
11 Jackson 5 *I'll Be There*
12 Paul McCartney & Wings *Silly Love Songs*
13 Rod Stewart *Maggie May*
14 Donna Summer *Bad Girls*
15 Donna Summer *It's Too Late*
16 Roberta Flack *Killing Me Softly*
17 The Osmonds *One Bad Apple*
18 Andy Gibb *I Just Want To Be Your Everything*
19 Bee Gees *Stayin' Alive*
20 Donna Summer *Hot Stuff*

Source: Billboard

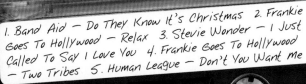

1. Band Aid — Do They Know It's Christmas 2. Frankie Goes To Hollywood — Relax 3. Stevie Wonder — I Just Called To Say I Love You 4. Frankie Goes To Hollywood — Two Tribes 5. Human League — Don't You Want Me

UK HITS OF THE 1980s

6. Wham! — Last Christmas 7. Culture Club — Karma Chameleon 8. George Michael — Careless Whisper 9. Jennifer Rush — The Power Of Love 10. Dexy's Midnight Runners — Come On Eileen

11. Survivor — Eye Of The Tiger 12. Soft Cell — Tainted Love 13. New Order — Blue Monday 14. Ray Parker Jr — Ghostbusters 15. Pink Floyd — Another Brick In The Wall 16. Irene Cara — Fame

17. Adam & The Ants — Stand and Deliver 18. Kylie Minogue & Jason Donovan — Especially For You 19. Billy Joel — Uptown Girl 20. Black Box — Ride On Time

Source: OCC

US HITS OF THE 1980s

1	Olivia Newton John *Physical*	**11**	Survivor *Eye Of The Tiger*
2	Kim Carnes *Bette Davis Eyes*	**12**	Irene Cara *Flashdance...What A Feeling*
3	Diana Ross & Lionel Richie *Endless Love*	**13**	Paul McCartney & Michael Jackson *Say Say Say*
4	The Police *Every Breath You Take*	**14**	Madonna *Like A Virgin*
5	Joan Jett & The Blackhearts *I Love Rock'n'Roll*	**15**	John Lennon *(Just Like) Starting Over*
6	Paul McCartney & Stevie Wonder *Ebony And Ivory*	**16**	Van Halen *Jump*
7	Michael Jackson *Billie Jean*	**17**	Prince *When Doves Cry*
8	Blondie *Call Me*	**18**	Michael Jackson *Rock With You*
9	Kenny Rogers *Lady*	**19**	Queen *Crazy Little Thing Called Love*
10	J. Geils Band *Centerfold*	**20**	USA For Africa *We Are The World*

Source: Billboard

185

LEADING CEMENT PRODUCERS

Country / Annual production (millions of short tons/metric tons)

1. China
1,530,427 /
1,388,380

2. India
195,100 /
177,000

3. USA
95,471 /
87,610

4. Japan
69,236 /
62,810

5. South Korea
59,415 / 53,900

6. Russia
58,422 / 53,000

7. Brazil
57,171 /
51,865

8. Turkey
56,694 /
51,432

9. Mexico
52,480 /
47,609

10. Iran
48,943 / 44,400

11. Italy
47,432 / 43,030

15. Indonesia
40,785 / 37,000

16. Vietnam
40,785 / 37,000

17. Thailand
39,242 / 35,600

12. Spain
46,394 / 42,088

13. Egypt
44,092 / 40,000

18. Germany
37,016 / 33,581

19. Saudi Arabia
35,078 / 31,823

20. France
21,700 / 23,920

14. Pakistan
42,990 / 39,000

BIGGEST AIR POLLUTERS

Country / Micrograms per cubic meter (average in cities of over 100,000)

1 Sudan 246

2 Mali 194

3 Pakistan 180

4 Iraq 178

5 Uruguay 173

6 Niger 164

7 Chad 161

8 Egypt 152

9 Bangladesh 147

10 Kuwait 134

11 Angola 125

12 Mauritania 113

13 Burkina Faso 108

14 Saudi Arabia 106

15 Bolivia 106

16 Oman 105

17 Nigeria 104

18 Indonesia 102

19 Syria 102

20 Azerbaijan 99

COCOA (CHOCOLATE) CONSUMERS

Country	lbs per person per year	kg per person per year
1. Switzerland	22.36	10.14
2. Austria	20.13	9.13
3. Ireland	19.47	8.83
4. Germany	18.04	8.18
5. Norway	17.93	8.13
6. Denmark	17.66	8.01
7. UK	17.49	7.93
8. Belgium	13.16	5.96
9. Australia	12.99	5.89
10. Sweden	12.90	5.85
11. USA	11.64	5.27
12. France	11.38	5.16
13. Netherlands	10.56	4.78
14. Finland	10.45	4.74
15. Italy	6.13	2.78
16. Greece	5.01	2.25
17. Japan	3.90	1.76
18. Spain	3.37	1.52
19. Portugal	2.67	1.21
20. Brazil	2.25	1.02

Source: F. H. Seligson et al., "Patterns of Chocolate Consumption," The American Journal of Clinical Nutrition

SALT PRODUCERS

Country	Annual production (tons)	Percentage share of world total
1. USA	46,500,000	22.1
2. China	37,101,000	17.7
3. India	15,000,000	7.4
4. Canada	14,125,000	6.7
5. Australia	11,211,000	5.3
6. Mexico	8,180,000	3.9
7. France	7,000,000	3.3
8. Brazil	6,500,000	3.1
9. Chile	6,000,000	2.9
10. UK	5,800,000	2.8
11. Netherlands	5,000,000	2.4
12. Italy	3,600,000	1.7
13. Spain	3,200,000	1.5
14. Russia	2,800,000	1.3
15. Iran	2,618,000	1.3
16. Romania	2,450,000	1.2
17. Egypt	2,400,000	1.1
18. Ukraine	2,300,000	1.1
19. Turkey	2,250,000	1.1
20. Bulgaria	1,800,000	0.9

WORST RAIL DISASTERS

	LOCATION	YEAR	FATALITIES		LOCATION	YEAR	FATALITIES
1.	SAINT-MICHEL-DE-MAURIENNE, FRANCE	1917	800-1,000	11.	NISHAPUR, IRAN	2004	320
2.	CIUREA, ROMANIA	1917	600-1,000	12.	SUKKUR, SINDH, PAKISTAN	1990	307
3.	BIHAR, INDIA	1981	500-800	13.	MONTEMORELAS, MEXICO	1915	300+
4.	GUADALAJARA, MEXICO	1915	600+	14.	TOLUNDA, ANGOLA	1994	300
5.	BALVANO. ITALY	1944	521-600+	15.	BAKU (METRO FIRE), AZERBAIJAN	1995	289
6.	UFA, RUSSIA	1989	575	16.	GAISAL, INDIA	1999	285
7.	TORRE DEL BIERZO, SPAIN	1944	200-500+	17.	IGANDU, TANZANIA	2002	281
8.	AWASH AFAR, ETHIOPIA	1985	428	18.	MONTGOMERY, PAKISTAN	1957	250
9.	AL AYATT, EGYPT	2002	383	19.	EL VIRILLA, COSTA RICA	1926	248
10.	FIROZABAD, INDIA	1995	358	20.	LAGNY TO POMPONNE, FRANCE	1933	230

Did you know?
The airlines with the best safety record are America West (USA), South West (USA) and Quantas (Australia), with no fatal accidents over 100,000 flights.

WORST AIRCRAFT ACCIDENTS

Location / Date / Airline / Aircraft / Fatalities

#	Location / Airline	Date / Aircraft	Fatalities
1.	Tenerife, Canary Islands	3/27/1977	
	Pan Am / KLM	B77 / B747	583
2.	Mt. Osutaka, Japan	8/12/1985	
	Japan Airlaines	B747	520
3.	New Delhi, India	11/12/1996	
	Saudi/ Kazakstan	B747 / Il 76	349
4.	Bois d'Ermenonville, France	3/3/1974	
	Turkish Airlines	DC10	346
5.	Atlantic Ocean, off W. Ireland	6/23/1985	
	Air India	B747	329
6.	Riyadh, Saudi Arabia	8/19/1980	
	Saudi Arabian Airlines	B747	301
7.	Persian Gulf	7/3/1988	
	Iran Air	A300	290
8.	Shahdad, Iran	2/19/2003	
	Islamic Guards Co.	Il-76MD	275
9.	Chicago, USA	5/25/1979	
	American Airlines	DC10	273
10.	Sakhalin Island, Russia	9/1/1983	
	Korean Airlines	B747	269
11.	Belle Harbor, New York City	11/12/2001	
	American Airlines	A300	265
12.	Komaki, Japan	9/26/1994	
	China Airlines	A300	264
13.	Jeddah, Saudi Arabia	7/11/1991	
	Nationair / charter		
	Nigeria Airways	DC8	261
14.	Mt. Erebus, Antarctica	11/28/1979	
	Air New Zealand	DC10	257
15.	Gander, Newfoundland, Canada	12/12/1985	
	Arrow Airways	DC8	256
16.	Buah Nabar, Indonesia	9/26/1997	
	Garuda Indonesian Airways		
		A300	234
17.	Off East Moriches, NY, USA	7/17/1996	
	Trans World Airlines	B747	230
18.	Off Nova Scotia, Canada	9/2/1998	
	Swissair	MD11	229
19.	Atlantic Ocean	6/1/2009	
	Air France	A330	228
20.	Agana, Guam	8/6/1997	
	Korean Airlines	B747	228

COUNTRIES WITH MOST
NATIVE ENGLISH SPEAKERS

Country / Native speakers (millions)

1 USA 214.8
2 UK 58.2
3 Canada 18.2
4 Australia 15.6

5 Ireland 4.4
6 South Africa 3.7
7 New Zealand 3.5
8 Philippines 3.4

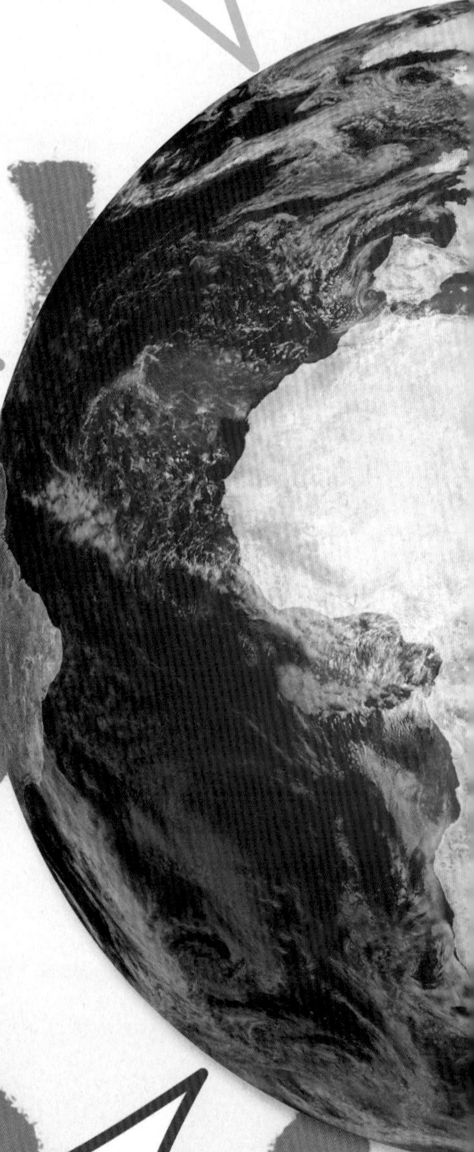

9 Jamaica 2.6
10 Trinidad & Tobago 1.2
11 Singapore 0.9
12 Guyana 0.7

13 Liberia 0.6
14 Sierra Leone 0.5
15 Malaysia 0.4
16 Germany 0.3

17 Barbados 0.26
18 Bahamas 0.26
19 Zimbabwe 0.25
20 India 0.23

PEOPLE

COUNTRIES WITH MOST NATIVE SPANISH SPEAKERS
Country / Native speakers (millions)

1 Mexico 103.5
2 Colombia 45.3
3 USA 44.5
4 Spain 41.9

5 Argentina 39.6
6 Venezuela 28.0
7 Peru 23.8
8 Chile 15.5

9 Ecuador 13.3
10 Cuba 11.2
11 Dominican Rep. 10.1
12 Guatemala 9.3

13 Honduras 8.0
14 El Salvador 6.2
15 Nicaragua 5.1
16 Bolivia 4.4

17 Costa Rica 4.4
18 Puerto Rico 3.8
19 Uruguay 3.3
20 Panama 2.6

Source: CIA World Factbook

191

LONGEST-RUNNING RADIO SHOWS WORLDWIDE

Title (Country) Start date (all are still running)

1. Laurdagsbarnetimen (Norway) 1925

2. Grand Ole Opry (USA) 1925

3. Shipping Forecast (UK) Jan 1926

4. Radioavisen (Denmark) Aug 1926

5. Choral Evensong (UK) Oct 1926

6. Hamburger Hafenkonzert (Germany) Jan 1926

7. Music & the Spoken Word (USA) Jul 1929

8. Metropolitan Opera (USA) 1931

9. Hockey Night (Canada) 1931

10. The Guilding Light (USA) Jan 1937

11. Desert Island Discs (UK) Jan 1942

12. Folksong Festival (USA) Dec 1945

13. Woman's Hour (UK) Oct 1946

14. Arbeidsvitaminen (Netherlands) Feb 1946

15. Letters from America (UK) Mar 1946

16. Gardeners' Question Time (UK) Apr 1947

17. The Reith Lectures (UK) 1948

18. Sports Report (UK) Jan 1948

19. Any Questions (UK) Oct 1948

20. Su Alegre Despertar (Puerto Rico) Jan 1949

150

165

HIGHEST-RATED TV SHOWS IN THE UK

	Title	Viewing figures (millions)	Broadcast date
1.	EastEnders	30.10	Dec 25 1986
2.	EastEnders	28.00	Jan 1 1987
3.	Coronation Street	26.65	Dec 25 1987
4.	Only Fools and Horses	24.35	Dec 29 1996
5.	EastEnders	24.30	Jan 2 1992
6.	Royal Variety Performance 1965	24.20	Nov 14 1965
7.	EastEnders	24.15	Jan 7 1988
8.	To the Manor Born	23.95	Nov 11 1979
9.	EastEnders	23.55	Dec 26 1985
10.	Panorama (Princess Diana)	22.78	Nov 20 1995
11.	Miss World 1967	23.76	Nov 19 1967
12.	Royal Variety Performance 1975	22.66	Nov 16 1975
13.	This is Your Life (Lord Mountbatten)	22.22	April 27 1977
14.	Sunday Night at the London Palladium	21.89	Dec 3 1967
15.	The Benny Hill Show	21.67	March 24 1971
16.	Dallas (Who shot JR?)	21.50	May 26 1980
17.	Coronation Street	21.60	Jan 8 1992
18.	Eurovision Song Contest 1973	21.56	April 7 1973
19.	Steptoe and Son	21.54	Feb 18 1964
20.	The Mike Yarwood Show	21.40	Dec 25 1977

Source: The Official UK Charts Company

HIGHEST-RATED TV SHOWS IN THE USA

	Title / Viewing figures (millions) / Broadcast date		
1.	The Ed Sullivan Show (Beatles' first appearance)	73.24	Feb 9 1964
2.	Super Bowl XLIV	53.6	Feb 7 2010
3.	M*A*S*H* (finale)	50.15	Feb 28 1983
4.	Super Bowl XIII	48.66	Feb 3 2008
5.	XVII Winter Olympics (Ladies figure skating short program—Nancy Kerrigan and Tonya Harding)	45.69	Feb 23 1994
6.	Super Bowl XXX	44.15	Jan 28 1996
7.	Super Bowl XXXII	43.63	Jan 25 1998
8.	Super Bowl XXXIV	43.62	Jan 30 2000
9.	Super Bowl XXVIII	42.86	Jan 30 1994
10.	Cheers series finale	42.36	May 20 1993
11.	Super Bowl XXXI	42.00	Jan 26 1997
12.	XVII Winter Olympics (Ladies figure skating long program—Kerrigan and Harding)	41.54	Feb 25 1994
13.	Super Bowl XXVII	41.99	Jan 31 1993
14.	Super Bowl XX	41.49	Jan 26 1986
15.	Dallas (Who shot JR?)	41.47	Nov 21 1980
16.	Super Bowl XVII	40.48	Jan 30 1983
17.	Super Bowl XXI	40.04	Jan 25 1987
18	Super Bowl XVI	40.02	Jan 24 1982
19.	Super Bowl XIX	39.39	Jan 20 1985
20.	Super Bowl XVIII	38.88	Jan 22 1984

Source: Nielsen Media Research

BESTSELLING ALBUMS WORLDWIDEOF ALL TIME

1 Michael Jackson
Thriller
(50 million+)

2 AC/DC
Back In Black
(49 million)

3 Pink Floyd
The Dark Side Of The Moon
(45 million)

4 Whitney Houston/*The Bodyguard* (soundtrack)
(44 million)

5 Meat Loaf
Bat Out Of Hell
(43 million)

6 Eagles
Their Greatest Hits
(1971–1975) (42 million)

7 Various Artists
Dirty Dancing (soundtrack)
(42 million)

8 Backstreet Boys
Millennium
(40 million)

9 Bee Gees   *Saturday Night Fever* (soundtrack)
(40 million)

10 Fleetwood Mac
Rumours
(40 million)

11 Shania Twain
Come On Over
(39 million)

12 Led Zeppelin
Led Zeppelin IV
(37 million)

13 Alanis Morissette
Jagged Little Pill
(33 million)

14 The Beatles *Sgt Pepper's Lonely Hearts Club Band*
(32 million)

15 Celine Dion
Falling Into You
(32 million)

16 Mariah Carey
Music Box
(32 million)

17 Michael Jackson
Dangerous
(32 million)

18 The Beatles
The Number Ones
(31 million)

19 Celine Dion
Let's Talk About Love
(31 million)

20 Elton John
Goodbye Yellow Brick Road
(31 million)

Thriller by Michael Jackson is generally accepted as the bestselling album in the world, with sales of between 50 million and 110 million depending on source!

BESTSELLING ARTISTS WORLDWIDE

1. The Beatles / 600 million–1 billion
2. Elvis Presley / 600 million–1 billion
3. Michael Jackson / 350–750 million
4. ABBA / 300–350 million
5. Madonna / 275–300 million
6. Led Zeppelin / 200–300 million
7. Queen / 150–300 million
8. Elton John / 250 million
9. Mariah Carey / 200 million
10. Celine Dion / 200 million
11. Pink Floyd / 200 million
12. AC/DC / 200 million
13. The Rolling Stones / 200 million
14. Whitney Houston / 170 million
15. Aerosmith / 150 million
16. Frank Sinatra / 150 million
17. Genesis / 150 million
18. Stevie Wonder / 150 million
19. U2 / 150 million
20. David Bowie / 140 million

BESTSELLING SINGLES WORLDWIDE

1. Bing Crosby *White Christmas* (50 million)
2. Elton John *Candle In The Wind 1997/Something About The Way You Look Tonight* (33 million)
3. Bing Crosby *Silent Night* (30 million)
4. Bill Haley & His Comets *Rock Around The Clock* (25 million)
5. USA For Africa *We Are The World* (20 million)
6. The Ink Spots *If I Didn't Care* (19 million)
7. Baccara *Yes Sir, I Can Boogie* (18 million)
8. Scorpions *Wind Of Change* (14 million)
9. Black Eyed Peas *I Gotta Feeling* (13.2 million)
10. Ke$ha *Tik Tok* (12.8 million)
11. The Beatles *I Want To Hold Your Hand* (12 million)
12. Village People *Y.M.C.A.* (12 million)
13. Whitney Houston *I Will Always Love You* (12 million)
14. Terry Jacks *Seasons In The Sun* (11.5 million)
15. George McCrae *Rock Your Baby* (11 million)
16. Mills Brothers *Paper Doll* (11 million)
17. Roger Whittaker *The Last Farewell* (11 million)
18. ABBA *Fernando* (10 million)
19. Cher *Believe* (10 million)
20. Middle Of The Road *Chirpy Chirpy Cheep Cheep* (10 million)

BUILDINGS AND STRUCTURES

CITIES WITH MOST SKYSCRAPERS

City	Country	Number of high-rise buildings	City	Country	Number of high-rise buildings
1. Hong Kong	China	7,685	11. Buenos Aires	Argentina	1,709
2. New York City	USA	5,899	12. St. Petersberg	Russia	1,538
3. São Paulo	Brazil	5,667	13. Kiev	Ukraine	1,531
4. Singapore	Singapore	4,364	14. London	UK	1,466
5. Moscow	Russia	3,017	15. Osaka	Japan	1,463
6. Seoul	South Korea	2,877	16. Mexico City	Mexico	1,366
7. Tokyo	Japan	2,702	17. Mumbai	India	1,173
8. Rio de Janeiro	Brazil	2,564	18. Madrid	Spain	1,124
9. Istanbul	Turkey	2,148	19. Chicago	USA	1.121
10. Toronto	Canada	1,820	20. Caracas	Venezuela	1,109

1. Burj Khalifa

2. Taipei 101

4. International Commerce Centre

TALLEST BUILDINGS

Name / Location / Height (feet) / Height (meters) / Year completed

Name	Location	Height (feet)	Height (meters)	Year completed
1. Burj Khalifa	Dubai, United Arab Emirates	2,717	828	2010
2. Taipei 101	Taipei, Taiwan	1,670	509	2004
3. World Financial Center	Shanghai, China	1,614	492	2008
4. International Commerce Centre	Hong Kong, China	1,588	484	2010
5. Petronas Towers	Kuala Lumpur, Malaysia	1,483	452	1998
6. Greenland Financial Centre	Nanjing, China	1,480	450	2010
7. Willis Tower	Chicago, USA	1,450	442	1974
8. Jin Mao Building	Shanghai, China	1,381	421	1999
9. Two International Financial Centre	Hong Kong, China	1,362	415	2003
10. CITIC Plaza	Guangzhou, China	1,283	391	1997
11. Shun Hing Square	Shenzhen, China	1,260	384	1996
12. Empire State Building	New York, USA	1,250	381	1931
13. Central Plaza	Hong Kong, China	1,227	374	1992
14. Bank of China Tower	Hong Kong, China	1,204	367	1990
15. Bank of America Tower	New York, USA	1,201	366	2009
16. Almas Tower	Dubai, United Arab Emirates	1,180	360	2009
17. Emirates Office Tower	Dubai, United Arab Emirates	1,165	355	2000
18. Tuntex Sky Tower	Kaohsiung, Taiwan	1,142	348	1997
19. Aon Center	Chicago, USA	1,135	346	1973
20. The Center	Hong Kong, China	1,135	346	1998

5. Petronas Towers

8. Jin Mao Building

MOST RECENT WINNERS OF THE GOLD DAGGER AWARD

Date / Title / Author

Date	Title	Author
2010	*Blacklands*	Belinda Bauer
2009	*A Whispered Name*	William Brodrick
2008	*Blood from Stone*	Francis Byfield
2007	*The Broken Shore*	Peter Temple
2006	*Raven Black*	Ann Cleeves
2005	*Silence of the Grave*	Arnaldur Indriðason
2004	*Blacklist*	Sara Peretsky
2003	*Fox Evil*	Minette Walters
2002	*The Athenian Murders*	José Carlos Samoza
2001	*Sidetracked*	Henning Mankell
2000	*Motherless Brooklyn*	Jonathan Lethem
1999	*A Small Death in Lisbon*	Robert Wilson
1998	*Sunset Limited*	James Lee Burke
1997	*Black and Blue*	Ian Rankin
1996	*Popcorn*	Ben Elton
1995	*The Mermaids Singing*	Val McDermid
1994	*The Scold's Bridle*	Minette Walters
1993	*Cruel and Unusual*	Patricia Cornwell
1992	*The Way Through the Woods*	Colin Dexter
1991	*King Solomon's Carpet*	Barbara Vine

MOST RECENT MAN BOOKER PRIZE WINNERS

Date / Title / Author

Date	Title	Author
2010	*The Finkler Question*	Howard Jacobson
2009	*Wolf Hall*	Hilary Mantell
2008	*The White Tiger*	Aravind Adiga
2007	*The Gathering*	Anne Enright
2006	*The Inheritance of Loss*	Kiran Desai
2005	*The Sea*	John Banville
2004	*The Line of Beauty*	Alan Hollinghurst
2003	*Vernon God Little*	D. B. C. Pierre
2002	*Life of Pi*	Yann Martel
2001	*True History of the Kelly Gang*	Peter Carey
2000	*The Blind Assassin*	Margaret Atwood
1999	*Disgrace*	J. M. Coetzee
1998	*Amsterdam*	Ian McEwan
1997	*The God of Small Things*	Arundhati Roy
1996	*Last Orders*	Graham Swift
1995	*The Ghost Road*	Pat Barker
1994	*How Late It Was, How Late*	James Kelman
1993	*Paddy Clarke Ha Ha Ha*	Roddy Doyle
1992	*The English Patient*	Michael Ondaatje
1991	*The Famished Road*	Ben Okri

MOST RECENT WINNERS OF THE NOBEL PRIZE FOR LITERATURE

2010 Mario Vargas Llosa

2009 Herta Müller

2008 Jean-Marie Gustave Le Clézio

2007 Doris Lessing

2006 Orhan Pamuk

2005 Harold Pinter

2004 Elfriede Jelinek

2003 John M. Coetzee

2002 Imre Kertész

2001 Sir Vidiadhar Surajprasad Naipaul

Günter Grass and Toni Morrisson

2000 Gao Xingjian

1999 Günter Grass

1998 José Saramago

1997 Dario Fo

1996 Wislawa Szymborska

1995 Seamus Heaney

1994 Kenzaburo Oe

1993 Toni Morrison

1992 Derek Walcott

1991 Nadine Gordimer

RISKIEST CONTAINERS AND PACKAGING

Container or packaging / Accidents per year*

1 Tin or can 15,979
2 Glass bottle 15,311
3 Cardboard box/wood packaging ..12,500
4 Plastic bottle 4,130
5 Plastic bag 3,345
6 Glass jar or pot 2,527
7 Other container 2,507
8 Corned beef tin 2,117
9 Aerosol spray can 1,871
10 Food case or crate 1,845
11 Metal container 1,599
12 Squeeze tube 1,228
13 Cardboard 1,223
14 Ring-pull 1,058
15 Foil, film, or paper wrap 937
16 Other wrapping 719
17 Plastic pot or tub 613
18 Blister pack 601
19 Carton 497
20 Sachet 129

According to a magazine survey, 60 percent of those polled have stabbed themselves while removing food packaging or prising the lid off food or drinks containers. Risky items include cheese in shrink-wrapped plastic, cellophane-covered sandwiches, jam jars and ring-pull cans. The most common injuries are cuts and bruises to the hands.

* Source: Yours magazine.

RISKIEST ITEMS OF CLOTHING AND FOOTWEAR

Item / Accidents per year*

1 Belt or buckle 5,544,990
2 Training shoes 267,748
3 Slippers 66,016
4 Sandal/flip-flop 52,256
5 Socks, tights or stockings 13,49
6 High-heeled shoes 12,77
7 Trousers 7,776
8 Coat 3,355
9 Plimsolls/pumps 3,148
10 Shirt or T-shirt 2,708
11 Gloves 2,398
12 Shorts 1560
13 Dress/skirt 1,459
14 Cardigan/pullover 1,359
15 Jacket/anorak 1,341
16 Dressing gown, housecoat, bathrobe 948
17 Hat, scarf or shawl 918
18 Buttons 790
19 Underwear 423
20 Night-dress 358

* Average number of accidents requiring hospital treatment per year. Source: Royal Society for the Prevention of Accidents.

RISKIEST ITEMS OF SPORT AND LEISURE EQUIPMENT (UK)

Equipment / Accidents per year*

1 Soccer ball or basketball 231,517

2 Cricket ball or bat 23,467

3 Rugby ball/ American football 23,270

4 Climbing frame 21,447

5 Roller blade/ in-line skate 16,058

6 Netball 13,542

7 Trampoline 10,928

8 Golf club or ball 10,701

9 Gymnasium mat 10,612

10 Bouncy castle 9,551

11 Indoor swimming pool 9,320

12 Roller skate/roller ski 7,923

13 Fishing rod, hook and line 6,594

14 Football goal post and net 6,229

15 Rope swing 5,155

16 Tennis racket, ball and net 4,378

17 Punch ball or bag 3,826

18 Bowling ball 3,244

19 Exercise machine 3,175

20 Toboggan or sledge 2,920

* Average number of accidents requiring hospital treatment per year.

201

HIGHEST MOUNTAINS

Name / Range / Country / Height in feet/meters

A view of the breathtaking Mount Everest

1 Everest, Himalayas (China/ Nepal)
29,029 / 8,848

2 K2, Karakoram (China/ Pakistan)
28,251 / 8,611

3 Kanchenjunga, Himalayas (India/ Nepal)
28,208 / 8,598

4 Lhotse, Himalayas (China/ Nepal)
27,940 / 8,516

5 Makalu, Himalayas (China/ Nepal)
27,824 / 8,481

6 Cho Oyu, Himalayas (China/ Nepal)
26,906 / 8,201

7 Dhaulagiri, Himalayas (Nepal)
26,811 / 8,172

8 Manaslu, Himalayas (Nepal)
26,758 / 8,156

9 Nanga Parbat, Himalayas (Pakistan)
26,660 / 8,126

10 Annapurna I, Himalayas (Nepal)
26,502 / 8,078

Gasherbrum I, Karakoram (China/ Pakistan)
26,469 / 8,068 **11**

Broad Peak, Karakoram (India)
26,414 / 8,051 **12**

Gasherbrum II, Karakoram (China/ Pakistan)
26,362 / 8,034 **13**

Shishapangma (Himalayas, Tibet)
26,335 / 8,027 **14**

Gyachung Kang, Himalayas (Nepal/ Tibet)
26,089 / 7,952 **15**

Gasherbrum III, Karakoram (China/ Pakistan)
26,070 / 7,946 **16**

Annapurna II, Himalayas (Nepal)
26,040 / 7,937 **17**

Gasherbrum IV, Karakoram
(China/ Pakistan)
26,024 / 7,932 **18**

Himalchuli, Himalayas (Nepal)
25,896 / 7,893 **19**

Distaghil Sar, Karakoram (Pakistan)
25,869 / 7,885 **20**

Cho Oyu, the sixth highest peak

LONGEST MOUNTAIN RANGES

Name/ Location / Length in miles/km

1 Mid-Ocean Ridge (Underwater range stretching around the globe) 40,000 / 64,374

2 Andes (Argentina, Bolivia, Chile, Colombia, Ecuador, Peru, Venezuela) 4,500 / 7,242

3 Rocky Mountains (Canada, United States) 3,750 / 6,035

4 Great Dividing Range (Australia) 2,250 / 3,621

5 Trans-Antarctic Mountains (Antarctica) 2,175 / 3,500

6 Himalays (China, Tibet, Nepal, India, Pakistan) 1,491 / 2,400

7 Brazilian Atlantic Coast Range (Brazil) 1,900 / 3,000

8 West Sumatra–Javan Range (Sumatra, Java) 1,800 / 2,900

9 Aleutian (Alaska) 1,650 / 2,650

10 Tien Shan (China, Pakistan, India, Kazakhstan, Kyrgyzstan, Uzbekistan) 1,400 / 2,250

11 Eastern Ghats (India) 1,300 / 2,092

12 Altai Mountains (Russia, China, Mongolia, Kazakhstan) 1,250 / 2,012

13 Central Range (Papua New Guinea) 1,250 / 2,012

14 Urals (Russia) 1,250 / 2,012

15 Carpathian Mountains (Czech Republic, Poland, Slovakia, Hungary, Ukraine, Romania, Serbia) 932 / 1,500

16 Alps (France Switzerland, Italy, Austria, Slovenia, Croatia, Bosnia, Serbia, Montenegro, Albania) 750 / 1,200

17 Apennine Mountains (Italy) 750 / 1,200

18 Caucasus Mountains (Russia, Georgia, Azerbaijan, Armenia, Iran, Turkey) 684 / 1100

19 Hindu Kush (Afghanistan, Pakistan) 500 / 804

20 Karakorum Range (Pakistan, India, China) 311 / 500

LARGEST DESERTS

Name /Location / Area in square miles/km

1 Antarctic (Antarctica) / 5,339,000 / 13,827,950

2 Arctic (Arctic Basin) / 5,300,000 / 13,726,940

3 Sahara (North Africa) / 3,513,530 / 9,100,000

4 Arabian (Middle East) / 899,618 / 2,330,000

5 Gobi (China, Mongolia) / 500,000 / 1,295,000

6 Patagonian (Argentina) / 260,000 / 673,400

7 Great Basin (South West USA) / 190,000 / 492,100

8 Great Victoria (Australia) / 163,707 / 424,000

9 Chihuahuan (Mexico, USA) / 140,000 / 362,600

10 Great Sandy (Australia) / 139,000 / 360,000

11 Karakum (Turkmenistan) / 135,000 / 349,650

12 Colorado Plateau (Western USA) / 130,000 / 336,70

13 Sonoran (Mexico, USA) / 120,000 / 310,800

14 Kyzyl Kum (West Asia) / 115,000 / 297,850

15 Taklamakan (China) / 105,000/ 271,950

16 Kalahari (Southern Africa) / 100,000 / 259,000

17 Syrian (Syria, Jordan, Iraq) / 100,000 / 259,000

18 Thar (India, Pakistan / 77,000 /199,420

19 Gibson (Australia) / 60,000 / 155,400

20 Simpson (Australia) / 56,000 / 145,040

Bedouin houses in the Syrian desert.

BIGGEST SELLING FEMALES IN THE USA

Artist / Albums sold

	Artist	Albums sold		Artist	Albums sold		Artist	Albums sold
1.	Barbra Streisand	71.5 million	10.	Enya	26.5 million	19.	Norah Jones	17 million
2.	Madonna	64 million	11.	Janet Jackson	26 million	20.	Amy Grant	17 million
3.	Mariah Carey	63.5 million	12.	Faith Hill	25.5 million			
4.	Whitney Houston	55 million	13.	Sade	23.5 million			
5.	Celine Dion	50 million	14.	Alanis Morisette	20.5 million			
6.	Shania Twain	48 million	15.	Mary J. Blige	19.5 million			
7.	Reba McIntyre	41 million	16.	Toni Braxton	19.5 million			
8.	Britney Spears	32 million	17.	Jewel	18.5 million			
9.	Linda Ronstadt	30 million	18.	Sarah McLachlan	18.5 million			

Source: RIAA

Did you know?
The Dixie Chicks have sold 30.5 million albums in the US, and TLC have sold 22 million.

BIGGEST SELLING MALES IN THE USA

Artist / Albums sold

	Artist	Albums sold
1.	Elvis Presley	129.5 million
2.	Garth Brooks	128 million
3.	Billy Joel	79.5 million
4.	Michael Jackson	70.5 million
5.	Elton John	70 million
6.	George Strait	68.5 million
7.	Bruce Springsteen	64.5 million
8.	Kenny Rogers	51 million
9.	Neil Diamond	48.5 million
10.	Kenny G	48 million
11.	Alan Jackson	43 million
12.	Eric Clapton	42.5 million
13.	Prince	39.5 million
14.	2Pac	37.5 million
15.	Rod Stewart	37 million
16.	Bob Dylan	37 million
17.	Tim McGraw	37 million
18.	Willie Nelson	35 million
19.	Phil Collins	33.5 million
20.	R Kelly	33 million

Source: RIAA

BIGGEST GROSSING TOURS

	Artist or band	Year	Tour	Gross
1.	U2	2009–11	*360 Degree Tour*	$750,000,000*
2.	Rolling Stones	2005–07	*A Bigger Bang Tour*	$558,255,524
3.	AC/DC	2008–10	*Black Ice World Tour*	$441,600,000
4.	Madonna	2008–09	*Sweet & Sticky Tour*	$408,000,000
5.	U2	2005–06	*Vertigo Tour*	$389,000,000
6.	The Police 2	2007–08	*Reunion Tour*	$358,825,665
7.	Celine Dion	2008–09	*Taking Chances Tour*	$279,200,000
8.	Cher	2002–05	*Living Proof Farewell Tour*	$260,000,000
9.	Bruce Springsteen	2007–08	*Magic Tour*	$235,000,000
10.	Bruce Springsteen	2002–03	*Rising Tour*	$221,500,000
11.	Bon Jovi	2007–08	*Lost Highway Tour*	$210,600,000
12.	Madonna	2006	*Confessions Tour*	$194,754,447
13.	U2	1997–98	*PopMart Tour*	$171,677,024
14.	Michael Jackson	1996–97	*HIStory World Tour*	$163,500,000
15.	P!nk	2009–10	*Funhouse Tour*	$150,000,000
16.	Tim McGraw & Faith Hill	2006–07	*Soul2Soul Tour*	$141,000,000
17.	Lady Gaga	2009–11	*Monster Ball Tour*	$133,600,000
18.	Britney Spears	2009	*Circus Tour*	$131,800,000
19.	Michael Jackson	1987–89	*Bad Tour*	$125,000,000
20.	Madonna	2004	*Re-Invention World Tour*	$124,000,000

Source: Billboard
* Estimated final gross

Did you know?
These are the reported actual gross figures for each tour and do not take into account inflation. The Rolling Stones figure for the Bigger Bang Tour would now be over $591,000,000).

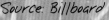
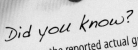

COUNTRIES WITH THE LOWEST BIRTH RATE

Country/Estimated birth rate (Live births per 1,000)

1 Japan 7.6

2 Italy 8.2

3 Germany 8.2

4 Austria 8.7

5 Singapore 8.9

6 Czech Republic 8.78

7 Bosnia Herzegovina 8.9

8 Macau 8.9

9 South Korea 8.9

10 Taiwan 8.9

11 Slovenia 9.0

12 Monaco 9.1

13 Lithuania 9.1

14 Serbia 9.2

15 Greece 9.5

16 Hungary 9.5

17 Bulgaria 9.5

18 Switzerland 9.6

19 Ukraine 9.6

20 San Marino 9.6

Source: CIA World Factbook

YEARS WITH THE MOST BIRTHS IN THE UK

Year	Births
1. 1920	957,782
2. 1903	948,271
3. 1904	945,389
4. 1902	940,509
5. 1908	940,383
6. 1906	935,081
7. 1901	929,807
8. 1905	929,293
9. 1899	928,646
10. 1900	927,062
11. 1898	923,165
12. 1895	922,291
13. 1897	921,683
14. 1907	918,042
15. 1896	915,331
16. 1893	914,572
17. 1909	914,472
18. 1891	914,157
19. 1884	906,750
20. 1886	903,760

Source: International Statistics

COUNTRIES WITH THE
HIGHEST BIRTH RATE

Country / Estimated birth rate (live births per 1,000)

1	Niger	51.1	**11**	Malawi	41.3
2	Uganda	47.6	**12**	Congo, Republic	
3	Mali	46.1		of the	41.0
4	Zambia	44.6	**13**	Chad	40.1
5	Burkina-Faso	44.0	**14**	Sao Tome Principe	39.1
6	Ethiopia	43.3	**15**	Sierra Leone	38.8
7	Angola	43.3	**16**	Mayotte	38.8
8	Somalia	43.3	**17**	Benin	38.7
9	Congo, Democratic		**18**	Liberia	38.1
	Republic of the	42.3	**19**	Afghanistan	38.1
10	Burundi	41.4	**20**	Madagascar	37.9

Source: CIA World Factbook

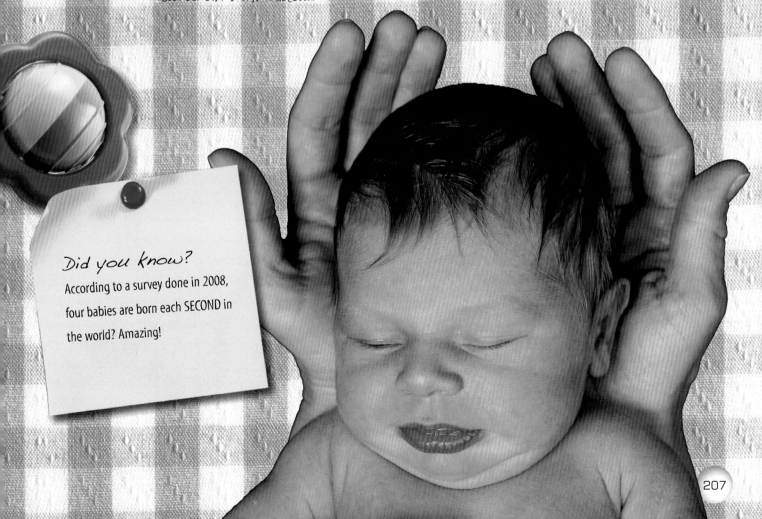

Did you know?

According to a survey done in 2008,
four babies are born each SECOND in
the world? Amazing!

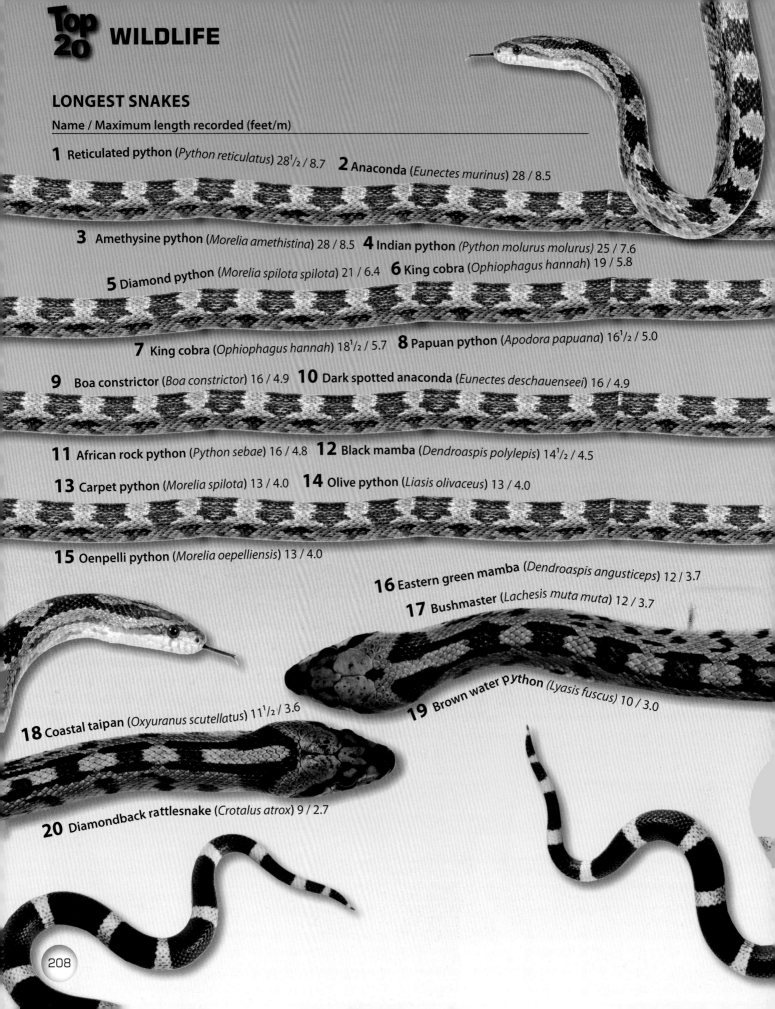

Top 20 WILDLIFE

LONGEST SNAKES

Name / Maximum length recorded (feet/m)

1 Reticulated python (*Python reticulatus*) 28$\frac{1}{2}$ / 8.7   **2** Anaconda (*Eunectes murinus*) 28 / 8.5

3 Amethysine python (*Morelia amethistina*) 28 / 8.5   **4** Indian python (*Python molurus molurus*) 25 / 7.6

5 Diamond python (*Morelia spilota spilota*) 21 / 6.4   **6** King cobra (*Ophiophagus hannah*) 19 / 5.8

7 King cobra (*Ophiophagus hannah*) 18$\frac{1}{2}$ / 5.7   **8** Papuan python (*Apodora papuana*) 16$\frac{1}{2}$ / 5.0

9 Boa constrictor (*Boa constrictor*) 16 / 4.9   **10** Dark spotted anaconda (*Eunectes deschauenseei*) 16 / 4.9

11 African rock python (*Python sebae*) 16 / 4.8   **12** Black mamba (*Dendroaspis polylepis*) 14$\frac{1}{2}$ / 4.5

13 Carpet python (*Morelia spilota*) 13 / 4.0   **14** Olive python (*Liasis olivaceus*) 13 / 4.0

15 Oenpelli python (*Morelia oepelliensis*) 13 / 4.0

16 Eastern green mamba (*Dendroaspis angusticeps*) 12 / 3.7

17 Bushmaster (*Lachesis muta muta*) 12 / 3.7

19 Brown water python (*Lyasis fuscus*) 10 / 3.0

18 Coastal taipan (*Oxyuranus scutellatus*) 11$\frac{1}{2}$ / 3.6

20 Diamondback rattlesnake (*Crotalus atrox*) 9 / 2.7

DEADLIEST CREATURES

Creature / Cause / Human deaths*

1	Mosquito	Malaria infection / 2 million+
2	Tse tse fly	Sleeping sickness / 250,000+
3	Sand fly	Disease/various / 60,000+
4	Dogs	Bite/rabies infection / 55,000+
5	Snake	Venomous bite / 20,000+
6	Kissing bug	Chagas disease / 20,000+
7	Scorpion	Venomous sting / 5000+
8	Flea	Disease/various / 1300+
9	Crocodile	Bite/predation / 1000+
10	Bee	Venomous sting / 500+
11	Elephant	**Goring/trampling / 300+**
12	Buffalo	Goring/trampling / 200+
13	Lion	Predation / 100+
14	Hippopotamus	Bite/trampling / 100+
15	Wasp	Venomous sting / 90–100
16	Hornet	Venomous sting / 80–90
17	Jelly fish	Venomous sting / 50+
18	Shark	Bite/predation / 50+
19	Bear	Bite/claw/predation / 30–40
20	Army Ant	Venomous bite / 20–40

* Approx. average deaths (worldwide per year). Source: World Health Organization

MOST VENOMOUS REPTILES AND AMPHIBIANS*

1 Belcher's sea snake (*Hydrophis belcheri*)
2 Beaked sea snake (*Enhydrina schistosa*)
3 Indian cobra (*Naja naja*)
4 Golden poison dart frog (*Phyllobates terribilis*)
5 Common Indian krait (*Bungarus caeruleus*)
6 Inland taipan (*Oxyuranus microlepidotus*)
7 Russell's viper (*Vipera russellii*)
8 Saw-scaled viper (*Echis carinatus*)
9 Philippine cobra (*Naja philippinensis*)
10 King cobra (*Ophiophagus hannah*)
11 Black mamba (*Dendroaspis polylepis*))
12 Yellow jawed tommygoff (*Bothrops asper*)
13 Multibanded krait (*Bungarus multicinctus*)
14 Tiger snake (*Notechis scutatus*)
15 Jararacussu (*Bothrops Jararacussu*)
16 Rattlesnake (*Crotalus sp.*)
17 Water moccasin (*Agkistrodon piscivorus*)
18 Coral snake (*Micrurus fulvias*)
19 Copperhead (*Agkistrodon contortix*)
20 Pit viper (*Bothrops asper*)

* Order indicates risk to average-sized man based on laboratory toxicity tests

MOST TEST MATCHES IN A CAREER

1	Sachin Tendulkar	(India)	177
2	Steve Waugh	(Australia)	168
3	Allan Border	(Australia)	156
4	Ricky Ponting	(Australia)	152
5	Rahul Dravid	(India)	150
6	Jacques Kallis	(South Africa)	145
7	Shane Warne	(Australia)	145
8	Mark Boucher	(South Africa)	139
9	Muttiah Muralitharan	(Sri Lanka)	133
10	Alec Stewart	(England)	133
11	Anil Kumble	(India)	132
12	Courtney Walsh	(West Indies)	132
13	Kapil Dev	(India)	131
14	Brian Lara	(West Indies)	131
15	Shivnarine Chanderpaul	(West Indies)	129
16	Mark Waugh	(Australia)	128
17	Sunny Gavaskar	(India)	125
18	Javed Mianded	(Pakistan)	124
19	Glenn McGrath	(Australia)	124
20	Viv Richards	(West Indies)	121

MOST WICKETS IN A TEST CAREER

1 Muttiah Muralitharan (Sri Lanka) 800

2 Shane Warne (Australia) 708

3 Anil Kumble (India) 619

4 Glenn McGrath (Australia) 563

5 Courtney Walsh (West Indies) 519

6 Kapil Dev (India) 434

7 Sir Richard Hadlee (New Zealand) 431

8 Shaun Pollock (South Africa) 421

9 Wasim Akram (Pakistan) 414

10 Curtly Ambrose (West Indies) 405

11 Harbhajan Singh (India) 393

12 Makhaya Ntini (South Africa) 390

13 Ian Botham (England) 383

14 Malcolm Marshall (West Indies) 376

15 Waqar Younis (Pakistan) 373

16 Imran Khan (Pakistan) 362

17 Dennis Lillee (Australia) 355

18 Chaminda Vaas (Sri Lanka) 355

19 Daniel Vettori (New Zealand) 345

20 Allan Donald (South Africa) 330

Source: cricinfo.com

Did you know?

Wisden, the cricketers' almanack, has been published every year since 1864. The very first Test match took place in 1877, between England and Australia, but was not covered in the almanack for a hundred years.

HIGHEST INNINGS IN ONE DAY INTERNATIONAL CRICKET

#	Score	Match
1	443/9	Sri Lanka v Netherlands (2006)
2	438/9	South Africa v Australia (2006)
3	434/4	Australia v South Africa (2006)
4	418/5	South Africa v Zimbabwe (2006)
5	414/7	India v Sri Lanka (2009)
6	413/5	India v Bermuda (2007)
7	411/8	Sri Lanka v India (2009)
8	402/2	New Zealand v Ireland (2010)
9	401/3	India v South Africa (2010)
10	399/6	South Africa v Kenya (1996)
11	397/5	New Zealand v Zimbabwe (2005)
12	392/6	South Africa v Pakistan (2007)
13	392/4	India v New Zealand (2009)
14	391/4	England v Bangladesh (2005)
15	387/5	India v England (2008)
16	385/7	Pakistan v Bangladesh (2010)
17	377/6	Australia v South Africa (2007)
18	376/2	India v New Zealand (1999)
19	374/4	India v Hong Kong (2008)
20	373/6	India v Sri Lanka (1999)

BIGGEST BEATLES CONCERTS
(NORTH AMERICAN TOURS OF 1964, 1965 & 1966)

The Beatles played a total of 73 shows during their three tours of North America, selling more than one million tickets during the process. Here are the top attendances they played before, where a date has a second entry, this is because the band played two shows at the same venue on the same day! By way of comparison, The Beatles played two shows at the Rizal Memorial Football Stadium in Manila in the Philippines on 4 July 1966; the first was watched by 30,000 and the second by 50,000. Unfortunately, the band were later accused of having delivered a snub to Philippine First Lady Imelda Marcos and left the islands a day later under something of a cloud.

1 — 15 August 1965 — Shea Stadium (55,600)

2 — 28 August 1966 — Los Angeles (45,000)

3 — 13 August 1966 — Shea Stadium (44,600)

4 — 20 August 1965 — Chicago (37,000)

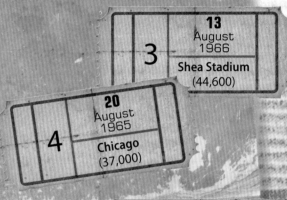

5 — 15 August 1966 — Washington DC (32,164)

6 — 11 September 1964 — Jacksonville (32,000)

7 — 18 August 1965 — Atlanta (30,000)

8 — 20 August 1965 — Chicago (25,000)

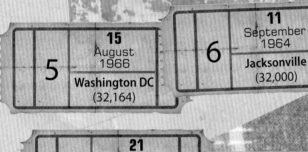

9 — 21 August 1965 — Bloomington (25,000)

10 — 18 August 1966 — Boston (25,000)

11 — 29 August 1966 — San Francisco (25,000)

12 — 21 August 1966 — St Louis (23,000)

13 — 16 August 1966 — Philadelphia (21,000)

14 — 22 August 1964 — Vancouver (20,621)

15 — 17 September 1964 — Kansas (20,124)

16 — 14 August 1966 — Cleveland (20,000)

17 — 30 August 1964 — New Jersey (18,000)

18 — 31 August 1965 — San Francisco (18,000)

19 — 17 August 1965 — Toronto (18,000)

20 — 17 August 1965 — Toronto (18,000)

POSTHUMOUS UK NUMBER ONE HITS

1. Buddy Holly *It Doesn't Matter Anymore*
2. Eddie Cochran *Three Steps To Heaven*
3. Jim Reeves *Distant Drums*
4. Jimi Hendrix *Voodoo Child*
5. Elvis Presley *Way Down*
6. John Lennon *(Just Like) Starting Over*
7. John Lennon *Woman*
8. Johnn Lennon *Imagine*
9. Jackie Wilson *Reet Petite*
10. Freddie Mercury (with Queen) *Bohemian Rhapsody/ These Are The Days Of Our Lives*
11. Freddie Mercury *Living On My Own*
12. Aaliyah *More than A Woman*
13. George Harrison *My Sweet Lord*
14. Elvis Presley (Vs JXL) *A Little Less Conversation*
15. Elvis Presley *Jailhouse Rock*
16. Elvis Presley *One Night/I Got Stung*
17. Elvis Presley *It's Now Or Never*
18. 2Pac Featuring Elton John *Ghetto Gospel*
19. Notorious B.I.G. (with Diddy, Nelly, Jagged Edge & Avery Storm) *Nasty*
20. Eva Cassidy (with Katie Melua) *What A Wonderful World*

This list has been compiled according to the year of the hit record. Buddy Holly was the first to have a number one hit after his death in 1959.

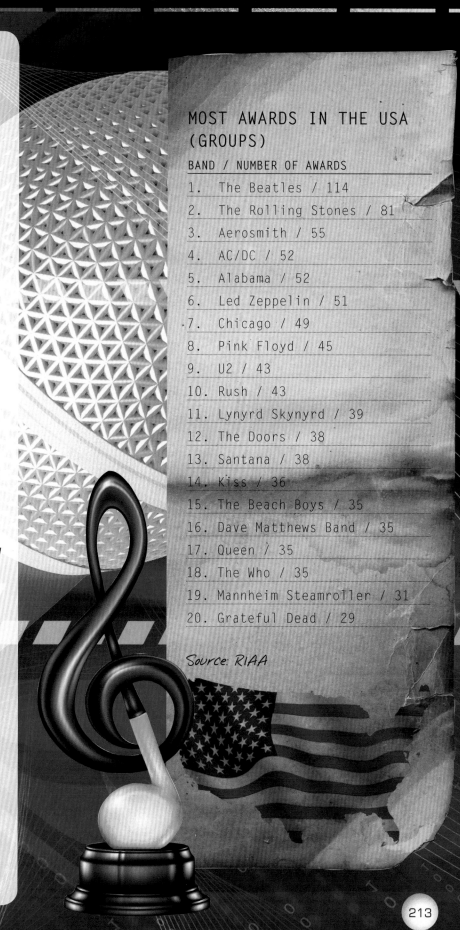

MOST AWARDS IN THE USA (GROUPS)

BAND	NUMBER OF AWARDS
1. The Beatles	114
2. The Rolling Stones	81
3. Aerosmith	55
4. AC/DC	52
5. Alabama	52
6. Led Zeppelin	51
7. Chicago	49
8. Pink Floyd	45
9. U2	43
10. Rush	43
11. Lynyrd Skynyrd	39
12. The Doors	38
13. Santana	38
14. Kiss	36
15. The Beach Boys	35
16. Dave Matthews Band	35
17. Queen	35
18. The Who	35
19. Mannheim Steamroller	31
20. Grateful Dead	29

Source: RIAA

RICHEST COUNTRIES BY GDP

Country / GDP per capita ($/£)

1 Luxembourg $104,390/£63,991		**11 Canada** $45,888/£28,129	
2 Norway $84,543/£51,825		**12 Ireland** $45,642/£27,979	
3 Qatar $74,422/£45,621		**13 Austria** $43,723/£26,802	
4 Switzerland $67,074/£41,116		**14 Finland** $43,134/£26,441	
5 Denmark $55,113/£33,784		**15 Singapore** $42,653/£26,146	
6 Australia $54,869/£33,635		**16 Belgium** $42,596/£26,111	
7 Sweden $47,667/£29,220		**17 Japan** $42,325/£25,945	
8 UAE $47,406/£29,012		**18 France** $40,591/£24,882	
9 USA $47,132/£28,892		**19 Germany** $40,512/£24,834	
10 Netherlands $46,418/£28,454		**20 UK** $36,298/£22,251	

Source: International Monetary Fund (IMF)

GDP (gross domestic product) per capita is the total value of goods and services produced in one year by each nation divided by head of population. It is used as an indication of a country's wealth.

COUNTRIES WITH THE MOST BILLIONAIRES

Country / Number of billionaires

1 USA 412 **2** China 115 **3** Russia 101 **4** India 55 **5** Germany 52 **6** Turkey 38

7 Hong Kong SAR, China 36 **8** UK 33 **9** Brazil 30 **10** Japan 26 **11** Canada 24

12 Indonesia 22 **13** Taiwan 18 **14** Italy 13 **15** Spain 13 **16** France 12

17 Switzerland 11 **18** South Korea 11 **19** Switzerland 11 **20** Australia 11

POOREST COUNTRIES BY GDP

Country / GDP per capita ($/£)

1 Burundi $177/£109

2 Congo $188/£115

3 Liberia $226/£139

4 Sierra Leone $325/£199

5 Malawi $354/£217

6 Ethiopia $364/£223

7 Niger $383/£235

8 Madagascar $391/£240

9 Guinea $420/£257

10 Eritrea $423/£259

11 Togo $441/£270

12 Central African Republic $468/£287

13 Mozambique $473/£290

14 Zimbabwe $475/£291

15 Guinea-Bissau $497/£305

16 Uganda $503/£308

17 Timor-Leste $535/£328

18 Nepal $536/£329

19 Tanzania $542/£332

20 Afghanistan $560/£343

LARGEST GOLD RESERVES BY COUNTRY
Country / Gold (tons)

Source: International Monetary Fund

1 USA 8,134

2 Germany 3,402

3 Italy 2,452

4 France 2,435

5 China 1,054

6 Switzerland 1,040

7 Russia 775

8 Japan 765

9 Netherlands 613

10 India 558

11 Taiwan 424

12 Portugal 383

13 Venezuela 364

14 Saudi Arabia 323

15 UK 310

16 Lebanon 287

17 Spain 282

18 Austria 280

19 Belgium 228

20 Philippines 176

COUNTRIES WITH MOST OLYMPIC GOLD MEDALS AT THE SUMMER GAMES

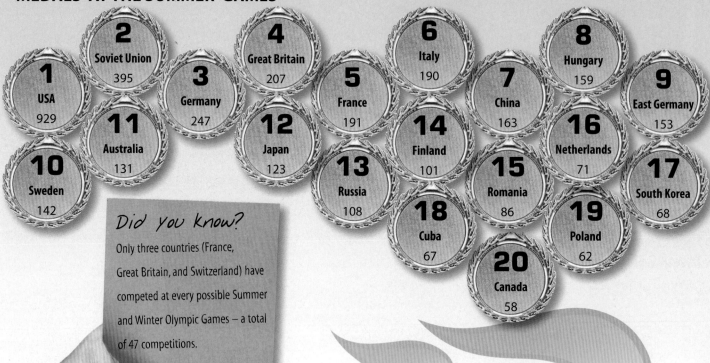

1 USA 929
2 Soviet Union 395
3 Germany 247
4 Great Britain 207
5 France 191
6 Italy 190
7 China 163
8 Hungary 159
9 East Germany 153
10 Sweden 142
11 Australia 131
12 Japan 123
13 Russia 108
14 Finland 101
15 Romania 86
16 Netherlands 71
17 South Korea 68
18 Cuba 67
19 Poland 62
20 Canada 58

Did you know?

Only three countries (France, Great Britain, and Switzerland) have competed at every possible Summer and Winter Olympic Games – a total of 47 competitions.

OLYMPIANS WITH MOST MEDALS AT THE SUMMER GAMES

Winner / Country of origin / Category / Number of medals

1 Larissa Latynina / Soviet Union / Gymnastics / 18

2 Michael Phelps / USA / Swimming / 16   **3** Nikolai Andrianov / Soviet Union / Gymnastics / 15

4 Boris Shakhlin / Soviet Union / Gymnastics / 13   **5** Edoardo Mangiarotti / Italy / Fencing / 13

6 Takashi Ono / Japan / Gymnastics / 13   **7** Paavo Nurmi / Finland / Athletics / 12

8 Birgit Fischer / Germany / Canoeing / 12   **9** Sawao Kato / Japan / Gymnastics / 12

10 Jenny Thompson / United States / Swimming / 12   **11** Dara Torres / USA / Swimming / 12

12 Alexei Nemov / Russia / Gymnastics / 12   **13** Mark Spitz / USA / Swimming / 11

14 Matt Biondi / USA / Swimming / 11

15 Vera Caslavska / Czech Republic / Gymnastics / 11

16 Viktor Chukarin / Soviet Union / Gymnastics / 11

17 Carl Osburn / USA / Shooting / 11   **18** Carl Lewis / USA / Athletics / 10

19 Aladar Gerevich / Hungary / Fencing / 10   **20** Akinori Nakayama / Japan / Gymnastics / 10

Source: IOC

OLYMPIANS WITH MOST MEDALS (SUMMER & WINTER GAMES COMBINED)

Winner / Country of origin / Category / Number of medals

1 Larissa Latynina / Soviet Union / Gymnastics / 18
2 Michael Phelps / USA / Swimming / 16
3 Nikolai Andrianov / Soviet Union / Gymnastics / 15
4 Boris Shakhlin / Soviet Union / Gymnastics / 13
5 Edoardo Mangiarotti / Italy / Fencing / 13
6 Takashi Ono / Japan / Gymnastics / 13
7 Paavo Nurmi / Finland / Athletics / 12
8 Bjorn Daehlie / Norway / Cross Country Skiing / 12
9 Birgit Fischer / Germany / Canoeing / 12
10 Sawao Kato / Japan / Gymnastics / 12
11 Jenny Thompson / USA / Swimming / 12
12 Dara Torres / USA / Swimming / 12
13 Alexei Nemov / Russia / Gymnastics / 12
14 Mark Spitz / USA / Swimming / 11
15 Matt Biondi / USA / Swimming / 11
16 Vera Caslavska / Czech Republic / Gymnastics / 11
17 Viktor Chukarin / Soviet Union / Gymnastics / 11
18 Ole Einar Bjorndalen / Norway / Biathlon / 11
19 Carl Osburn / USA / Shooting / 11
20 Carl Lewis / USA / Athletics / 10

Source: IOC

The youngest person to win an Olympic gold medal will never be known. In 1900, in Paris, the Dutch Minerva/Amsterdam rowing team decided after a heat in the coxed pairs that their coxswain was too heavy and recruited a seven-year-old French boy to take his place. They won the event, but the coxswain's name is still unknown.

The youngest recorded gold medallist is Marjorie Gestring of the United States, who was 13 years and 268 days old when she won the three metre springboard diving event at the 1936 Olympics in Berlin. The youngest medalist is Dimitrios Loundras, who helped Greece win silver in the parallel bars event, aged 10 years and 218 days old in 1896. Since the minimum age to compete in the Olympics has been raised to 16 years of age, neither record will be broken.

MUSIC

MOST PLATINUM AWARDS IN THE UK (MALE)

BPI certified awards were introduced into the UK in April 1973 with qualification based on the revenue received by the manufacturers. In 1978 this was replaced by the unit system whereby a platinum disc is presented for sales in excess of 300,000 copies. Multi-platinum awards were introduced in February 1987.

Source: BPI

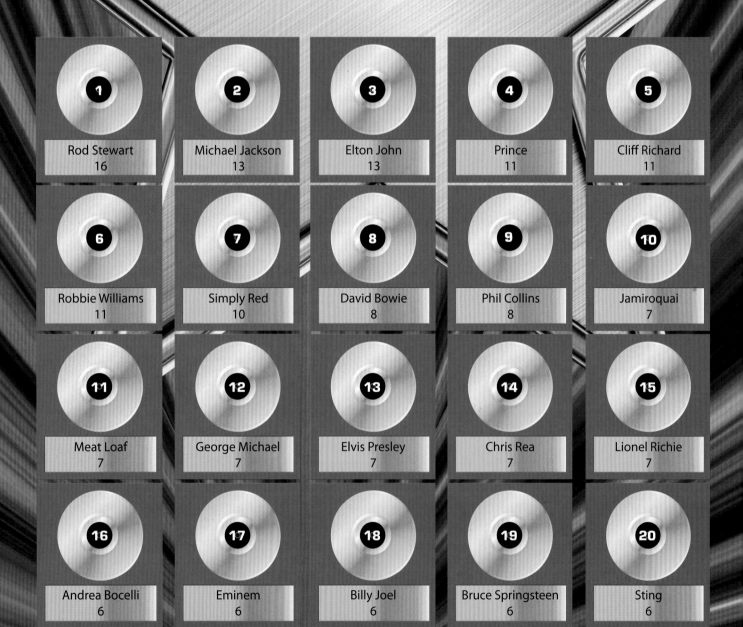

#	Artist	Awards
1	Rod Stewart	16
2	Michael Jackson	13
3	Elton John	13
4	Prince	11
5	Cliff Richard	11
6	Robbie Williams	11
7	Simply Red	10
8	David Bowie	8
9	Phil Collins	8
10	Jamiroquai	7
11	Meat Loaf	7
12	George Michael	7
13	Elvis Presley	7
14	Chris Rea	7
15	Lionel Richie	7
16	Andrea Bocelli	6
17	Eminem	6
18	Billy Joel	6
19	Bruce Springsteen	6
20	Sting	6

218

MOST AWARDED MALE ARTISTS USA

Artists / Number of awards

1. Elvis Presley 159
2. George Strait 84
3. Elton John 76
4. Neil Diamond 72
5. Kenny Rogers 58
6. Bob Dylan 57
7. Rod Stewart 54
8. Bruce Springsteen 49
9. Frank Sinatra 48
10. Garth Brooks 47
11. Billy Joel 47
12. Prince 46
13. Eric Clapton 45
14. Willie Nelson 45
15. Barry Manilow 43
16. Luther Vandross 41
17. John Denver 40
18. Alan Jackson 40
19. James Taylor 39
20. Ozzy Osbourne 36

Source: RIAA

Did you know?
RIAA (Recording Industry Association of America) launched gold awards in 1958, initially for singles, before awarding the first album award to Gordon MacRae for the soundtrack to Oklahoma. Platinum awards were introduced in 1976 to signify sales in excess of one million units (gold was then set at 500,000 units), with multi-platinum awards, signifying sales of more than two million units, introduced in the mid 1980s. Elvis Presley's tally of 159 awards therefore is made up of 86 gold, 48 platinum and 25 multi-platinum discs.

Michael Jackson is probably the most awarded male artist of all time if you include critic's awards, such as MTV awards, American Music awards, Grammys, etc. He has won over 392 major awards!

WORST MARITIME DISASTERS

Vessel	Location	Year	Fatalities
1. MV *Dona Paz*	Philippines	1987	*4,400
2. SS *Kiangya*	East China Sea	1948	*3,920
3. MV *Joola*	Senegal	2002	1,863
4. SS *Sultana*	Mississippi River, USA	1865	1,547
5. RMS *Titanic*	North Atlantic	1912	1,517
6. RMS *Lusitania*	Atlantic, off south coast of Ireland	1915	1,198
7. *Toya Maru*	Tsugaru Strait, Japan	1954	1,159
8. SS *General Slocum*	East River, New York City	1904	1,021
9. MS *al-Salam Boccaccio 98*	Red Sea	2006	1,018
10. RMS *Empress of Ireland*	St Lawrence River, Canada	1914	1,012
11. SS *Hong Moh*	South China Sea	1921	*1,000
12. MV *Bukoba*	Lake Victoria, Tanzania	1996	894
13. MS *Estonia*	Baltic Sea	1994	852
14. SS *Eastland*	Chicago, USA	1915	844
15. MV *Princess of Stars*	Sibuyan Island, Philippines	2008	832
16. SS *Camorta*	Irrawaddy Delta, Burma	1902	737
17. SS *Princess Alice* / SS *Bywell Castle*	River Thames, London	1878	*640
18. SS *Norge*	North Atlantic Ocean	1904	627
19. SS *Ramdas*	Arabian Sea	1947	625
20. *Novorossiyk*	Sevastopol, Ukriane	1955	608

* Estimated figures

BIGGEST OIL SPILLS
Name / Location / Dates / Tons of crude oil

1
Kuwait Oil Fires
Kuwait
January–November
1991
136–205 million

2
Kuwait Oil Lakes
Kuwait
January–November
1991
3,409,000–6,818,000

3
Lakeview Gusher
California USA
May 1910–
September 1911
1,200,000

4
Gulf War oil spill,
Persian Gulf, Kuwait,
January 1991
818,000–1,091,000

5
Deepwater Horizon
US, Gulf of Mexico
April–July 2010
560,000–585,000

6
Ixtoc I
Mexico, Gulf of Mexico
June 1979–March 1980
454,000–480,000

7
Atlantic Empress/ Aegean
Captain
Trinidad and Tobago
July 1979
287,000

8
Fergana Valley
Uzbekistan
March 1992
285,000

9
Nowruz Field
Platform
Iran, Persian Gulf
February 1983
260,000

10
ABT Summer
offshore Angola
May 1991
260,000

11
Castillo de
Bellver, South Africa,
Saidanha Bay
August 1983
252,000

12
Amoco Cadiz
Brittany, France
March 1978
223,000

13
MT Haven
Mediterranean nr
Genoa, Italy
April 1991
144,000

14
Odyssey
off Nova Scotia,
Canada
November 1988
132,000

15
Sea Star
Iran, Gulf of Oman
December 1972
115,000

16
Irenes Serenade
Pylos, Greece
February 1980
100,000

17
Urquiola,
Coruña, Spain
May 1976
100,000

18
ExxonMobil oil spill
Niger Delta, Nigeria
May 2010
95,500

19
Torrey Canyon
Scilly Isles, UK
March 1967
80,000–119,000

20
Greenpoint oil spill
New York City, USA
1940–1950s
55,000–97,000

USEFUL WEBSITES

THE ARTS

nobelprize.org
Nobel Foundation official website
nationalgallery.org.uk
Website for The National Gallery, London

HISTORY

royal.gov.uk
The official website of the British Royal family
rulers.org
Information on rulers around the world

TRANSPORT

uic.org
Railway facts and figures
railwaygazette.com
Railway business information
airports.org
Statistics on the world's airports
baaa-acro.com
Database on air accidents

PEOPLE

statistics.gov.uk
For UK population figures
who.int.en
World Health Organization
cia.gov/library/publications/the-world-factbook/
Information on history, people, and governments around the world
unesco.org
Information on education and culture
forbes.com
Website of Forbes magazine, with lists of the world's rich

SPORT

iaaf/org
Website of the governing body of athletics
fifa.com
Official website of the governing body of soccer
olympic.org/uk
The official Olympics website
lta.org.uk
Official website of the British Lawn Tennis Association
cricinfo.com
Cricket online information

LANGUAGE AND LITERATURE

bl.uk
The British Library
ethnologue.com
Reference on languages of the world
themanbookerprize.com
Website of the literary prize

INTERNET AND PHONE

twitterholic.com
For information on the twittersphere

internetworldstats.com
Facts and figures on the internet

itu.int/en
Website for information and communication technologies

EARTH AND SPACE

nasa.gov
The official NASA website

emdat.be
International disaster database

fao.org
Information from the Food and Agriculture Organization

fishbase.org
Website with global fish information

ENERGY AND RESOURCES

usgs.gov
US Geological Survey with information on climate, energy, and resources

geology.com
News and information about geology and science

www.caverbob.com
Lists of caves

worldatlas.com
Online maps and atlases

bp.com
British Petroleum website with information and statistics

MUSIC

billboard.com
US chart information

BRIT Awards
Website for the BRIT music awards in the UK

naras.org
The Grammys website

mtv.co.uk
The MTV website

theofficialcharts.com
Weekly present and past chart information

PETS AND ANIMALS

fao.org
Agriculture statistics

thepigsite.com
The website for the global pig industry

thepoultrysite.com
Statistics on global chicken and egg trends

petplace.com
Pet information

thekennelclub.org.uk
The largest organization dedicated to the health and welfare of dogs in the UK

FILM, TV, AND ENTERTAINMENT

oscars.org
The official Academy Awards website
bafta.org
Information on the British film awards
imdb.com
The Internet Movie Database with a wealth of movie information
londontheatre.co.uk
Reviews and information on London theater shows
screendaily.com
Website with daily film news and information

WILDLIFE

zsl.org
London Zoological Society website
nhm.ac.uk
Natural History Museum, London, website
amnh.org
The American Museum of Natural History website
shark.org.au
Site for the Shark Research Institute in Australia

PLACES

nationsonline.org
An online guide to the countries of the world
esa.un.org
United Nations population information

BUILDINGS AND STRUCTURES

un.org
The United Nations website
tallestskyscrapers.info
Facts on skyscrapers
higestbridges.com
Information on the highest bridges around the world
lotsberg.net
Facts on the longest rail, road, and canal tunnels

PICTURE CREDITS